# Theology & Violence
## The South African Debate

Edited by Charles Villa-Vicencio

GRAND RAPIDS
WILLIAM B. EERDMANS PUBLISHING COMPANY

Library of Congress Cataloging-in-Publication Data

Theology & violence : the South African debate
edited by Charles Villa-Vicencio.
p.   cm.
ISBN 0-8028-0359-8
1. Violence — Religious aspects — Christianity.   2. South Africa — Race relations.
3. Race relations — Religious aspects — Christianity.
I. Villa-Vicencio, Charles. II. Title: Theology and violence.
BT736.15.T47  1988
241.6′21′0968 — dc19          87-37524
CIP

# Contents

**INTRODUCTION** ........................................................................ 1

**CONTRIBUTORS** ....................................................................... 11

## CONTOURS OF SOUTH AFRICAN HISTORY

| | | |
|---|---|---|
| Greg Cuthbertson: | THE ENGLISH-SPEAKING CHURCHES AND COLONIALISM .......... | 15 |
| Jaap Durand and Dirkie Smit: | THE AFRIKANER CHURCHES ON WAR AND VIOLENCE ............................... | 31 |
| Allan Boesak and Alan Brews: | THE BLACK STRUGGLE FOR LIBERATION: A RELUCTANT ROAD TO REVOLUTION ...................................... | 51 |

## THE CONTEXTUAL DEBATE

| | | |
|---|---|---|
| Desmond Tutu: | FREEDOM FIGHTERS OR TERRORISTS? ............................................. | 71 |
| Buti Tlhagale: | CHRISTIAN SOLDIERS ............................. | 79 |
| Malusi Mpumlwana: | LEGITIMACY AND STRUGGLE .............. | 89 |

## CLASSICAL TRADITIONS

| | | |
|---|---|---|
| Itumeleng Mosala: | VIOLENCE AND THE PROPHETS ........ | 103 |
| Ephraim K. Mosothoane: | VIOLENCE IN THE GOSPEL TRADITION ...................................... | 111 |
| Seqibo Dwane: | EARLY CHRISTIANS AND THE PROBLEM OF WAR .................................. | 133 |
| Douglas Bax: | FROM CONSTANTINE TO CALVIN: THE DOCTRINE OF THE JUST WAR ................................................... | 147 |
| John de Gruchy: | RADICAL PEACE-MAKING: THE CHALLENGE OF SOME ANABAPTISTS ............................................. | 173 |

## CONTEMPORARY DEBATE

Robin Petersen: NATIONALISM AND REVOLUTION: THE NINETEENTH CENTURY AND KARL BARTH ............... 189

Albert Nolan and Mary Armour: ARMED STRUGGLE AS A LAST RESORT: THE ROMAN CATHOLIC POSITION ......................... 209

Paul Germond: LIBERATION THEOLOGY: THEOLOGY IN THE SERVICE OF JUSTICE ......................... 215

Charles Villa-Vicencio: THE ECUMENICAL DEBATE: VIOLENT REVOLUTION AND MILITARY DISARMAMENT ...................... 233

Denise Ackerman: WOMEN, VIOLENCE AND THEOLOGY ..................... 255

Sheena Duncan: RADICAL PACIFISM: AN OPTION FOR PEACE? .................................. 271

Lois Law, Chris Lund and Harald Winkler: CONSCIENTIOUS OBJECTION: THE CHURCH AGAINST APARTHEID'S VIOLENCE ..................... 281

## BEYOND DEBATE

Frank Chikane: WHERE THE DEBATE ENDS ............... 301

# Introduction

Churches and theologians have never agreed completely on the use of violence in political struggle. The dominant tradition of the church has, however, tended to bless the state's use of violence while condemning violent revolution against the ruling authorities. This predisposition in favour of the state is a phenomenon which first emerged in an institutional sense with the Edict of Milan in 313 C.E. Constantine had found it expedient to negotiate with the church, bringing to an end a period of sporadic but intense persecution of Christians. Hardly a decade later he emerged as the sole ruler of the empire, Christianity practically becoming a state religion, and in the centuries that followed the church was transformed from a persecuted sect into a community of wealthy and powerful people. The church's origins as a persecuted minority soon became a distant memory as it found itself socially located on the side of the dominant rulers of each successive age, and by the high Middle Ages it had become the single most despotic political force in Europe.

By this time new economic and political forces were beginning to transform the identity of European society, and this too took its toll on the character of the church, leading to the Protestant Reformation and the Catholic Counter-Reformation. Whatever the causes of these reform processes, the consequence was the emergence of a bourgeois church. The control of the church shifted from the imperial aristocracy to bourgeois princes, with the peasants continuing to be relegated to the subservient position in the church that they occupied in the wider social formation. This process is nowhere shown more clearly than in 1525 when the peasants of Germany sought to extend the Protestant affirmation of spiritual freedom to socio-political liberation and Martin Luther sided with the princes, counselling them to kill the peasants. Christianity has since then been appealed to in a variety of situations to legitimate violence in the interests of maintaining law and order — not least of all in South Africa.

A detailed history of the shift in the ideological identity of the church from a church of the subversive poor in pre-Constantinian days to a church of the ruling class cannot be told here. It is

1

addressed at various points in the essays that follow, and has become the subject of several other studies. Suffice it to say that held captive to the dominant forces of what has come to be known as 'Western Christian civilisation', the Christian religion has come to be an important part of the ideological framework that has supported the existence of successive regimes in different parts of the world who affirm the dominant values of the West. And the inclination of the church to legitimate the use of violence by these regimes, while opposing revolutionary violence to overthrow such regimes, is a natural consequence of this ideological captivity.

It would be quite wrong, however, to suggest that for some extraneous reasons it is only in our time that some Christians have resorted to revolutionary violence. Throughout its history the church has never quite managed to deny or suppress a residual revolutionary theology which obliges it to be on the side of the poor and the oppressed. It is what Metz calls a 'dangerous memory' which theologically contradicts the institutional church's social location on the side of the dominant classes of history. It is this residual theology, which exists adjacent to the dominant theology of the church, which has obliged the church, in response to the demands of its socially marginalised and politically oppressed members, to allow for revolutionary forces to emerge at crisis points in history. It is this tradition that allows for a theological understanding and at times a theological legitimation of revolutionary struggle and violence.

It is this alternative theological tradition that is affirmed in the *Kairos Document* which questions the institutional church's condemnation of 'all violence', its refusal to distinguish between oppressive state violence and the use of violence in self-defence against aggressors and tyrants, while at the same time providing tacit support for the growing militarisation of the South African state. It is this same tradition which is affirmed in the Lusaka Statement (May 1987) of the World Council of Churches' consultation on Justice and Peace in Southern Africa, which recognises that 'the nature of the South African regime which wages war against its own inhabitants and neighbours compels the movements to use force along with other means to end oppression.'

Desmond Tutu adopts a cautious stance in this regard, but one firmly located in the historic tradition of the church. This is clear from his essay included in this volume, in which he writes:

> We are driven ... to invoke a non-violent method which we believe is likely to produce the desired result. If this option is denied us, what then is left? If sanctions should fail there is no other way but to fight.
>
> Should the West fail to inspire sanctions it would, in my view, be justifiable for blacks to try to overthrow an unjust system violently. But I must continue to work to bring an end to the present tyranny by non-violent means.

What is 'new' in recent theological debate is the re-affirmation of this alternative tradition within Christianity which stands in contradiction to the dominant tradition that has for so long been imposed on adherents to the faith. A closer reading of what the *Kairos Document* calls 'church theology' shows, however, that this alternative tradition which has been reclaimed by an increasing number of Christians since the 'discovery' of Third World liberation theologies by the ecumenical church has been clearly although never overtly present throughout history. Dominant classes do not have a monopoly over the theology of the church, which they have so consistently employed as an instrument of domination. This alternative tradition is read with growing interest by Christians who are oppressed and by those who seek in solidarity with them to reconstitute the revolutionary character of Christianity once the cultural and political accretions of the ruling class in the West have been removed.

The subject under consideration in this study, 'theology and violence', brings together two important theological debates. These concern the use of historical texts in contemporary theological and ethical formulations, and an understanding of the place of violence within the political process. Not all who have contributed essays to this book agree on all aspects of these debates. Yet, despite the known and obvious differences discerned in the pages that follow, a certain broad presuppositional consensus can be identified in most essays. An attempt is made in what follows simply to note the broad parameters of this consensus as it relates to the two debates being considered.

## THE USE OF HISTORY IN CONTEMPORARY DEBATE

The essays included in this book are largely of an historical nature, each seeking to uncover the way in which past generations have wrestled theologically with the clash between classes and nations in conflict, especially regarding the question of violence. The purpose of the study is not, however, an exercise in historical erudition for its own sake, but rather historical enquiry as a basis for analysing contemporary existence. As such, no attempt is made to disguise the hermeneutical lens through which texts, often located in ages and situations very different to that which prevails in contemporary South Africa, are read. It would be ridiculous to expect to find in the history of Christian thought simple theological answers to complex contemporary questions on state and revolutionary violence in South Africa. However, to the extent that there is some continuity between contemporary debate and past tradition — a *sine qua non* for legitimate theology — the possibility exists that we can learn something from past experiences of suffering, violence, death and victory. It is this presupposition which persuades most theologians that Hegel is probably wrong in his estimation that all history teaches us is that we can learn nothing from history, and that Santayana is possibly right in suggesting that those who ignore history are often condemned to become its victims. Yet when a society resolutely clings to self-affirming and legitimating myths about the past, refusing to become self-critical in its historical consciousness, it is unlikely to be able to control its present or to creatively shape its future.

A constant reassessment of historical identity is therefore a pre-requisite for social renewal. This is a process that acquires a soteriological function, requiring more than a summation of what a particular theologian or age believed about a particular issue. It demands a more thoughtful answer to the question of how that theologian or age would have responded to a contemporary problem, involving the more profound discovery of the latent meaning within a tradition that has perhaps become sterile, seen to be far removed from and unrelated to an issue of burning contemporary significance. It is essentially this understanding of history and historical theology that constitutes the unifying identity of the essays included in this book. Particular historical periods and contemporary problems are each considered in their own right, while an enduring concern is to equip Christians to live *now* rather than merely learn how others lived *then*.

No attempt is made to provide a systematic answer to the question of violence in the South African situation, and while certain definite themes emerge from these essays, it is expected that readers will reach their own conclusions concerning the implications of the historical material for the South African situation. As such the essays provide an open-ended contribution to the need for Christians to respond thoughtfully to what has emerged as perhaps the most pertinent debate in the area of religion and society in South Africa today. For those confronted with the daily reality of state violence and compelled to live with revolutionary violence as a responsive reality, the naïve response of the churches in their rejection of 'all violence' has acquired a hollow and embarrassing sound. At least since the Constantinian settlement between church and state, Christians have not been particularly squeamish about the use of violence. The church has, however, felt itself constrained to allow that the resort to violence should, *inter alia* be an *ultima ratio* (a last resort) and that it should be restrained and employed only in pursuit of a just end. Historical reality has indicated, however, that in practice the church has more often than not been forgetful of these restraints and has usually been drawn into violent conflict on the side of the ruling class.

Submitting by default to the dominant ideology of the time, churches have in most places on most occasions contributed to the sabre-rattling milieu which has taken more than one nation to war for less than a just or justified cause. Yet, as already argued, an alternative option has continued to haunt the church in its forgetful co-option into the ruling ideology of the dominant classes. It is an option which affirms that tradition of the church whose origins reach back to a community of oppressed and alienated people. As such it is an option which affirms a preferential option for the poor (rather than the rich and powerful). In so doing it necessarily resists the dominant ideology of rulers who resort to arms to protect and maintain what is theirs. It also allows that if violence be justified at all it can only be justified as a limited and dangerous means towards establishing a society which is to the benefit of those who suffer most in the existing order.

There is a sense, however, in which debate on the justification of violence is both futile and morally unacceptable. The present situation in South Africa is one in which the church has no choice whether to engage in violence or not. Its members have already been engulfed by the war. And certainly black Christians living in townships and rural areas cannot afford the luxury of debate on such matters. An essay by Frank Chikane which is included in this study shows that the priority for blacks is not theoretical debate about violence, but the elimination of the fundamental causes of violence, whether by counter-violence or the most effective non-violent means available. It is from this perspective that the historical studies within this book need to be read and interpreted. Bluntly stated, it is a perspective which suggests violence to be an inevitable part of a conflictual political situation.

## VIOLENCE AND THE POLITICAL PROCESS

If politics be the art of the possible, then those seriously engaged in politics and/or the pursuit of social justice are inevitably faced with the question of how to ensure that those who resist a proposed program of action can be persuaded to conform. This involves what has been defined as 'force', 'coercion', or 'violence'. Much debate has been entered into with a view to distinguishing between these concepts, and some have preferred to reserve the term 'violence' only for the most extreme forms of statecraft while using it quite freely to describe the activity of those who oppose what they prefer to call state 'force' or 'coercion'. One therefore reads of the police being compelled to use force to disperse students engaging in violent protest. Such semantic differences often contribute towards confusing rather than clarifying debate. Language is a carrier of value, and there is a case to be made for using violence as an all-inclusive act of compulsion or restraint even though such inclusive language would fail to distinguish between what constitutes acceptable and unacceptable degrees of violence. But to suggest that 'violence' constitutes the improper use of force, while 'force' is violence sanctioned by law raises as many questions as it answers. Against this broad definition of violence certain propositions follow:

*1. Some form of violence is an inherent part of the political process.*

Constraint and restraint constitute the essentials of all but the most utopian understandings of social existence. The most avid pacifist social reformers are, in turn, likely to have their non-violent action programs provoke a violent situation. Events surrounding the campaigns of Mahatma Gandhi and Martin Luther King as well as the history of non-violent initiatives in South Africa are enough to make this point. The restraint of some is no guarantee that all will exercise equal restraint, and furthermore provides no incentive for civil authorities to respond in a similar manner. In India Gandhi faced a colonial power that fell short of being a ruthless tyranny. In the United States of

America Martin Luther King was engaged in a civil rights campaign. In South Africa the struggle is of a different kind, and the extent of the brutality unleashed on children and defenceless people is perhaps still to be revealed.

2. *There is a difference between state violence and tyranny.*

When a state fails to secure the consent and respect of the governed and loses its moral legitimacy, having to rely solely on military force to maintain power, its legalisation of violence degenerates into a licence to enforce tyranny. Morality aside, it is this situation which suggests that if it is legitimate to use violence to support such a regime it is also legitimate to use force to destroy it — a situation which constitutes rule by the barrel of a gun.

3. *Revolution is an inevitable response to state tyranny.*

History and theology both suggest that the will to liberation is part of what it means to be a human being. Sustained oppression and imposed servitude have relentlessly given rise to protest, resistance and revolution throughout history. When normal democratic channels are denied to people who seek to realise the will to be free such people do not remain silent nor do they remain in subjection. They resort to violence. And the story of South African history is no exception. The churches have at times been part of this oppression, and only with the greatest reluctance in extreme cases have they shown a measure of understanding for those who have resorted to armed resistance. Christians have traditionally concerned themselves with the morality of violence and been particularly troubled by, revolutionary violence. They continue to be so troubled, but must also allow that their own tradition requires them to condemn violence less harshly than indifference, even if only because the latter can never be an expression of love.

4. *Not all violence is revolutionary violence.*

Obviously there is institutional and repressive violence, which includes the sustained effects of apartheid laws, cross-border raids, police violence, the excesses of vigilante groups, and much more. But careful analysis also shows that not all violence by oppressed people is necessarily revolutionary violence. Sporadic, unco-ordinated violence simmers just below the surface among the oppressed classes of society and, as is shown in at least one essay in this book, it is at times this kind of spontaneous resistance that becomes the focus of revolutionary violence. Ultimately, however, revolutionary violence is goal-oriented and

purposeful. The tragedy is that the quality of life for the oppressed
can degenerate to the point where anarchic violence is seen by
some to be more acceptable than the existing form of oppression.
Indeed for some this too (like the violence debate itself) is no
debate at all, it is merely a consequence of a spiral of violence
resulting from their efforts to eradicate the fundamental causes of
institutional violence, which activity is responded to with further
repression.
*5. The spiral of violence needs to be broken.*
     The only reasonable way to do this is to eliminate the
fundamental cause of political violence in South Africa. To fail to
do this is to fail to address the problem of violence. Karl Marx was
correct regarding the inevitability of violence in certain situations.
Writing to his daughter Jenny in 1881 he suggested that violence
was 'a historically inevitable means of action, the morality or
immorality of which it was as useless to discuss as that of the
earthquake at Chios'. While oppression endures, violence is
inevitable. It is this that convinces some that the violence issue is
not the primary political-ethical question for the church to
consider. Violence, suggests Mpumlwana in his contribution to
this book, is 'a subsidiary question of method and tactics' in
dealing with a far greater problem, and such methods can only be
addressed by people 'who, at the very least have a common
diagnosis of the problem'. The obdurate problem facing the
church concerns an inability to agree on the nature of the South
African society. It is this that separates the analysis of the Kairos
theologians from that of 'church theologians'. And there is a
sense in which serious theological debate on issues such as
violence can only begin after the analytical debate is completed.
     Not all who are responsible for the essays included in this
volume would agree about the precise theological or political
nature of the South African regime. What does unite them is a
deep conviction that this regime needs to be replaced with a
radically and fundamentally different kind of society.

## THEOLOGY IN DIALOGUE
The decision to engage in the study which has culminated in the
publication of this book emerged at more or less the time of the
publication of the *Kairos Document*, as a contribution to the
'open-ended' debate which that document initiated. A wide
spectrum of South African theologians were approached to write

essays in areas of their own speciality and interest with a view to providing a background document making the tradition of the church more accessible to people doing theology in their own situations today. As such the book is intended to be a contribution to dialogue — between past and present, traditional and contextual theologies and people of different theological persuasions who are committed to see the dawning of a new, liberated South Africa. Not all who have contributed would regard themselves as liberation theologians, but all find themselves drawn deeper and deeper into what might be called liberation work.

Recognising that context strongly shapes content, the first three essays provide an historical analysis of the role of violence in British imperialism, Afrikaner nationalism and the black liberation struggle. The first of these studies is written by Greg Cuthbertson, Jaap Durand and Dirkie Smit contribute an essay on Afrikaner nationalism, and the essay on black liberation is written by Allan Boesak and Alan Brews. These are followed by three contextual reflections on violence within the contemporary situation written by Archbishop Desmond Tutu, Buti Tlhagale and Malusi Mpumlwana. The third section of essays constitutes a history of doctrine approach within which the theme of violence is considered theologically from biblical times to the present. Itumeleng Mosala and Ephraim Mosothoane provide essays on the Old and New Testaments. Seqibo Dwane writes on violence in the early church, Douglas Bax addresses the period extending from Augustine to Calvin, and John de Gruchy considers the Radical Reformation. Moving towards more contemporary debate, Robin Petersen considers nineteenth-century nationalism and revolution with a special focus on Karl Barth. Albert Nolan and Mary Armour identify violence as a last resort in the Roman Catholic just war tradition, Paul Germond gives his attention to the response of Latin American theologians to the problem of violence, and the apparent contradiction in the ecumenical debate on violent revolution and military disarmament is tackled by myself. Sheena Duncan writes on pacifism as a radical alternative to violence, Denise Ackermann comments on women and violence, and Lois Law, Chris Lund and Harald Winkler consider conscientious objection in a militarised state. The final essay in the book belongs to Frank Chikane and provides a thoughtful conclusion to a long debate.

The manuscript took much longer to put together than was

anticipated. Dilisa Matshoba was tragically killed while writing a contribution to the book. Some who had undertaken to write essays have been detained and others driven underground, while the crisis that presently racks South Africa placed enormous additional burdens on a number of contributors. All this extended the deadline for publication three times. As authors we are grateful to Mothobi Mutloatse and Jaki Seroke of Skotaville Publishers, and to Bill Eerdmans from Wm. B. Eerdmans Publishing Co. for their co-operation and for agreeing to publish the book. Many people have contributed to this publication who deserve our gratitude. Some have read drafts of essays making valuable suggestions, others have drafted outlines. Authors have, in turn, in many instances been most gracious in agreeing to changes to their manuscripts. Shaan Ellinghouse typed the manuscript with immaculate precision, Mary Armour facilitated the editorial process with skill and Pat Lawrence toiled away at the many secretarial functions involved in pulling together nineteen essays from twenty-four contributors located in virtually every corner of South Africa. Arlene Stephenson assisted with proof-reading the final manuscript.

One final word. The Institute of Contextual Theology (ICT) has provided the inspiration for a number of theological projects since its inception in September 1981, and the contributors to this volume have agreed that such royalties as may accrue from the sale of *Theology and Violence: The South African Debate* be paid to ICT.

Charles Villa-Vicencio
Cape Town, May 1987

# Contributors

| | |
|---|---|
| Denise Ackerman: | Lecturer in the Department of Practical Theology, University of South Africa |
| Mary Armour: | Postgraduate Student in the Department of Religious Studies, University of Cape Town |
| Douglas Bax: | Minister, United Congregational Church of Southern Africa, Rondebosch |
| Allan Boesak: | President of the World Alliance of Reformed Churches and Moderator of the NG Mission Church |
| Alan Brews: | Minister, Methodist Church of Southern Africa, Buitenkant Street, Cape Town |
| Frank Chikane: | General Secretary, South African Council of Churches |
| Greg Cuthbertson: | Senior Lecturer in the Department of History, University of South Africa |
| John de Gruchy: | Professor of Christian Studies, Department of Religious Studies, University of Cape Town |
| Sheena Duncan: | Former President of the Black Sash and Vice-President of the South African Council of Churches |
| Jaap Durand: | Deputy Vice-Chancellor, University of the Western Cape |
| Seqibo Dwane: | Bishop, Order of Ethiopia, Church of the Province of South Africa |
| Paul Germond: | Teaching Assistant, Department of Religious Studies, University of Cape Town |
| Lois Law: | Postgraduate Student, Department of Sociology, University of Cape Town |
| Chris Lund: | Postgraduate Student, Department of Religious Studies, University of Cape Town |

Itumeleng Mosala:            Lecturer, Department of Religious
                             Studies, University of Cape Town

Ephraim K. Mosothoane:  Associate Professor, Department of
                             Biblical and Religious Studies,
                             University of the Transkei

Malusi Mpumlwana:            Minister, Order of Ethiopia, Church of
                             the Province of South Africa

Albert Nolan:                Priest of the Dominican Order, Adviser
                             to the Institute for Contextual Theology,
                             Johannesburg

Robin Petersen:              Minister, United Congregational Church
                             of Southern Africa, Heideveld, Cape
                             Town

Dirkie Smit:                 Professor of Systematic Theology,
                             Theological Faculty, University of the
                             Western Cape

Buti Tlhagale:               Catholic priest and Liaison Officer in
                             the Education Opportunities Council

Desmond Tutu:                Archbishop of Cape Town, Church of
                             the Province of South Africa

Charles Villa-Vicencio:      Associate Professor, Department of
                             Religious Studies, University of Cape
                             Town

Harald Winkler:              Postgraduate Student, Department of
                             Religious Studies, University of Cape
                             Town

# CONTOURS OF SOUTH AFRICAN HISTORY

# The English-Speaking Churches and Colonialism

## GREG CUTHBERTSON

During the nineteenth century southern Africa was one of the most active missionary fields in the colonial world. British missionaries of the mainline Protestant denominations (those churches which are today commonly referred to as the English-speaking churches) were instigators and proponents of the dismantling of African societies through the introduction of capitalism and the extension of imperial control. The theme of missionaries and violence is therefore a broad one and for the purposes of this article three levels of violence are emphasised. First, the violence against the individual as a result of proselytisation; secondly, the structural violence of British imperialism; and finally the physical violence unleashed in full-scale colonial warfare. My focus in this latter category is specifically on the attitudes and reactions of British missionaries to the South African war of 1899-1902, and only limited reference will be made to other colonial wars.

The missiological debate has produced many formative and authoritative monographs and articles since the 1950s,[1] and the issue of missionary conquest in Africa is at the heart of the discussion. Consequently, all I can attempt is a synthesis of the most influential views on the impact of missionaries and specifically their culpability in perpetrating or acquiescing in violence against subject and unconquered peoples. My main argument is that missionaries in southern Africa both used and defended violence. The structural violence of imperialism forms the backdrop of my analysis and the forces of capitalism and militarism are shown to impinge on missionary motivation and conduct. Moreover, I take issue with those writers who claim that missionaries were revolutionaries, especially those who insist that there is a structural parallel between Marxian revolutionaries and imperialist missionaries.[2] On the contrary, missionaries were not anti-establishment activists, but rather the 'natural associates of

the Colonial government'. While they may have had interests
peculiar to their calling, they usually acted in conjunction with
other contemporary agents. As Legassick puts it, 'they were
shapers and manipulators of the interests of others'.[3] Indeed, it is
contended here that missionaries were the harbingers of capitalist
exploitation and prime-movers in the expansion and consolidation
of white political power.

As custodians of the 'religion of the status quo',[4] missionaries
served the prevailing ideology of imperial expansionism. The
ideology they propagated was a selective Christianity consciously
modified and adapted for export to the colonies:

> Colonial expansion is ... cast as an altruistic crusade, bringing
> hope    of    salvation    to    those    otherwise    irrevocably
> lost ... Salvation is thus presented as an exclusive club,
> admission to which is European-controlled ... we see an
> ideology that serves the interests of the dominant party, spread
> by an institution that the dominant party supports, and this
> (is) ... the hallmark of the religion of the status quo.[5]

It is clear therefore that ideological hegemony was the ultimate
goal of the religion of the status quo.

## THE VIOLENCE OF 'CONVERSION'

Richard Elphick has explained 'conversion' to Christianity in terms
of 'the clash and interchange' between European and African
cultures in southern Africa and avers that

> ... by severing history from nature, the missionaries, in part
> unwittingly, unleashed powerful forces in Africa ... they closed
> nature down; they silenced and deadened it by eliminating
> personalist and magical strategies of explanation and offering
> instead the simplifications of mathematics which makes
> possible the technology of industrialism ...[6]

The single-minded dedication to 'conversion' caused
missionaries to disrupt the mores of 'indigenous' communities
through concerted efforts to discredit and undermine any system
of belief which conflicted with Christian dogma. And because the
dynamics of 'conversion' were decidedly not politically,
economically or ideologically neutral, missionary 'religious
onslaught reinforced the confusion, breakdown, and
victimisation ... that land loss and political pressures created ...'.[7]

'Conversion' strategy centered on a concerted assault on values
and the religious or spiritual sanctions underlying them. So
missionaries consciously confronted what they regarded as the
'pagan' worship of spiritual forces, which destroyed the social

cohesion of communities based on kinship relationships, with the peculiar individualism of western Christianity. In sum, 'conversion' meant a rejection of an African religion world-view and a denial of traditional social custom.

Elphick suggests that missionaries strove to replace what they perceived as the 'false consciousness' of the indigenes with a 'true' one 'so that the converts could destroy an old order and create a new . . .'.[8] As a result, the impact of 'conversions' on black communities was dislocating and often caused irrevocable schisms in families: 'The kraal was becoming the scene of disagreement, of arguments, of indecision, where authority for patterned behaviour was lost'. 'Conversion' was therefore the initial phase in the subversion of African societies by Europeans. For this reason blacks increasingly resisted the premeditated attempts by missionaries to enforce 'conversion' to Christianity, which they regarded as 'simply an act of treachery'.[9] By the latter half of the nineteenth century many blacks in southern Africa realised the extent to which missionary activity was creating political cleavages in their communities, which divisions had then been vigorously exploited by the expansionist thrust of the white colonists. Moreover, resistance to 'conversion' signalled the unwillingness of blacks to submit to missionary attempts to control them 'through socialisation to a new order'. Blacks came to see that through conversion strategy missionaries were instrumental in creating the 'psychological basis for the politics of colonialism' by persuading them to 'submit humbly even to the worst indignities'.[10]

The proselytising spirit of missionary endeavour rested on an inherent spiritual imperialism which dictated that the primary purpose of the missionary was to preach that 'the God of Europe was superior to the Gods of Africa'. Such cultural arrogance was conceived in the Victorian synthesis of 'God, church and British empire'[11] in which the virtues of Christianity were identified with those of the empire; 'empire and the sway of the church were seen as two sides of the same coin'.[12] Therefore, 'conversion' to Christianity was equally 'conversion' to westernism and imperialism which, according to Guy, 'had nothing to do with the grand principles of justice, and everything to do with the forcible extension of power for some, and its extinction amongst others, with economic change, exploitation and oppression'.[13] For the missionary, 'conversion' was not an option but an imperative because he assumed the superiority not only of his religion and culture, but also his economic and political system.

If at one level 'conversion' entailed a subversion of values, then
at another it meant segregation from the communities which
clung to the 'traditional' order. Consequently missionaries insisted
that 'converts' move to mission stations so that they could
practise their new faith unhindered by 'the continuous influence
of ... traditional beliefs and social controls'. Hutchinson argues
further that mission stations also provided 'converts' with
protection from the 'consequences of social disapproval' which
were bound to accompany any defection from African society.[14]
Such removal from 'traditional' communities to mission stations
highlights how significant missionaries were as a source of social
disruption and dislocation. There can be no doubt that the
upheaval of 'conversion' effected far more than merely a change
in ideology; it coerced blacks into an entirely new lifestyle in an
alien environment. This violence of segregation and alienation
underpinned the establishment of the 'missionary state'. Villa-
Vicencio concludes that it was the missionaries' sense of religious
and cultural superiority 'which caused African converts to be torn
out of their traditional social structure, yet at the same time they
were never allowed to fully enter into the western social structure
of the missionaries'.[15]

Certainly, missionary motivation is sometimes difficult to
fathom, but the evidence is overwhelming that their conduct was
profoundly influenced by the powerful prevailing secular forces of
capitalist imperialism and militarism which distorted purely
religious motives. Despite the apologetic defence of missionaries
in Monica Wilson's 'Conquerors or servants of God?',[16] it is
nevertheless true that they were the most articulate proponents of
western capitalism. As Beidelman points out, they 'were keen to
present most aspects of European life as integrally related, as
though the kind of minds that theologized about sin and salvation
were necessarily those which could develop vaccines, lead
conquering troops, or organise a productive textile mill'.[17]

It should however be emphasised that missionary attempts to
convert blacks to Christianity were often singularly unsuccessful.
African resistance to western religion remained resilient
throughout the nineteenth century and led to feelings of
frustration among missionaries, who increasingly adopted a more
imperialist stance as a result. Because blacks proved less than
amenable to their preaching, missionaries were driven to favour
British expansion as a means of creating a more conducive
climate for the acceptance of their gospel. That blacks were not

passive in the 'missionising' process is evident from the way they sometimes manipulated missionaries for their own economic and political purposes; 'conversion' could be expedient. Moreover African initiative and adaptability is clearly demonstrated by religious syncretism, which response in itself challenged the ideological strait-jacket missionaries hoped to enforce.

## MISSIONARIES AND THE STRUCTURAL VIOLENCE OF COLONIAL SUBJUGATION

Precisely because the secular power to which missionaries looked was the British empire, they were inclined to attribute imperial importance to their activities. Therefore, as Bundy has stated, 'duty and self-interest co-incided'.[18] For them the intrusion and expansion of British administration in southern Africa was a pre-requisite for peace and a sure means of preserving racial harmony. And, of course, imperial expansion and missionary advance were synonymous. In fact, missionary conquest was seen to be conditional upon the establishment of British hegemony. Such reliance on imperial protection for their work made missionaries keen agents, with traders and administrators, of 'alien political expansion':

> By their settlement they threatened independence; by their methods they eroded custom, integrity and authority; by their connexions they invited the imperial replacement of resistant African rule.[19]

The 'brutality and dishonesty of colonialism' is a theme explored by Guy, and in considering the role of mission stations in fracturing Zulu society after 1879 he declares them to be catalysts of political foment, where missionaries were able to instigate opposition to chiefly authority.[20] As resistance mounted against colonial incursion, so missionaries became more inclined to the view that the overthrow of 'traditional' rule by the imposition of British government was 'the necessary precondition for African acceptance of the gospel'.[21] Consequently missionaries became accomplices in the advance of capitalism which was 'pursued by means of racial domination as traditional African societies were incorporated, manipulated, or annihilated for Christianity, commerce and civilisation', and mission stations provided the springboard for this advance.[22] Thus, according to Trapido, the notion of missionaries as the tribunes of African freedom was confined to their own rhetoric.[23]

Missionaries were vociferous in their attacks on chiefly power,

rain-making and initiation ceremonies, but the 'debilitating effects
of Christianity' were especially felt where practices of courtship
and marriage were systematically undermined. Little wonder then
that chieftains saw in Christianity a threat to the political order
which they represented. They resented the violence of
missionaries against accepted social practices such as *lobola* and
polygamy, and the removal of black 'converts' to mission stations
where they were removed from the ambit of chiefly authority and
incited to political activism. Another category of missionary
violence hinted at by Hutchinson is that of expulsion if 'converts'
infringed rigidly-imposed regulations. Such sanctions were used
to exercise social control on mission stations. Defaulters were
summarily banished and found themselves alienated from the
westernised African élite on the one hand and regarded on the
other with suspicion by the 'traditional' community from which
they had originally come. The violence of European technological
change was also evident where missionaries had acted as
'mediators of modernity' in agriculture and industrialisation.
African lifestyle had been profoundly modified as a result and the
population was gradually transformed into 'a reservoir of labour
for the growing European economy'. By ensuring an amenable
labour supply, missionaries became facilitators of industrialisation
in South Africa.

The concomitant surrender of economic independence by
indigenous communities points to a fifth category of missionary
violence: individualisation associated with capitalism's intrinsic
preoccupation with profit and competition. As missionaries
recruited black labour they contributed to peasantisation in
southern Africa and their servicing of the needs of mercantile and
mining capital meant that they played a crucial role 'in the
penetration of the market system into the traditional economy:
through the plough, trading stores and cash crops'.[24] And they
fostered class formation which arose from relatively greater
access by missionised blacks to the market. This has led Trapido
to assert that missionaries have done more than any other
institution to alter the relations of production in the nineteenth
century. Such an analysis is consistent with that formulated by
Majeke as early as 1952:

> It is against this background of vast economic forces that the
> influx of missionaries to the colonies acquires
> meaning ... (They) came from a capitalist christian civilization
> that unblushingly found religious sanctions for inequality, as it

does to this day, and whose ministers solemnly blessed its wars of aggression.[25]

During the course of the nineteenth century it became more and more difficult for blacks to distinguish missionaries from the armoury of imperial bureaucracy, especially as missionaries 'willingly served colonial regimes as channels of communication, agencies for the recruitment and training of lower level administrative staff' and 'inculcators of appropriate values'.[26] It was therefore possible for colonial authority to be mediated through the missionaries precisely because of the 'broad ideological assumptions they shared about policies to be followed towards 'heathen' and non-white peoples in general'.[27] Clearly, the political aims of the British government coincided to a remarkable degree with the goals set by missionaries. Both were engaged in state formation, as in the specific case of the Griqua, which was construed as the 'furtherance of missionary enterprise' and promoting 'civilisation'. Missionaries were doing the government's work for it — through the creation of black élites, for example that at Lovedale in the eastern Cape. It is ironical, however, that these mission-educated élites should have reacted against the structural violence of missionary intrusion by re-establishing their links with the people from which they had been removed and who 'through non-violent protest, through strikes, boycotts and civil disobedience, through sabotage, and ... through armed revolutionary struggle' are attempting to end white supremacy in South Africa. It could be argued, however, that without the missionary influence in black politics of the early twentieth century, the African National Congress may not have constituted itself in such an élitist mould in 1912. It took more than thirty years for the ANC to rid itself of its mission-educated image and establish firmer links with working people.

Significantly, then, missionary violence contributed to resistance. First, 'religions of resistance' emerged in order to counter the 'religion of the status quo'. Ethiopianism was the most powerful expression of religious resistance to white rule and it carried within it the germ of a larger political nationalism. Secondly, resistance came in the form of a complete rejection of Christianity. The corpus of material on 'indigenous' resistance to missionary endeavour by the Nguni, Griqua and Tswana illustrates the catalysing effect of missionaries in the growth of black nationalism.[28]

## MISSIONARIES AND COLONIAL WARFARE

Missionaries no less than anyone else believed that the British
empire was the greatest force for good in a world ripe for
Christianity. And most accepted that because the empire had
been won by war, it could legitimately be extended by war. It
seems that the military virtues were thus considered part of the
essence of a Christian imperial race — 'the aggregate of
imperialism, militarism and racism'.[29]

The extent to which missionary thinking was incorporated into
imperialist ideology is shown by the involvement of missionaries
in colonial warfare. They proved to be militarily useful in many of
the wars and uprisings in southern Africa in the late nineteenth
century. Earlier in the 1800s they had been important suppliers of
firearms to African polities, particularly on the Cape's northern
frontier.[30] The distribution of guns heightened the chances of
conflict and it is significant that smaller chiefdoms looked to
missionaries for a means of protection. The best example of the
military involvement of missionaries is provided by Robert Moffat
of the London Missionary Society (LMS), who was stationed at
Kuruman. In 1823 the Tlhaping, among whom Moffat had been
working as a missionary, were threatened with invasion and
therefore he appealed to the Griqua for aid. Owing to their
possession of firearms the missionised Griqua were dramatically
successful in saving Kuruman.[31] The military importance of
missionaries was therefore emphasised by their access to firearms
and superior armed troops and their influence with British
authorities at the Cape to provide weaponry. The proliferation of
firearms in the interior led to an escalation of violence in the
region and missionaries continually called for military intervention
by the British administration to restore political equilibrium.
Shillington argues, moreover, that the introduction of firearms had
a major impact upon the southern Tswana economy and society
because it produced a 'fundamental shift of emphasis in the
productive basis of the pre-colonial economies of many of the
southern Tswana polities'. And it was the missionaries who
vigorously encouraged the arms trade across the Cape colony's
border during 1858-59.

It has also been demonstrated in recent historical writing that
missionaries were a valuable source of military intelligence. For
instance, they were regarded as a 'virulent source of information
on happenings in the Zulu kingdom' before the Anglo-Zulu war of
1879.[32] It was often alleged that they acted as informers for the

colonial government and certainly mission stations were used as the headquarters of invading British soldiers, especially during the Tswana uprising of 1878. In that conflict the southern Tswana rose in opposition to the extension of alien rule and they rejected the social and economic changes which had accompanied missionary settlement. Typical of the anti-imperialist sentiment was the complaint of the Tlhaping at Kuruman: 'We accepted the Word of God in our youth ... but we did not know all that was coming behind it'. The Tswana conflict epitomised the struggle between a newly emergent Christian leadership and 'traditional' Tswana rulers — it reflected a widespread disillusionment with missionary activity, which was deepened when the LMS mission station at Kuruman gave refuge to the expelled chief, Jantje. Once again the mission station became an island within a kingdom and the struggle 'took place around the missionaries as the symbol of a new order of things'. The missionaries therefore welcomed the British military expedition against the Tswana and the Kuruman station was put at its disposal; 'and symbolically the mission press printed the notices calling on the Tswana to surrender'. When military intervention did not achieve all that the missionaries had hoped for, they campaigned for imperial rule by influencing the 'official mind' and mobilising the support of the churches in Britain. Clearly, the informal religious imperialism of the missionaries had been transformed into the formal imperialism associated with European political expansion.

The ideological captivity of British missionaries to the imperialist cause is evident in Christian support for the Anglo-Zulu war. Missionaries had chosen to relinquish their rather tenuous links with the nineteenth-century peace tradition as they advocated the idea of empire. They increasingly preached a militaristic gospel which had the effect of sanctifying war. Only the controversial Anglican bishop of Natal, John Colenso, condemned war against the Zulu in 1879. In a powerful sermon delivered shortly after the British defeat at Isandhlwana, Colenso declared that vengeance was the wrong response and remonstrated with his congregation not:

> merely to lift up our hands — to make vague professions of penitence, if we do not amend our doings — to keep a day of humiliation and prayer, if it leaves us as thoughtless and headstrong, as regardless of the good, the true, and the just, as vainglorious and self-confident, as reckless of bloodshedding and deeds of violence done in our name, as ready to triumph

boastfully in acts of slaughter and plundering, ravaging and
burning, as before.[33]

Almost without exception, missionaries also endorsed the
British cause during the South African War of 1899 – 1902. What
were the issues at stake in the war as far as missionaries were
concerned? The major preoccupation was British supremacy. In
this sense missionaries were just like any other imperialists. But
they put forward a special reason for wishing to see the triumph
of British arms in South Africa — the spread of their own
missionary work. British hegemony was a pre-requisite for the
smooth and effective expansion of Christianity in the region. Many
missionaries also thought that the fortunes of blacks were
inextricably bound up with the necessity to extend British imperial
rule. Therefore, the plight of Africans under Boer government
became important not for their own sake but as a moral pretext
for imperialist espousal of 'better treatment for the oppressed'
once the Boers had been conquered. The supremacy of the
British would ensure that African as well as *uitlander* grievances
would be redressed, although not in that order. For many
missionaries, blacks merely provided an excuse for imperialist
aims. John Hobson, the anti-war activist, exposed the propaganda
value of claims by missionaries that the war was being fought to
secure justice for blacks in South Africa. He accused them of
masking naked imperialism in the guise of a 'sacred war'. He also
criticised missionaries for serving the interests of capitalism
during the war. There was little doubt in his mind that
missionaries were incapable of speaking their minds freely
because of the hold exercised over them by finance capitalism,
and so they had acquiesced in the face of pressure from mining
magnates, *uitlanders*, politicians and the tide of jingoism which
was swelled by territorial expansion.[34]

Of all the missionary societies operating in South Africa the
LMS did most to generate the myth that the second Anglo-Boer
war was being waged on behalf of the black population. But to
suggest that this was the primary concern of its missionaries
would be an over-simplification. Even John Moffat, the champion
of black interests during the war, conceded that what was more
crucial was 'the preservation of British influence and civilization in
South Africa'.[35] Nevertheless, LMS missionaries focused attention
on the future of blacks after the war. Moreover, the treatment of
blacks by the Boers was a popular missionary theme throughout
the conflict, and the involvement of blacks in the war was

# The English-Speaking Churches and Colonialism

# English-Speaking Churches and Colonialism# The English-Speaking Churches and Colonialism
emphasised. It was the view of some LMS missionaries that the# The English-Speaking Churches and Colonialism# The English-Speaking Churches and Colonialism
# The English-Speaking Churches and Colonialism

emphasised. It was the view of some LMS missionaries that theemphasised. It was the view of some LMS missionaries that the political rights of blacks would be the most pressing issue facing the British authorities after the war. But the LMS struggle to make blacks an important justification for war against the Boers met with little success and missionaries found it increasingly difficult to persuade the former that they would benefit after the war. As the conflict dragged on into 1902 many blacks lost faith in the British forces. They realised to a greater degree than the missionaries the truth of Hobson's challenge:

> Let those who believe that this war is going to result in benefit to the natives read the avowals of native policy made by leading capitalists of the Rand, expressing their intention to reduce Kaffir wages, and to introduce hut and labour taxes, in order to compel natives to offer large quantities of labour to mining companies . . . [36]

Perhaps LMS missionaries failed to canvass support on the question of black rights precisely because they were party to capitalist ambitions. Had they distanced themselves from the mining magnates they may have served the interests of blacks with a more religious motivation. Missionaries lost their independence through alliance with mining and mercantile capital which favoured an extension of imperial control. They had not distanced themselves from capitalist strategies in South Africa and so increasingly came to be identified with them in the minds of many.

Missionary endeavour was therefore seen as, and indeed became part of, the larger imperialist ideology which encountered growing hostility from blacks whose own perceptions of Christianity found expression in separatist churches. Blacks soon realised that their political fortunes had not been central to British policy during the South African war and they became disillusioned with the post-war Native Affairs Commission which proved to them the complicity of Christian missionaries in the extension of capitalist domination.

Missionaries were sometimes also active participants in the British war effort, serving as army chaplains. It was a field of 'Christian mission' which opened naturally to them after many — particularly those in the Transvaal — had been compelled to leave their mission stations when war broke out in 1899. They therefore became part of the military machine and fulfilled a powerful function by endorsing the actions of the British forces. Being at the front and experiencing war at first-hand injected a stronger militarism into their religious brand of imperialism. Their evangelism exploited military imagery and the troops literally became the 'soldiers of Christ'. Furthermore, they reinforced the popular belief that the war against the Boers was the 'Lord's battle' in which a British victory would bring 'glory to his name', and they preached that 'Jehovah is a man of war' and 'the God of armies', citing the Old Testament record.[37] The chaplains' role as the moral conscience of the army gave considerable weight to their pronouncements. Therefore, they tended to confirm in the mind of the ordinary British soldier the justice of the imperialist cause and provided an ethical rationalisation to screen the true motives of empire.

In assessing the part played by missionaries in promoting a militaristic spirit during the South African war, it is suggested here that they actually gave active military involvement a religious respectability which served to quieten troubled consciences. Most missionaries were uncritical of the motives and the conduct of the war and preached a pro-war dogma couched in moral platitudes. This military dimension in the missionary experience in South Africa helps to explain their almost unanimous and implacable opposition to the anti-war lobby in Britain.[38]

An index of the attitudes of missionaries towards violence during the Anglo-Boer war is provided by an evaluation of their opinions about concentration and refugee camps. One might, for example, have expected the Wesleyan Methodist conference which met in Pietermaritzburg in 1901 to have pronounced on conditions in the camps and commented on other aspects relating to the guerilla stage of the war. However, the delegates — many of whom were missionaries — were more concerned about the death of Queen Victoria and the divisive impact of Ethiopianism within their denomination than about the mortality rate in the camps. Increased membership aroused more interest than the plight of Boer women and children or black refugees. Indeed, what seemed to worry most Wesleyan missionaries in 1901 was the impact that the war was having on their urban mission stations. The Diamond Fields' Native Mission, for instance, had been affected by the siege of Kimberley. African labour had declined on the mines and fewer blacks were to be found in the compounds. Therefore the mission contracted. The missionaries looked forward to the final cessation of hostilities so that De Beers could begin work on the Bultfontein and Du Toitspan mines, thereby attracting a large black labour force. This, they hoped, would 'increase the opportunity of the Mission' in terms of proselytisation and financial well-being.

Other missionaries were equally silent on the issue of concentration camps. James Stewart, the eminent Presbyterian principal of Blytheswood and Lovedale, did not even acknowledge that 'methods of barbarism' were employed by the British and there is no mention of 'scorched earth' tactics in his private or official memoranda. The Lovedale mouthpiece, *Christian Express*, also fails to give any detailed accounts of concentration camp conditions and only fleeting mention of relief measures in certain black refugee camps is made in a report found among the Stewart papers.[39] One can only speculate about this 'blind spot' in Stewart's outlook on the conflict. Perhaps he preferred to remain uninformed. This is the more significant in the light of recent research which has shown that conditions in black refugee camps were as severe, if not worse, than in white concentration camps.[40] It is apparent that missionaries were generally willing to ignore the atrocities of the British war effort in the belief that they were the price to be paid for imperial victory and therefore an assured future for Christian penetration.

## MISSIONARIES: REVOLUTIONARIES OR 'SHAPERS OF THE INTERESTS OF OTHERS'?

In conclusion, it remains to consider the extent to which missionaries may be compared with revolutionaries. I have tried to demonstrate in my analysis that missionary ideology was part of the apparatus of capitalist intrusion in southern Africa and was therefore inextricably involved in the structural violence associated with it. The main thrust of my discussion is therefore opposed to Richard Elphick's very generalised proposition that

> ... missionaries, like revolutionaries, were a self-conscious élite, enjoying considerable financial, legal, and social autonomy within their target society; they clearly articulated and debated the scope, nature, and the order of change they wanted; and they aspired to comprehensive upheavals that would affect all groups, all regions, and all aspects of life in South Africa.[41]

Rather, I would submit that missionaries were not separate from the ruling class in South Africa. Indeed, they were an elemental feature of it and therefore did not enjoy such wide 'autonomy' as Elphick allows. Secondly, it is an exaggeration to allege that they could have had a blueprint for massive social upheaval that was intrinsically their own original creation. Is it not also too sweeping an insinuation that missionaries could in fact precipitate a social transformation which would 'affect *all* groups, *all* regions, and *all* aspects of life in South Africa'? Missionary impact was essentially confined to mission stations which were often very isolated and extremely insular. The widespread resistance to missionary work among blacks also curbed its influence and even where Christianisation occurred, missionary authority was increasingly rejected. Religious separatism led to an 'indigenisation' of Christianity and was an effective means of at least containing the invasion of western ideology.

By giving prominence to the structural violence of imperialism, I have essentially accepted a counter-argument to Elphick's, namely, that missionary efforts 'seldom made much headway until other political and economic changes had been imposed' and thus the presence of Christian missionaries 'can hardly be regarded as an independent motor of social change'.[42] The nub of my hypothesis has therefore centred on the subservience of missionaries to the British imperial status quo; their activities were in keeping with the official policy of colonial subjugation and consequently they were permitted to be an extension of imperial rule. In other words, missionaries were under the tutelage of the political decision-makers and were important agents of western capitalism. In this sense, the fears of LMS missionary David Carnegie were well founded: in 1889 he wrote that 'Gold and the gospel are fighting for ... mastery and I fear gold will win'.[43] Once capitalism had assumed pre-eminence, the missionary gospel proved useful in condoning and legitimising mercantile exploitation. Moreover, as Ranger has astutely observed:

> After the conquest and the imposition of colonial rule missionaries were not liberated from the necessity of having to take political and social structures into account, or enabled to concentrate upon purely religious activity. Missionaries now operated within the total context of colonial white activity.[44]

Having preached imperialist religion so faithfully in the various phases of colonialism, it became functional for missionary Christianity to continue bolstering the political status quo. This inherent conservertism of the English-speaking denominations in South Africa has meant that they have been able to resist the dictates of capitalist ideology and have therefore remained consistently submissive even to the strictures of apartheid policy in more recent times.

# NOTES

1.  The most provocative and influential work on missionaries in southern Africa has been N. Majeke's *The Role of Missionaries in Conquest,* (Johannesburg: Ravan, 1952). And B. Hutchinson's 'Some social consequences of nineteenth-century missionary activity among the South African Bantu', in *Africa,* 27(2), 1957 is perhaps the most formative article in the early missiological debate.
2.  R. Elphick, 'Africans and the Christian campaign in southern Africa', in H. Lamar & L. Thompson (eds.), *The Frontier in history, North America and Southern Africa compared,* (New Haven, 1981), pp.270-307.
3.  M.C. Legassick, *The Griqua, the Sotho-Tswana, and the missionaries, 1780-1840: the politics of a frontier zone,* (Ph.D. thesis, UCLA, 1969), p.661.
4.  B. Lincoln, 'Notes toward a theory of religion and revolution', in B. Lincoln (ed.), *Religion, rebellion, revolution: an interdisciplinary and cross-cultural collection of essays,* (London: SPCK, 1985), p.271.
5.  Lincoln, *Religion, rebellion and revolution,* pp.271-272.
6.  Elphick, 'Africans and the Christian campaign', p.278.
7.  J.R. Cochrane, 'The Role of English-speaking Churches in South Africa; A Critical Historical Analysis and Theological Evaluation with Special Reference to the Church of the Province and the Methodist Church, 1903-1930',(Unpublished Ph.D. thesis, University of Cape Town, 1982), p.129.
8.  Elphick, 'Africans and the Christian campaign', p.282.
9.  R. Cope, 'Christian missions and independent African chiefdoms in South Africa in the 19th century', *Theoria,* 52, 1979, p.11.
10. T. Gladwin and A. Saidin, *Slaves of the White Myth: The Psychology of Neo-colonialism,* (Atlantic Highlands: Newman, 1980), p.42.
11. C. Villa-Vicencio, 'Race and class in the English-speaking churches', (Conference on Economic Development and Racial Domination, University of the Western Cape, unpublished paper, October 1984), p.7.
12. C. Bundy, *The Rise and Fall of the South African Peasantry,* (London: Macmillan, 1979), p.38.
13. J. Guy, *The Heretic: a study of the life of John William Colenso 1814-1883,* (Johannesburg: Ravan, 1983), p.219.
14. Hutchinson, 'Social consequences of missionary activity', p.162.
15. Villa-Vicencio, 'Race and class', p.10.
16. M. Wilson, 'Missionaries: conquerors or servants of God?', *South African Outlook,* 110(1258), March 1976, pp.40-42.
17. Beidelman, 'Social theory and missions', p.244.
18. Bundy, *Rise and Fall,* p.38.
19. *Ibid.,* p.658.
20. Guy, *The Heretic,* p.348.
21. Cope, 'Christian missions', p.1.
22. Guy, *The Heretic,* pp.256,348.
23. See S. Trapido, '"The friends of the natives": merchants, peasants and the political and ideological structure of liberalism in the Cape, 1854-1910' in S. Marks & A. Atmore (eds.), *Economy and Society in Pre-industrial South Africa,* (Oxford: OUP, 1980), pp.247-274.
24. Cochrane, 'English-speaking churches in South Africa', p.120.
25. Majeke, *Role of missionaries,* p.4.
26. R. Strayer, 'Mission history in Africa: New perspectives on an encounter', *African Studies Review,* 19(1), 1976, p.9.

27. Legassick, *Griqua, Sotho-Tswana and Missionaries*, p.157..
28. See for example the works by Guy, Legassick and Dachs above, as well as J.T. du Bruyn, *Die Aanvangsjare van die Christelike sending onder die Tlhaping*, (unpublished M.A. thesis, Unisa, 1980).
29. See M. Howard, 'Empire, race and war in pre-1914 Britain', in H. Lloyd Jones, V. Pearl & B. Worden (eds.), *History and Imagination: Essays in Honour of H.R. Trevor-Roper*, (London: Methuen, 1981), pp.340-355.
30. See E. Bradlow, 'The Significance of arms and ammunition on the Cape's northern frontier at the turn of the 18th century', *Historia* 26(1), 1981, pp.59-68.
31. Cape, 'Christian missions', pp.4-5.
32. Guy, *Heretic*, p.256.
33. *Ibid*, p.215.
34. J.A. Hobson, *The Psychology of Jingoism*, (London, 1901), pp.130-133.
35. R.U. Moffat, *John Smith Moffat: Missionary — A Memoir*, (London, 1921), p.330.
36. *British Weekly*, 12 April, 1900.
37. See for example the reminiscences of O.S. Watkins, *Chaplains at the front: incidents in the life of a chaplain during the Boer war, 1899-1900*, (London, 1901).
38. The extent of the anti-war movement in Britain is dealt with in my thesis, 'The Non-conformist Conscience and the South African War 1899-1902', (Unpublished Ph.D. thesis, Unisa, 1985), particularly in chapters 2 and 3.
39. Stewart Papers, BC 106 (J.W. Jagger Library, University of Cape Town).
40. P. Warwick, *Black People and the South African War 1899-1902*, (Johannesburg: Ravan, 1983), pp.145-162.
41. Elphick, 'Africans and the Christian campaign', p.285.
42. Strayer, 'Mission history in Africa', p.12.
43. B. Sundkler, 'The Churches' hinterland', in M.G. Whisson & M. West (eds.), *Religion and Social Change in southern Africa: Anthropological Essays in Honour of Monica Wilson*, (Cape Town & London, 1975), p.99.
44. T.O. Ranger & J. Weller (eds.), *Themes in the Christian History of Central Africa*, (London: Longman, 1975), p.86.

# The Afrikaner Churches on War and Violence

JAAP DURAND AND DIRKIE SMIT

The term 'violence' can be understood in many ways. A distinction is often made between structural or institutional violence and behavioural violence. Another useful distinction is the well-known idea of a 'spiral of violence', according to which structural violence attracts the violence of resistance or revolt, which in turn incurs repressive violence.

In terms of this last distinction, apartheid is fundamentally a violent system, as has often been argued. This means that any comprehensive account of the position of the Afrikaner churches towards violence would necessarily have to take into account, for instance, the Afrikaner churches' response to the diverse racial and discriminatory laws, and the ways they are enforced. In this essay we shall be specifically concerned with the attitude of the Afrikaner churches towards the violence of repression and the violence of resistance.

The Afrikaner churches, like most other churches, do not have a well-defined, authoritative and essentially timeless position on issues of war and violence. They have responded to these issues, like most other churches, in a variety of particular circumstances and therefore with differing voices.

Accordingly, one must approach questions like this cautiously. Church documents, decisions and actions can only be understood properly when they are placed against the backdrop of the time, and viewed within their particular social, political, economic and public contexts. Churches never proclaim timeless ethical guidelines, but respond to specific issues within a very specific discourse in society. Only when one takes note of this discourse, and takes into account the 'real' or underlying questions that are being asked, as well as noting the interests at stake, is one able to grasp something of what the church is really trying to say and what options the church is able to exercise. In many instances, therefore, a church's silence may be even more

noteworthy than what it says, in that it may be a more accurate
reflection of the interests that the church is trying to serve!

In view of this, we focus briefly[1] on certain official responses of
the Afrikaner churches, especially the influential Dutch Reformed
church (DRC), to issues involving war and violence in three
different socio-political contexts, namely

— the First World War and the 1914 rebellion;
— South Africa's participation in the Second World War,
  including the internal resistance to this participation;
— the so-called 'border war', especially in Namibia; responses to
  the establishment of the Program to Combat Racism and its
  Special Fund and the debate within the South African
  churches on conscientious objection, as well as the present
  so-called 'people's war', including the State of Emergency
  and township violence.

During the first two periods there were, of course, strong
sentiments within Afrikanerdom favouring resistance, while during
the third and current period, Afrikaner sentiments to a large extent
have favoured war and the repression of resistance. When viewed
together, attitudes prevalent during these periods may reflect
something of the views of the Afrikaner churches.

## REBELLION AND UNITY (1914-1915)

The formation of the Union of South Africa in 1910 did not help
to bring about the longed-for unity amongst the Afrikaner people.
The conciliatory policy of Prime Minister Louis Botha towards
Britain was resented by a considerable number of Afrikaners with
the Anglo-Boer War and the concentration camps still fresh in
their memories. In January 1914 the Nationalist Party was formed
under Hertzog. Seven months later Britain went to war against
Germany and Botha was requested to occupy the harbours and
radio stations of German South-West Africa. Botha's English-
speaking followers and many Afrikaners were anxious to get
involved in the war, but Botha's nationalist opponents were
equally determined not to get involved in a war for the benefit of
the British empire. When Lieutenant-Colonel Maritz, the
commanding officer of the Union forces in the north-west Cape,
was ordered by Smuts to cross the border of German South-West
Africa, Maritz rebelled and crossed over to join the Germans on
the grounds that the government had promised to make use of
volunteers only. Furthermore, he called on Hertzog, Beyers, De

Wet and other ex-Boer generals to join him. The government responded to this action by declaring martial law. What followed was an abortive armed uprising led by Maritz, De Wet and Beyers which was eventually crushed in February 1915.

The first unofficial reactions in the Dutch Reformed church were decidedly against the rebels. In the Cape a number of professors of theology and ministers published a letter condemning the rebellion, and in the 15 October 1914 issue of *Die Kerkbode,* the official publication of the Cape church, the editorial stated clearly that the insurrection had been unjustified. The circuits of Tulbagh, Colesberg and Cape Town also condemned the rebels for their actions. But these criticisms were all Cape-based and it was soon clear that in the Orange Free State and the Transvaal the DRC was split on the issue of the rebellion. It must be kept in mind that the sufferings of the Anglo-Boer War were still fresh in the memories of the members of the Orange Free State and Transvaal churches. Because of this war and its after-effects of extreme poverty on the one hand and a rampant nationalism on the other hand, there was a growing tendency to consider the Dutch Reformed church as the spiritual bastion of the Afrikaner people, called to identify itself with the people's suffering and their destiny. The rebellion therefore put the church in an extremely difficult position. Theological considerations alone would have forced it to condemn the rebellion and to discipline the rebels, but in doing so it would have been taking sides with the *volk.* By doing this the church would have been instrumental in jeopardising the unity of the Afrikaner people and could even have incurred a split in its own ranks.[2]

Two prominent church members and acknowledged leaders of the Afrikaner *volk,* Dr D.F. Malan and the Rev. Kestell of Bloemfontein, now appeared on the scene in an effort to guide the Dutch Reformed church through this difficult period with a view to preventing a split in the church itself. Through their initiative a special meeting of the Council of Churches (a body which bound together the different provincial Dutch Reformed churches on a federal basis) was convened in Bloemfontein in January 1915.

The document presented at this meeting as a basis for discussion is remarkable for the way in which it identified the fate of the Afrikaner people with the destiny and mission of the church: the unity of the Afrikaner people, torn apart by the

rebellion, could only be brought about by the church. The various
Dutch Reformed churches were therefore exhorted not to take
action against members who participated in the rebellion. With
reference to the ethical issue of the rebels' use of violence against
the state, the document remained true to its ideal of unity in the
church and amongst the people. The armed insurrection was
neither approved nor condemned. The document contented itself
with the general observation that the Word of God expects the
citizens of a country not to resist the legitimate government,
unless for very profound reasons.

The Council of Churches accepted this document in substance,
with a few minor changes of no real consequence. In other words,
the Council did no more than state generally accepted 'Christian
principies', refusing to apply these principles to the matter-at-
hand. The question of whether, in fact, there were legitimate and
profound reasons for the insurrection was not asked, nor were the
rebels admonished for their participation in the rebellion. Indeed,
church bodies were asked not to proceed hastily with disciplinary
action against the rebels because, according to the Council,
armed resistance could not be equated with grave sins against
religion and morality.

For the sake of the unity of the Afrikaner people and their
church, the Council, to paraphrase Dr Malan, refused to take sides
because the church was not called to be a judge in political
matters.[3] He, and others like him, clearly did not realise that the
Council ultimately made a political choice, not perhaps for or
against the rebellion as such, but for the unity of the Afrikaner
people. In making this choice they did not realise that the real
issue at stake for the church was not that of political expediency
but of obedience to the Word of God in matters concerning
violence and the attempted overthrow of a legitimate government.

The different Synods of the DRC subsequently ratified the
resolutions of the Council of Churches. Only within the Dutch
Reformed church of the Orange Free State was there evidence of
a significant opposition led by a Rev. Hefer from Parys, who called
for disciplinary action against the unrepentant rebels in the
church. The response of the Synodical Commission of the
Orange Free State church to the Rev. Hefer's submission gives
one further insight into the reasoning of the church leaders. The
church, it was stated, could not accept the opinion that the rebels
defied the constitution of the church or the Word of God, because
they had acted 'under abnormal circumstances with the light they

had'. Furthermore, the Rev. Hefer and his followers were admonished for attempting to cause friction in the church, because the unity of the church could only be jeopardised by such action.[4]

The reaction of the Reformed Church (Gereformeerde Kerk) did not differ in substance from that of the Dutch Reformed church. At a meeting of its Synod at Potchefstroom in 1916, a lengthy document was tabled in which an effort was made to give a comprehensive overview of the traditional Reformed approach to the problem of resistance against the state.[5]

When one compares this document with the original Reformed writings alluded to, however, a few significant facts come to the fore. Without making a clear distinction between the different phases in the development of Reformed thinking on the matter, the document clearly expresses support for the post-Calvin period of the Monarchomachi, in which the idea of active resistance against the government, as opposed to a passive non-violent resistance, played a more important role. In accordance with this preference for the 'resistance writers' in the early history of the Reformers, the document is far more liberal than Calvin in condoning violent resistance. Whereas Calvin accepted only religious considerations as valid reasons for resistance (for example, a tyrannical government's deliberate abuse of the law of God), the Dutch Reformed church added to this the criterion of the basic 'rights and liberties' of the people. Even more significantly the DRC document accepted the fact that 'the leaders of the people' *(volkshoofde)* could lead active resistance against the government, whereas it is clear in the writings of Calvin that only the 'popular magistrates', who were themselves members of the government, could lead such a revolt against a tyrannical government. In the case of the Monarchomachi, Calvin's 'popular magistrates' became 'inferior magistrates', indeed lesser magistrates than those contemplated by Calvin, but still part of the government and not merely 'leaders of the people'. The Dutch Reformed church was put in the invidious position of somehow having to create a theological and ethical background to justify, not openly but by implication, the actions of men such as De Wet and Beyers who were 'leaders of the people' but did not occupy seats of authority or government. The 'inferior magistrates' of the Monarchomachi provided the 'loophole' and they made full use of it. At no time does the document specifically identify Afrikaner rebel leaders with these 'leaders of the people', but reading

between the lines it is not difficult to discover an implicit
identification. On the basis of the tabled report the Synod of the
Dutch Reformed church neither approved of the rebellion nor
condemned the actions of the rebels, but the theological
exposition in the report was clearly intended to exonerate their
actions.[6]

To sum up: Within Reformed theology the ethical problem of
the justification of violence on the part of the people against the
state has always been addressed against the background of the
idea of the 'last resort' *(ultima ratio)*. When all else has failed and
there is no hope that any other measure could succeed, violence
may be justified as the means by which an unjust government
can be overthrown or forced to end its injustice.

The judgement of the Afrikaner churches with regard to the
rebellion of 1914-1915 must be viewed against this background,
because these churches emerge from the Reformed tradition and
must be judged accordingly. In the final analysis, the questions
that need to be asked about the rebellion from a historical
perspective are the following:
— Did the government act in such an unjust way that its
   overthrow became a necessity?
— Had all other avenues been explored and did violence remain
   the only means for achieving this coup?

Of these two questions the first is more relevant, in that if it is
not possible to answer it in the affirmative, the second question
falls away.

It is not necessary to look far for an answer to the first
question. In no official meeting or document of the Afrikaner
churches were attempts made to justify the rebellion on the basis
that the actions of the government necessitated its overthrow.
Excuses were made for the rebels, and their actions were even
rationalised to a certain degree, but never was it stated clearly and
unequivocally that the rebellion as such was justified on ethical
grounds. The conclusion to be drawn from this seems obvious;
the rebellion could be condemned as an unjustified act. But this
did not happen, despite efforts by individual ministers and
members of the churches to persuade their church authorities to
take disciplinary actions against those who participated in the
rebellion. The Afrikaner churches, for obvious political and
strategic reasons, tried to remain as 'neutral' as possible in the
whole controversy, but by this very attitude condoned a violent
insurrection.

# WAR AND PEACE (1935-1948)

In order to fully understand the attitude prevalent in the DRC during this period, some background information is essential. A brief summary, however, can suffice, since the activities of such Afrikaner organisations as the *Ossewabrandwag* and the *Broederbond* are well-documented, and can be obtained elsewhere.

The following facts should be mentioned:

— The 1930s were marked by a deep political rift within the Afrikaner community caused by Hertzog's Nationalist Party's alliance with Smuts. Those nationalists who, under the leadership of Malan, did not support Hertzog considered themselves the true proponents of Afrikaner nationalism. This rift, however, did not seriously affect the life of the Dutch Reformed churches, where the *smelters* (those who supported the fusion of Hertzog's and Smuts' parties) and the 'purified' nationalists of Malan worshipped together.

— The declaration of war by Smuts in support of the British empire intensified the existing opposition within Afrikanerdom, and the issue of participation in the war became a serious threat, not only on a congregational level, but also due to the varying approaches of the different synods of the DRC towards the issues of war and violence.

— The emergence of an extreme right-wing Afrikaner group, the *Ossewabrandwag,* with its own militant and subversive wing, complicated matters even further for the DRC, especially in the Orange Free State where opposition to Smuts and his war effort was strongest. How could the church denounce violent and subversive actions without being accused of damaging the Afrikaner cause?

The dilemma of the DRC during the war is brought out in sharp relief if we examine a document tabled at the Council of Dutch Reformed churches in 1937 by the Cape Synod.[7] At that time the dark clouds of war were gathering in Europe, but locally there was little suspicion that South Africa would be involved if war should break out. After all, Hertzog was still Prime Minister and nobody could have foreseen Smuts' manoeuver in neutralising Hertzog's opposition to participation in the war, thereby ousting him as Prime Minister and bringing South Africa into the war.

The document is therefore not controversial in itself, but rather provides a well-balanced theological treatise on war and peace, blaming existing tensions in the world on 'apostasy' and pointing out that an armaments race would be to nobody's benefit. The government is called upon to work with the League of Nations to remove the causes of enmity between nations. At the same time the church pledges itself to work together with other churches and organisations seeking peace.

Although the document expresses bias in favour of peace, it is not pacifist in its contents. Christian ethics, it claims, have always maintained the right to self-defence and the possibility of a war waged for the sake of justice and undertaken only as a last resort. Romans 13 gives the state the right to wage war, although in principle war is an evil which should be resisted.

In 1939 war broke out and in the face of strong Afrikaner opposition against supporting England, the South African government of Smuts nevertheless joined the Allies. This altered situation confronted the DRC with the same two problems present during the rebellion: the unity of the Afrikaner people and their church and the issue of the legitimacy of the government, with the concomitant idea of the right of resistance. In the following paragraphs we shall take a look at the varied responses in the DRC to these two issues.

Concern for the unity of the Afrikaner people had prevented the Afrikaner churches from taking a clear and unequivocal stand during the rebellion against violent insurrection. The policies and statements of these churches during the Second World War reflect the same concern. The overall impression is that the churches considered division amongst the Afrikaner people to be the biggest danger resulting from South Africa's participation in the war. A number of instances can be cited to substantiate this impression:

— Days of prayer for the war and those involved in it became a controversial activity. A request for a day of prayer for the 'fighting youth' was initially rejected by the Orange Free State Synod of 1944. A subsequent public storm of protest forced the Synod to reconsider, but ultimately the Synod declared that a day of prayer for the forces in the field could only be held if at the same time prayers were offered for those Afrikaners interned or imprisoned under the emergency regulations.[8] Similarly, the Moderature of the Transvaal DRC Synod expressed their unwillingness to accede to a request of the Governor-General for a day of prayer on behalf of the British empire. Instead they advised ministers to give their

congregations time for intercession, thus allowing for those
who wished to intercede for Britain and the Allies, but also for
those who held opposite views. The Moderature, despite its
own pro-Afrikaner sentiments nevertheless sought to
accommodate those with a different viewpoint for the sake of
unity.[9]

— Despite the resistance of the majority of their members to the
war effort, the Afrikaner churches neither withdrew their
chaplain services to the army, nor questioned the legitimacy
of such a service.[10] At the same time pastoral care of those
Afrikaners interned for political reasons remained a high
priority for the churches. Two meetings between the DRC
and the Prime Minister are on record, in which the
representatives of the church obtained the right to
unimpeded spiritual care and other privileges for the political
prisoners. The Orange Free State Synod of 1944 also
petitioned the Prime Minister either to release all political
prisoners forthwith or to bring them to trial without further
delay.[11]

Even more significant perhaps are specific statements on the
theme of war made by DRC church bodies indicating the different
synods' responses to the changing war situation. During the years
of the war when Germany was regarded as likely to win, the
church showed remarkable restraint in its language and an
obvious primary concern not to play a divisive role in
Afrikanerdom. As the years passed and the fortunes of war
changed, some of the DRC synods showed less concern about
Afrikaner unity and the cause of Afrikaner nationalism was taken
up more openly, the central theological issue being seen as the
legitimacy of a government which had forced the Afrikaner into
an unpopular war.

A comparison of various statements, two by the Orange Free
State Synod (in 1940 and 1944) and one made by the Cape
Synod in 1940, is indicative of this change in attitude. At the 1940
Orange Free State Synod, conscientious objection against
participation in the war by the people of South Africa was raised
as a point of discussion. There was also a request for a message
to the government by the church on the war issue. The Synod
responded by producing a statement called *A Scriptural
Exposition on War.*[12]

The content of this statement does not differ in essence from
the document presented by the Cape Synod in 1937. It is a well-

balanced theological treatise which stressed the following:
— the fact that the state receives its authority from God;
— the responsibility of the subjects of the state to give the state
  the necessary obedience;
— the limitations of obedience to the state insofar as the
  Christian conscience and the demands of the Word of God
  forbid an absolute and unlimited obedience to anyone but
  God;
— the fact that the Bible does not absolutely prohibit war, nor
  rule out the possibility of a just war.

This document is remarkable for the things left unsaid. The
existing war situation is not directly addressed nor is an
ideological stand taken, despite the fact that such a statement
would have had the support of the majority in the Synod. The
Synod was clearly reluctant to force an issue that could easily lead
to controversy, thereby endangering the unity of the church and
that of Afrikaners.

In the same year (1940) at the Cape Synod, a few members
asked for a special sitting at which they tabled *A Message to the
Church on the World Situation*. After what must have been a
heated debate, the message was eventually accepted by the
Synod, although quite a number of representatives abstained or
voted against it on the grounds that the differences of opinion in
congregations on the war issue made such statements
inappropriate.[13]

Just as with the Orange Free State Synod's statement, the
wording of the Cape Synod's message is noteworthy because of
its absence of political argumentation. The document is very
specific in its refusal to evaluate the reasons for the war and the
policies of the participants. In no way, it says, can any of the
parties claim to be waging a holy war for the sake of Christianity.
Having made clear the virtual impossibility for the church of Christ
to take sides in a war between nations, the message proceeds on
a pastoral note, regretting the divisions, intolerance and
embitterment in South African society and exhorting the members
of the church to conduct themselves with dignity, calmness and
faith in God.

Against this background the Synod makes use of a two-edged
sword, condemning irregularities and violent actions perpetrated
by Afrikaners on the one hand, but on the other hand censuring
any action through which the government attempts to force
anyone to act against his or her own conscience.

The ultimate concern of both the documents has to do with the unity within the church and amongst the Afrikaner people. But there is also mention of something that was to become a vehement controversy: the problem of the legitimacy of the government itself.

At the 1944 Synod of the Orange Free State an open attack on the legitimacy of the government disregarded all previous considerations of the unity within the Dutch Reformed churches. With an unprecedented forthrightness the Synod made a political choice in support of the Afrikaner nationalists. This document, *A Message to the Government Concerning the Present War*,[14] is overtly political in its reasoning and language and no effort is made to disguise the civil religion which forms its basic point of departure. The church which in its obedience to God is called on to disobey the government under certain circumstances is clearly identified with the Afrikaner people *(volk)*, and the criterion for this disobedience is the conscience of the people *(volksgewete)*. The argument developed in the document can be summarised as follows:

— Although the *volk* were able to take part in the democratic process according to the Statutes of Westminster, they were outvoted by the English-speaking South Africans and forced into the war against their will.
— Because the war was therefore against the will of the *volk*, they feel assailed in their conscience insofar as the *volk* have their own confession, voice and calling, situated in the holy sphere of the conscience and given to them by God.
— The *volk* therefore only acknowledge a government that under oath would uphold these basic rights and liberties of the *volk*, and in actual fact does so.

The Synod's opposition to the government's war effort was clearly not motivated on theological or ethical grounds, but was political in nature, despite all efforts to give it a religious flavour. At the same time the old Reformed idea of the right to resist was altered beyond all recognition as the church came to be replaced by the *volk*, and the will of God by the will of the *volk*. It is not the deliberate abuse of the law of God by a tyrannical government, but the 'rights and liberties' of the people that forms the basis of resistance.

The 1944 message of the Orange Free State Synod can be considered as significant in the Afrikaner churches' thinking on war. It is even more extreme than the statement of the Dutch

Reformed church at Potchefstroom in 1916 (which it echoes in its
emphasis on the rights and liberties of the people as a reason for
resistance) because of the more overt role that civil religion
played in 1944. What was intended as a prophetic voice in a very
concrete situation became a travesty because of deep
undercurrents of nationalistic resentment. Not surprisingly, the
arguments used in the document were never affirmed in official
statements on the war, and in 1945 at the Cape Synod the DRC
was able to redeem itself theologically to a certain degree. But by
then the war in Europe was over and the issues of war and peace
could be looked at more objectively and less emotionally.

The 1945 Cape Synod expressed a firm option for peace on
the grounds of the deep suffering caused by the war and the
threats of a general world catastrophe through the availability of
inhumane weapons such as war missiles (the V-2) and nuclear
bombs.[15] With this the Cape Synod prepared the way for the
Council of 1947, when the DRC spoke out definitively against war
on theological and ethical grounds.[16] This latter document is of
great importance although it was never fully accepted as the
official standpoint of the DRC.

The document in question tries to answer two questions:

— Is war justified as a means of settling international disputes?
— What should Christians do if their government undertakes an
   unjust war?

The answers can be summarised as follows:

The possibility of a just war is acknowledged, but with serious
reservations. Not only does the Bible clearly place emphasis on
non-violent resistance against injustice, with violence seen only as
a last resort, but the existence of modern technology capable of
mass destruction makes it almost impossible to translate the
theory of a just war into practice.

Because of the nature of modern warfare it is almost
impossible for Christians to escape inhumane repercussions in
which the guilty as well as the innocent suffer. Even in a 'just war'
they may lose their souls. Therefore they have no option but to
resist war in general even though they will suffer for their
convictions, in that few governments are lenient towards
conscientious objectors.

Here we have the prophetic voice of practical pacifism, but
although the Cape and the Transvaal Synods accepted the
argument pertaining to the virtual impossibility of a just war, they
did not commit themselves to any kind of pacifism.

# RESISTANCE, MILITARISATION AND REPRESSION (1970-1986)

During the 1970s an important 'debate on violence' took place in South African church and political circles. An important catalyst to debate was the decision of the World Council of Churches to provide funds for liberation movements through a Special Fund of the Program to Combat Racism (PCR), which is discussed in detail elsewhere in this volume. The issue grew in importance along with the escalation of the war in Angola, the intensification of civil war in Zimbabwe (then Rhodesia), the events in Mozambique, and the local resurgence of African nationalism in the form of the Black Consciousness Movement. Generally speaking, this led to increased polarisation in South Africa and to intensified political turmoil and repression. More assertive political attitudes and activism as well as labor unrest and strikes gave rise to harsh police actions, detentions and increased state repression.

During the 1970s the controversial Special Fund of the PCR led to the DRC's breaking off relations with other churches. By now the different synods of the DRC were joined together in a General Synod, making it consequently simpler to gauge the official reaction of the DRC as a whole towards war and violence.

The General Synod of 1970 expressed its deepest abhorrence of the WCC's 'financial support of terrorist movements'. The example of Christ, says the Synod, teaches us to suffer injustice; it is therefore not the calling of the church to encourage insurrection and violence. Four years later the General Synod severed all official relations with Reformed churches in the Netherlands, giving as the main reason for this action the Reformed churches' support of the Special Fund.[17]

The early 1970s are also marked by a growing consciousness of what the government termed 'total onslaught' against South Africa with its concomitant 'bush wars' in Namibia, Angola and Mozambique.[18] However, no official pronouncements on the subject of war and violence were forthcoming during this period. The attitudes and sentiments of the DRC were rather expressed through its sermons, prayers and pastoral care.

A gradual process of *militaristic conscientisation* set in, however, which culminated in a publication authorised by the Moderature of the DRC and accepted at its General Synod of 1982 as an official church document on conscientious objection.[19] This document provides us with the most up-to-date and comprehensive exposition of the DRC's views on war and the implications of these for both the South African government and the people of this country.

Conscientious objection became the central point of debate for one obvious reason. With increasing urgency, questions were being asked not only about the legitimacy of the government's military actions, but even about the legitimacy of the government itself. But now, in contradistinction to the previous war period, the Afrikaner wielded the sceptre and it was people of other groups who in increasing numbers expressed resentment of their forced involvement in what they saw as an unjustified war for the sake of preserving white domination. The theological response of the DRC to this challenge is most revealing and indicative of the fact that theology and theological ethics are more often a reflection of the perspective from which a specific situation is viewed than an honest evaluation of biblical options within that situation.

The document, not surprisingly, starts off by rejecting total pacifism as contrary to the Christian tradition. But it soon becomes clear that such pacifism is not the issue at hand. What is at stake is so-called 'selective pacifism', the refusal to do military service under certain conditions of war.

One might have expected the authors of the document to take seriously the argument used by selective pacifists and to develop counter-arguments. The argument is widely understood: The option to become a conscientious objector is undertaken because one does not want to take sides in what is considered a civil war as one is convinced that an enduring solution can only be found by non-violent means. However, instead of taking the argument seriously, the authors of the document attack its proponents as being enemies of the state who support 'the so-called freedom fighters', thus being, by implication, militarists posturing as pacifists. The possibility that someone in good conscience can experience the struggle in South Africa and Namibia as a civil war is not considered at all in the document. The existing conflict is a war, not rebellion, and anybody who refuses to fight for 'his country' is a traitor.

Having stated as its premise that South Africa is involved in a state of war with external forces, the conclusions drawn by the document are predictable. The state has the right to defend itself and to this purpose it can call upon its citizens. The citizens for their part are bound to obey and no differences of opinion concerning the way in which the government of the day exercises its duties can relieve them of that obedience. From this viewpoint, civil disobedience in the form of conscientious objection is not directed against a political system but against the existence and orderly function of the state. Neither political arguments nor objections on ethical grounds (such as helping to preserve an unjust social system) are regarded as valid and therefore cannot be used as an excuse for granting an alternative form of national service.

At the time of the rebellion in 1914 and during the Second World War the idea of overriding obedience to God vis-à-vis the state, and accompanying this the acceptance of the possibility of a right to resist formed an intrinsic part of the DRC's line of argument. In its 1982 document on conscientious objection the argument is virtually reversed, to such a degree that neither the church nor individual Christians are allowed to challenge the state in the name of God on the issue of an unjust war. According to the report the ruling party has its own conscience which accepts the normative function of the Word of God. If the government therefore appeals to the basic values and principles of the Bible, nobody, not even the church, can interfere or set itself up as a conscience for the state. This extraordinary argument not only negates the Reformed tradition on the right to resist but also rejects the idea of the church's prophetic voice over against the state, an idea accepted by the majority of Christian groupings and more often than not propounded in the DRC itself!

We have described the DRC's document on conscientious objection as the culmination of a process through which an atmosphere conducive to support for war was created. This process was developed by various DRC studies on themes such as the 'theology of revolution',[20] the 'onslaught against South Africa', 'communism', etc. At the same time, however, the late 1970s and the early 1980s were marked by increasing resistance to the apartheid regime within South Africa, not only politically but also theologically. The DRC came under extreme pressure, not least because it was challenged concerning its stand on apartheid by almost all the Christian churches in South Africa, including members of the DRC family and theologians within its own ranks.

Ambivalence developed within the DRC reflecting a similar ambivalence in the political situation of South Africa, the crumbling edifice of apartheid on the one hand and the extreme and totalitarian measures for the safeguarding of the state on the other hand. This ambivalence manifested itself clearly at the 1986 meeting of the General Synod. A closer look at this Synod is therefore called for, but in order to come to a better understanding of what really transpired in terms of resolutions on war, revolution and violence, we must again, briefly, remind ourselves of what happened during those traumatic years leading up to the 1986 Synod.

During the 1970s the South African military scene was dominated by conflict on the border of Namibia. For the average white South African there was something 'unreal' about a war that was in many ways distant, with relatively few reported casualties. The Soweto uprising of 16 June 1976 was the first concrete indication that the conflict in South Africa would move closer to home. The 1980s heralded this new phase. The ANC replaced SWAPO as official enemy number one, even as the black townships of South Africa replaced the Namibian border as the focal point of attention.

A State of Emergency was declared and the armed forces were called in to assist the police in their efforts to repress the black uprising. These developments inevitably led to a greater militarisation of life in South Africa on the one hand, but on the other hand to a more profound awareness of the ethical challenges of a situation characterised by a spiral of violence and counter-violence.

The DRC responded to these things with deep concern, appealing for peace and calm,[21] but also showing a definite bias towards the forces of law and order and a lack of understanding for the struggle of the oppressed people. An appeal by the National Initiative for Reconciliation to Christians to stay away from work for a day of prayer on' 9 October 1985 was turned down by the Moderature of the DRC. About a month earlier the same Moderature had asked Dr Allan Boesak to cancel a planned march to Pollsmoor jail (demanding the release of Nelson Mandela) for the sake of order, peace and mutual relationships, and 'above all for the Kingdom of God'.[22] Emergency funds were also established by the Moderature for the victims of unrest, but with the clear 'condition' that these funds were meant for those law-abiding people who tried to preserve an orderly community life and for the security forces who suffered or were injured in the course of their duties.[23] A number of examples of the DRC's attitude can be listed, but of greater importance are resolutions taken at the General Synod of 1986.[24]

In a previous paragraph we referred to the ambivalence of the 1986 DRC Synod with regard to the issues under discussion. This ambivalence was the direct result of the church's desire not to lag behind in the process of dismantling selective aspects of the apartheid policy on the one hand, but on the other hand to its determination not to succumb to any real or imagined threat to the white-dominated western way of life in South Africa.

This is the reason why the most important document of the Synod, the report entitled *Church and Society*,[25] combines outspoken criticism of racism, injustice and oppression and a qualified condemnation of apartheid with an almost complete subservience to the state in matters of security. This becomes clear in the report's emphasis on the right and obligation of the state to defend itself and accordingly its right to impose compulsory military training. In this instance, the report says, the citizens of a country have no option but to obey. No indication is given of the moral dilemma that such compulsory participation in military action can cause for those citizens who do not wish to defend a 'way of life' precisely because of those aspects of it that the report itself has rejected. No mention is made of the possibility of conscientious objection. That problem had been dealt with at the 1982 Synod and the report saw no cogent reason to re-open such a debate, even though military action had by now moved into the black townships of South Africa, possibly intensifying the moral dilemma of members of the security forces.

The report does mention the necessity of replacing in an orderly way a government whose legitimacy has become suspect, and it even acknowledges the right to resist under special circumstances, but it is clear that the report only considers these possibilities in theoretical terms. It says so in as many words: 'As a last resort for resistance against injustice, non-violent resistance and civil disobedience cannot be ruled out from an ethical perspective, at least not in theory'. The addition 'at least not in theory' is tantamount, in the times in which the report was tabled, to making the accepted principle almost worthless.

*Church and Society* is clear in its preference for peaceful reform and the total rejection of revolution, violation and anarchy. This is also in line with the way in which the Synod dealt with the *Kairos Document*. A report by the Moderature on the *Kairos Document* in which the document was rejected on the basis of its alleged advocacy and justification of violence was accepted by the Synod, although willingness was expressed for dialogue with the authors. An appeal was accordingly made to all office-bearers and members of the church not to participate in any action that could

cause polarisation, violence, anarchy and 'revolutionary' disobedience to the legitimate authority of the state.[26]
More could be added to point out the shift in the DRC's theological emphasis pertaining to the issues of war and violence subsequent to the Second World War and in the immediate period following the war. Of course circumstances changed, and the relative positions of the different social groups changed. Theology reflects biases and perspectives that are sometimes a matter of life and death. This statement is not meant as an excuse to relativise the sincerity and necessity for theological reflection on these issues, but rather as a challenge to theology to strive constantly towards obedience to the Word of God within the circumstances in which it finds itself, fully aware of the deviousness of the human heart and the self-interest that it serves. Theological reflection and self-criticism should be the two sides of the same coin.

## NOTES
1.  The detailed background information for this analysis will be published separately.
2.  C.F.A. Borchardt, *Die Afrikaanse Kerke en die Rebellie, Teologie en Vernuwing,* (Universiteit van Suid-Afrika, 1975), pp.85-116.
3.  D.F. Malan, *Afrikaner-volkseenheid en my ervarings op pad daarheen,* (Nasionale Boekhandel, 1961), p.30.
4.  J.C. Hefer, *Kerk en Rebellie,* (Paarl), pp.8-9.
5.  *De handelingen van de achtiende algemeene synodale vergadering van Gereformeerde gemeenten in Zuid-Afrika,* 9 Maart 1916, e.v.d., pp.93-100.
6.  Compare Calvin's *Institutes* 4, XX, 31, with the *Vindiciae contra Tyrannos* of Junius Brutus, (ed.) Treitsche.
7.  *Handelinge Raad van Kerke 1935,* pp.23,84-86. It can also be found in the documents of the separate provincial Synods of the Cape in 1936, and Transvaal and Orange Free State in 1940.
8.  *Handelinge OVS 1944,* Verslag A.1. 2(b), p.3; Verslag A.4. 61, p.31; p.362 punt 61; pp.454-455 punt 3; p.467, 'protes-telegramme'; pp.481-482 punt 8; p.483 'biddag-voorstel'.
9.  *Handelinge Transvaal 1944,* Verslag van die Moderatuur 3 (b), p.49.
10.  All the Synods repeatedly discussed the role of the so-called *veldpredikers,* and although it was sometimes an emotional issue, the principle itself was never put to debate.
11.  *Handelinge OVS 1944,* Verslag A.1. punt 6 p.5; Bylae (1) A.1. (6) p.10; Verslag A.4. punt 58 p.31; draft resolution B.33 p.269 with decision on p.365; *Handelinge Transvaal 1944* Bylae by Verslag van Moderatuur punt 13 p.243; p.281 punt 12 en 13; Handelinge Kaap 1945 Addisionele Verslag van die Moderatuur punt 126 p.40 en punt 135 p.41; *Handelinge OVS 1948* Verslag van die Moderatuur punt 7 p.11 met p.289; punt 13 p.12 met p.391.
12.  *Handelinge OVS 1940,* pp.498-501.
13.  *Handelinge Kaap 1940,* pp.283-285.

14. *Handelinge Sinode OVS 1944,* Verslag A.4. punt 59 p.31, and appendix 6, pp.49-53, accepted on p.362.
15. *Handelinge Kaap 1945,* pp.423-424.
16. *Handelinge Raad van Kerke 1947,* pp.44-50. For the reactions of the provincial Synods, c.f. *Handelinge Kaap 1949,* pp.422-423; *Handelinge Transvaal 1948,* p.354.
17. *Handelinge Algemene Sinode 1970,* p.824; *Handelinge Algemene Sinode 1974,* pp.562-563; *Handelinge Algemene Sinode 1978,* pp.33-43,82-127,798-799,955; *Handelinge Algemene Sinode 1982,* p.108. In 1978 the Synod noticed with appreciation the fact that the conference of the Methodist Church in East London also strongly disapproved of the WCC's grant to the Patriotic Front, *Handelinge,* p.927.
18. Compare *Handelinge Kaapse Sinode 1975,* A.2. punt 7 p.160; *Agenda Algemene Sinode 1978,* p.490 en *Handelinge* p.879; also *Agenda Algemene Sinode 1978,* pp.489-490; and *Handelinge Algemene Sinode 1974,* p.582.
19. *Geloofsbeswgare teen diensplig en verbandhoudende sake,* 1980 NGKB: Pretoria.
20. See for example the extensive study in the well-known *Ras, Volk, Nasie.*
21. *Agenda Algemene Sinode 1986,* Verslag van die Bree Moderatuur 2.9.1. p.45.
22. *Ibid.*
23. *Agenda Algemene Sinode 1986,* Verslag van die Bree Moderatuur 2.9.2.10. p.45; 3.2.6. p.60; p.321; *Handelinge,* pp.48-49.
24. For example, the decisions on *banning and detention without trial, Agenda Algemene Sinode 1986;* Verslag van die Bree Moderatuur 2.8.2. p.42; *Handelinge,* p.35; on the *right of resistance, Agenda Algemene Sinode 1986,* Verslag van die Bree Moderatuur 2.8.4. p.43; Verslag AKLAS p.154; *Handelinge* pp.36,82; on *violence and the sanctity of life, Agenda Algemene Sinode 1986,* Verslag AKLAS 4.5. p.91; *Handelinge,* p.62; and *capital punishment, Agenda Algemene Sinode 1986,* Verslag AKLAS 4.14. pp.95-101; *Handelinge,* pp.64-65.
25. The text as accepted will be published separately after the Synod.
26. *Agenda Algemene Sinode 1986,* Verslag van die Bree Moderatuur 3.2.7. pp.60-65; *Handelinge,* pp.49,58,76-77.

# The Black Struggle for Liberation: A Reluctant Road to Revolution

ALLAN BOESAK AND ALAN BREWS

The escalation of violence in recent years and the prospects of the intensification of the violent conflict between those who repress others and those who fight for their survival and liberation in South Africa compel us to again consider the attitudes of the liberation movements concerning violence as a means toward political change. Under consideration is the period in which these movements publically opted for armed struggle as a viable strategy toward the removal of apartheid.

## THE EVOLUTION OF ORGANISED BLACK POLITICS

Contemporary organised black politics was born in 1912 when several political groups were consolidated into the South African Native National Congress, later to be called the African National Congress (ANC). Prompted by the establishment of the Union of South Africa in 1910 the Congress sought to provide direct and independent channels through which the grievances and needs of black people could be communicated to the white government. There was no thought of assuming or sharing power, only the modest aim of facilitating consultation, with the Congress emerging by all standards as moderate and cautious, petitions and delegations being the major focus of its political protest.

Despite the emergence of more radical black political movements such as the Industrial and Commercial Workers Union (ICU) in 1919, and the Communist Party of South Africa (CPSA) in 1921, the first forty years of ANC existence were characterised by an exercise of constitutional options for political change and a consistent rejection by leadership of more militant strategies. Alliances were formed for pragmatic reasons and little

51

effort was made to mobilise mass political support. This meant that ANC policy and tactics usually lagged behind the growing spirit of resistance in the black community. Yet in time, in no small measure due to the involvement of black workers in the ANC (especially in the wake of the 1919-21 black miners' and ICU strike and the increasing militancy of urban and rural blacks in the face of the consolidation of white domination), black leaders were compelled to look to more radical political options. It was not, however, until the fifties that the ANC showed signs of becoming a mass organisation.

# THE PERIOD OF TRANSITION

## TOWARD MASS MOBILISATION

In 1952 Albert Luthuli, the Natal leader of the ANC, in a public statement made after his dismissal as a chief by the white government, assessed the results of the moderate approach of the ANC up to that time[1]:

> ... who will deny that thirty years of my life have been spent knocking in vain, patiently, moderately and modestly at a closed and barred door? What have been the fruits of my many years of moderation? Has there been any reciprocal tolerance or moderation from the Government, be it Nationalist or United Party? No! On the contrary, the past thirty years have seen the greatest number of laws restricting our rights ... In short, we have witnessed in these years an intensification of our subjection to ensure and protect white supremacy ...

By implication a change of approach was required. Luthuli continued:

> It is with this as background and with a full sense of responsibility that, under the auspices of the African National Congress (Natal), I have joined my people in the new spirit which moves them today, the spirit that revolts openly and boldly against injustice and expresses itself in a determined and non-violent manner.

This 'new spirit' was not only the result of intensified government repression following the National Party's 1948 election victory, but also of the new spirit of aggression within the ANC, primarily from the ANC Youth League, formed by a group of young ANC members in April 1944 under the guidance of Anton Muziwakhe Lembede. Driven by a growing militancy in the urban workers' movements the Youth League focused on what it identified as the inadequate and weak organisation within the ANC. It regarded dominant sections of the ANC leadership to be 'a body of gentlemen with clean hands', providing 'an overwhelmingly negative' direction to the prevailing struggle, and the activity of the Youth League slowly began to galvanise the ANC leadership, their emphasis being on 'Africanism' and their goal a popular mass movement. Lodge summarises the essential characteristics of this approach as follows:

> ... this involved a belief in the 'divine' destiny of nations, a rejection of 'foreign leadership', an insistence that leadership should express 'popular sentiments and ideals'.[2]

In a word, the emergence of the Youth League, with its more militant ideology, radically transformed the ANC. The emphasis was not on black leadership, and the awakening of popular consciousness. Strategies of mass action such as economic boycotts, strikes, civil disobedience and non-co-operation were to replace the reactive efforts of the past. The Youth League's Africanist ideology struck deep chords in the experience of working-class blacks and prepared the ground for a liberation movement that, although still firmly non-violent, was less afraid to directly confront the evils of white domination and violence.

This transition was by no means an easy one and was not readily embraced, and a period of internal conflict followed between the old guard 'liberals' and the more militant 'Africanists' who sought to give the black person 'guiding principles which he could feel in his soul'.[3] Whatever the ideological cross currents, the Youth League created within the ANC a new spirit that was to lead to the Defiance Campaign of 1952 in which white supremacy was to be challenged by a disciplined program of civil disobedience. This action heralded the beginning of the new strategy to which Luthuli gave his support.

Inspiration for the Defiance Campaign, found in the practical moral effectiveness of Gandhi's pacifist strategies, and fuelled by the new militancy within the ANC, provided a clear ideological and practical option for non-violence.[4] A disciplined, peaceful initiative against unjust laws was planned and because of the desire of the leadership to maintain control of the campaign, it was to be conducted by trained volunteers with the masses encouraged not to participate.

Again the ANC leadership was criticised for its restraining influence on the enthusiasm of its grassroots membership. Clearly by this time the ANC leadership, despite the influence of the Youth League, lagged behind the determination and militancy of its membership. But confronted by intransigent state oppression the spontaneous anger of the people could not be contained, leading to major riots and rebellions in Port Elizabeth, East London and Kimberley that exceeded the intentions and control of ANC leadership. Luthuli saw these events as the breaking of the chain which restrains black anger.

> What follows when the chain breaks is not riot and the restoration of order. It is riot and counter-riot. That was certainly true of the series which broke out in 1952 . . . [5]

This breaking of the chain prompted the ANC leadership to call off further acts of defiance. Despite careful planning and the involvement of disciplined volunteers, the campaign could not be controlled. The irony is that notwithstanding the ambivalence of ANC leadership, the Defiance Campaign dramatically increased the credibility of the ANC in the eyes of the masses. The movement's card-carrying membership rocketed from 7 000 to 100 000 within a year. This mass awareness was the new spirit of which Luthuli had spoken. And the reaction of the state was predictable. Determined to destroy the 'new spirit', it unleashed a program of repressive violence without precedent. Fifty-two ANC leaders were served with indefinite banning orders and others were restricted. This was followed in subsequent years by increased police brutality, the harassment of popular leaders and ultimately the treason trials. The story of the extent and nature of this period of repression is told elsewhere.[6]

In the meantime both the ANC and the mainstream Youth League had rejected important aspects of the radical ideology of Lembede which insisted on the exclusion of whites and favoured a strategy of popular militancy. It was a period of ideological re-alignment for the ANC within which the more moderate old guard and radical nationalists could co-exist. From this emerged the Congress of the People in June 1955 which adopted the Freedom Charter, providing a vision for a non-racial, democratic South Africa.

This did not satisfy the radical Africanists who claimed that the 'slogans' of the Freedom Charter were not being translated into concrete political programs capable of realising the envisioned goal. In other words, they regarded the principles of the Charter to be ideals suspended above the political struggle without becoming material forces within black politics. They demanded a more revolutionary approach in the name of true African Nationalism.[7] It came in the form of the Pan-Africanist Congress (PAC). The Africanist movement, an identifiable, yet unstructured group within the ANC formally constituted itself as the Pan-Africanist Congress (PAC) in April 1959 under the leadership of Robert Mangaliso Sobukwe.[8]

Ideologically, the position of the PAC brought into stark relief the reality of power in South Africa. In the words of Sobukwe:

> We have been accused of blood-thirstiness because we preach 'non-collaboration'. I wish to state here tonight that it is the only course open to us. History has taught us that a group in power has never voluntarily relinquished its position. It has always been forced to do so. And we do not expect miracles to happen in Africa.

Unfortunately the ideological implications of another sentence in the same speech of Sobukwe would prove fatal to the PAC. He also said:

> All we are required to do is show the light and the masses will find the way.[9]

The major ideological difference between the ANC and the PAC and one which was to affect their praxis in armed struggle revolved around the issue of spontaneity and organised leadership. The PAC approach was characterised by the belief that all they had to do was provide the spark and the fire would automatically catch alight. This naturally meant that little energy was devoted to organisation and discipline. The ANC, on the other hand, held that even the spontaneous responses of the masses require careful direction:

> when a spontaneous movement takes place the duty of leadership is not just to follow spontaneously but to give it proper direction.[10]

The danger inherent in the political realism of the ANC with its emphasis on organisation, discipline and direction was that resistance could become the domain of leadership. The movement could become élitist and isolated from the masses. The opposite is true of PAC, whose emphasis on spontaneity could lead the undisciplined masses to take suicidal risks in an inadequately co-ordinated campaign. It was these ideological divergences which influenced the thoughts and actions of these two organisations during the Sharpeville period and beyond.

## TO SUBMIT OR FIGHT

The violence at Sharpeville, a black township in the south-eastern Transvaal, occurred within the context of a campaign against the pass laws announced by both the ANC and PAC in December 1959. The PAC's campaign began on 21 March 1960, ten days before the scheduled protest of the ANC, the demonstrators being urged to remain strictly non-violent. Their task was not to engage in a sustained campaign of resistance but to 'touch off the initial spark, giving a tottering and explosive situation one well-placed shove'.[11] This meant, in the PAC's analysis, that if the initial impetus was provided, the grassroots masses were ready for a final showdown with the white oppressors.

Violence erupted at Sharpeville when police opened fire on a crowd of protestors, killing 67 (the great majority shot in the back), and wounding 186 others, including children. This not only elicited widespread international outrage but sparked off a chain reaction of internal protest and upheaval throughout South Africa. Much of the unrest was beyond both the intention and control of the protest organisers. Once again, as in 1952, the latent violence always present amongst oppressed people, sparked by police action within the context of sustained state violence, erupted.

The response of the state was again swift and violent. On Wednesday 30 March a State of Emergency was declared and the leadership of the ANC, PAC and others were detained. The viciousness of state repression was nowhere more clearly shown than in the breaking of a strike in the Cape Peninsula, although this is but one example. The strike followed the planned pass law protests and culminated in a mass march of 30 000 blacks from Langa township to the city centre of Cape Town. Led by Phillip Kgosana, the marchers peacefully reached the Caledon Square police station where Kgosana agreed to end the march, convinced that the demonstrators had made their point and after being promised, in negotiation with the police chief, an appointment with the Minister of Justice on the following afternoon. Despite being warned not to keep the appointment Kgosana insisted, and his unexpected arrest provided the initial step in the state's cruel determination to crush this challenge to white power. Restrained and non-violent protest was met with an increase of systematic police violence and the detention of about 1 750 people:

> It took the police four days of continuous brutality to break the strike. They used sticks, batons, crow bars, guns and Saracen armoured cars to comb the township and force men back to work.[12]

Finally, on 8 April 1960 the ANC and PAC were banned in terms of the Unlawful Organisations Act. The leadership that was not in detention either went underground within South Africa or left the country to make plans for the operation of the liberation movements in exile. Both organisations were scattered and a long period of regrouping and restructuring around a different approach to resistance was to follow.

Some have suggested that the Sharpeville crisis represented a historical movement in which 'extraordinary' opportunities relating to both the revolutionary potential of urban confrontation with the state and the vacuum created in the rural areas were missed:

> All over rural South Africa small and even medium-sized towns were suddenly denuded of their police, who were rushed to the urban centres. In almost no case did local Africans attempt to exploit the vacuum thus created in the countryside.[13]

Admittedly the emphasis of the popular movements of the time was primarily on the urban situation, possibly because of the massive urbanisation of the black population since the 1940s, and the rural context, which was of great significance in the early part of the century, only received greater prominence after the advent of the United Democratic Front (UDF) in 1983. However, at that time, neither the rural nor urban situations could be exploited because of the lack of organisational structure and planning. The plan had been to set alight the spontaneous fire by providing a spark. The willingness of the state to use repressive violence had, once again, been severely underestimated and the government used Sharpeville as a pretext to increase its security legislation to include provision for indemnified police action and extended detention without trial.

Sharpeville was a critical moment in the history of South Africa when, confronted by an intransigent oppressive state determined not to tolerate any protest at all, black political leaders were forced to begin thinking in terms of a revolutionary strategy. This was not so much the result of hard-nosed political analysis but rather

> the sense of crisis generated by the Sharpeville shootings and their aftermath appeared to be a vindication of a programme of armed insurgency.[14]

All other political alternatives had been foreclosed. The violence of white South Africa had created the conditions under which counter-violence was inevitable. What remained to be resolved was the precise nature of the armed resistance. An extract from the testimony of Nelson Mandela at his trial in 1962 illustrated this point:

> *They (the white government) set the scene for violence by relying exclusively on violence to meet our people and their demands . . .* We have warned repeatedly that the government,

by resorting continuously to violence, will breed, in this country, counter-violence amongst the people, till ultimately, the dispute between the government and my people will finish up being settled in violence and by force.[15]

In 1964, again on trial, Mandela would use the words of the document which introduced the armed struggle of the ANC:

The time comes in the life of any nation when there remain only two choices — submit or fight. That time has now come to South Africa. We shall not submit and we have no choice but to hit back by all means in our power in defence of our people, our future and our freedom.[16]

## APPROACHES TO ARMED RESISTANCE

The situation out of which the organised armed struggle was born was already violent. The perception that a well-directed strike would provide the impetus for a mass uprising led to a multiplicity of isolated small groups making their own plans for violent political struggle. This phenomenon is of vital importance because of the near-parallels we find on the internal black political scene today, some 26 years later. Mandela described these groups at his 1964 trial:

Small groups had arisen in the urban areas and were spontaneously making plans for violent forms of political struggle. There now arose a danger that these groups would adopt terrorism against Africans, as well as whites, *if not properly directed.*[17]

### *UMKHONTO WE SIZWE*

The impetus for the birth of *Umkhonto we Sizwe* ( 'Spear of the Nation') as the military wing of the ANC was therefore provided not only by the need to counter state violence but also by a desire to provide clear direction for the energies and mood of militant blacks. As Mandela put it:

Unless responsible leadership was given to canalise and control the feelings of our people, there would be outbreaks of terrorism which would produce an intensity of bitterness and hostility between the various races of this country.[18]

The decision to launch *Umkhonto* was taken with great reluctance. Not only were Mandela and his colleagues distressed at the need for this change, but initially some distance was kept between the ANC as a mass political organisation and the armed forces of *Umkhonto*. Tensions that developed between Mandela and Luthuli, the ANC leader at the time, took some years to resolve. Further, the ANC did not immediately alter its traditional non-violent position but suggested that it would 'no longer disapprove of such acts if "properly controlled"'.[19]

For *Umkhonto,* the options were fourfold: sabotage, guerilla warfare, terrorism, and open revolution. Because of the desire to avoid bloodshed and loss of life they chose the sabotage of economic installations and targets of economic and political significance as the way ahead. The campaign of sabotage was launched on 16 December 1961 and was intended as a forceful invitation to change directed towards the South African government. *Umkhonto* expressed its hope as follows:

> our first actions will awaken everyone to a realisation of the disastrous situation which the nationalist policy is leading. We hope we will bring the government and its supporters to its senses before it is too late, so that the government and its policies can be changed before matters reach the desperate stage of civil war.[20]

The intention was not the violent overthrow of the government but the more modest aim of creating a climate of urgency that would emphasise the necessity of a negotiation process. This strategy, according to Mandela, offered the most hope for future race relations.

This does not mean that the ANC abandoned non-violent forms of resistance. The primacy of political leadership and the subordination of all use of armed force to that leadership has always been affirmed by the movement.

The long-term political analysis of the *Umkhonto* strategists was that the sabotage campaign would initiate, if necessary, a period of ongoing armed struggle in which guerilla warfare would be the next stage. Realism persuaded the ANC that it was necessary to prepare for the intensification of an extended struggle. Whether the prepared strategies would be used depended on the willingness of the white government to negotiate. Mandela envisaged a process of conversation and concession in which the black majority would gradually attain greater participation in central government in a unitary South Africa. As the moment for such negotiations was allowed to pass, black determination to attain political power could only intensify.

State repression resulted in the 1960s becoming a decade in which political resistance in the form of mass mobilisation was almost non-existent. It was essentially with the protests which began in Soweto in 1976 that mass-based political action re-emerged. However, three factors are important for our purposes.

Firstly, whether the ANC *caused* the 1976 upheavals or not, it certainly emerged with renewed popularity and credibility.[21] Secondly, it is doubtful whether the ANC would have been in a position to experience a resurgence of popularity were it not for the armed struggle pursued over the previous one-and-a-half decades. Thirdly, the ANC saw the resistance of 1976 and the subsequent riots and repression as a sign of the need to intensify its guerilla strategy. In 1981 the ANC president, Oliver Tambo, warned that the officials of apartheid were to be regarded as targets and that combat situations might arise in which civilians could be caught in the crossfire.

There has been extensive debate on whether the current armed strategy of the ANC continues to include an unwillingness to directly strike at civilian or 'soft' targets. Targets of insurgent attacks have primarily been state, police and military institutions. Armed attacks have also been directed against border farmers, who are seen by the ANC as having been incorporated into the South African security network. There have, however, also been explosions in shopping centers and other 'soft' targets, causing further questions to be raised concerning the possibility of a shift in ANC strategy. Some reports suggest that these actions have caused a measure of concern to ANC leadership because of the contradiction with official policy.[22] Similar confusion has been created by the use of the 'necklace' method of dealing with those believed to be traitors to the black struggle. As in 1952, 1960 and 1976, the ANC has not always been able to exercise control over all the violent activities of angry, oppressed people.

## SOUTH AFRICAN COMMUNIST PARTY INFLUENCE

The criticism that Mandela originally and later *Umkhonto we Sizwe*, were heavily under the control of the South African Communist Party (SACP) needs comment. Suffice it to say that Mandela was never a communist. He was, by his own admission, influenced by Marxist thought and accepted 'the need for some form of socialism' in the future of South Africa.[23] The document, written in Mandela's handwriting, that has been extensively quoted by the South African propagandists reads:

> We Communist Party members are the most advanced revolutionaries in modern history.[24]

What both P.W. Botha and the Department of Information booklet, which has made extensive use of the quote, fail to mention is that it is a direct quote from a Chinese book in a manuscript on which Mandela was working. He neither composed the words nor did he appropriate them as his own.[25]

In the final analysis, it is difficult not to concur with Karis' conclusion in this regard:

> Most students of South African black politics do not believe that the ANC is dominated or controlled by the South African Communist Party. Their key premise, grounded in South African history, is that non-Communist African leaders work with Communists for their common end of opposing white domination ... The allegation of outright Communist control over the ANC cannot be substantiated ... [26]

## POQO

There were those who from the initiation of armed struggle acted with less restraint. The PAC too gave birth to an armed resistance movement, which because of its more militant ideology, was less controlled than *Umkhonto*. The movement was known as *Poqo*, which meant 'alone' or 'pure', denoting the separatist nature of the Africanist perspective. Lodge comments:

> Poqo was the first African political movement in South Africa to adopt a strategy that explicitly involved killing people and it was probably the largest active clandestine organisation in the 1960s.[27]

*Poqo*, in accordance with the PAC approach, did not place a great deal of emphasis on organisation and discipline. The vision of a spontaneous mass uprising initiated by the heroic actions of a few cadres remained compelling. Potlako Leballo, the leader of *Poqo*, aiming for 'independence by 1963', outlined the process of this uprising. It would begin with mass recruitment, followed by attacks on strategic targets on a prescribed day, accompanied by the indiscriminate killing of whites. Needless to say, due to the infiltration of informers and impulsive actions by leaders the uprising never materialised. *Poqo*, or the Azanian Peoples Liberation Army (APLA), as it was known from 1968 onwards was all but destroyed and the PAC has struggled to find its revolutionary feet in an exile which has extended long beyond its initial expectations. The less militant, but no less revolutionary, and more structured approach resulting from the ANC perception of a protracted struggle has proven more realistic.

The ideological perspective represented by the PAC continues, however, to hold great popular appeal and relevance. The Black Consciousness Movement (BCM), in the form of the South

African Students Organisation (SASO), the Black Peoples Convention (BPC) and others took up where the Africanists left off. Leaders such as Steve Biko became the ideological heirs of Lembede and Sobukwe. Gerhardt makes the point:

> Almost point for point, SASO had arrived anew at the diagnosis and cure originally devised by Lembede and Mda in the 1940s under the rubric of Africanism.[28]

The emphases of black consciousness have recurred with relentless persistence in recent South African history. The mobilisation of the masses is impossible without a profound rediscovery of the dignity of being black.

## TOWARD AN EVALUATION

The three standard criticisms of the ANC option for armed struggle can be summarised as follows: Firstly, the option for the sabotage of strategic targets by trained guerillas is said to have the effect of 'isolating the vanguard from the masses', tending to leave the majority of blacks as observers to a struggle being conducted *for* them.[29] The question is posed whether the exile movement would not do better to spend its energies on internal conscientisation. The ANC has, of course, never lost sight of the importance of mass politicisation, and when state repression has prevented all legitimate black politics from taking place it has been the reality of the armed struggle that has contributed to the kind of conscientisation required. A second criticism suggests that the remoteness of the exiled leadership from the impoverished workers has isolated them from the urgency and militancy of people living in the townships under the continued threat of suffering and death. Whether this was ever the case is debatable, but clearly the influx of exiles into the movement in the post-1976 period has re-established direct contact between those in exile and those in the townships.

A third standard criticism is that the ANC has not always been able to predict or control the excessive violence which inevitably arises from mass action. Analyses have shown that such 'excesses' have at times been instigated through *agents provocateurs*. Nonetheless, the violence latent in an angry community, long the victims of repressive legislation and always holding within it the possibility of anarchical dimensions, compounded by the readiness of a criminal element to exploit any disturbed situation, inevitably presents problems of control for a movement-in-exile. More recently, the emergence of vigilante groups *(Mabangalala)*, characterised by implicit or explicit police support and direct violent opposition to anti-apartheid activists and organisations, is for example, a sinister aspect of 'excess' violence for which the state has much to answer.[30]

Violence has also increased where responsible leadership has been prevented from fulfilling its role. Eager to destroy all organised resistance, the state has created a situation within which unco-ordinated small groups or individuals, determined not to submit to repression, resort to acts of violence that the exiled leadership is simply not able to oversee. While not all these groups would claim allegiance to the ANC, evidence suggests that the ANC leadership has tried to ensure that the use of violence in the pursuit of freedom remains disciplined and directed. It may not always have succeeded.

Positively, the armed struggle has despite its apparent lack of objective results become a symbol of resistance which has enabled the ANC to maintain considerable influence within South Africa through 25 years of exile.[31] It can, for example, be argued that the decline of the visible profile and popularity of the PAC is partly the result of its failure to be engaged in high-profile armed attacks on the state. The ANC has walked a tightrope between the growing tide of anger within black South Africa on the one hand, and a desire to avoid racial divisions and maintain international credibility as a movement worthy of being a government-in-exile on the other. On the international level at least, the disciplined and limited use of violence has been an important ingredient in the equation that has enabled at least one seasoned journalist of the western liberal tradition (who is not uncritical of the ANC) to suggest that the ANC remains 'the broad, true church of black politics'.[32]

Nonetheless, there remain those who ask whether all non-violent options of political struggle have been explored. Whilst it is difficult to comprehensively analyse the attempts at non-violent resistance in the past, indications are that favourable conditions for the exercise of these options do not exist. For instance, the effectiveness of non-violent strategies assumes a responsive government and a press which can freely communicate the rationale behind resistance. It is further necessary to have the backing of some basic reference such as a constitution or an independent judiciary which can test and challenge state action and also to be able to point to concrete victories won by such non-violent tactics. Clearly the South African government has consistently failed to respond positively to non-violent action. On the contrary, through repressive violence and State of Emergency clampdowns it has relentlessly denied people all recourse to passive resistance, thus making revolutionary counter-violence inevitable. In fact it is precisely the lengths to which the state has been prepared to go in order to preserve white privilege and power that has continued to alarm its opponents. The words of a former saboteur illustrate the point:

> Having talked of fascism for a decade and more, the movements were nevertheless caught by surprise when the police behaved like fascists.[33]

A full analysis of the violence of the South African state is impossible here, but some brief statistics indicate its brutality.[34] Between 1960 and 1983 more than 3,5 million people were victims of forced removals with a further 1,8 million under threat. From the introduction of detention-without-trial in 1963 until June 1985, at least 72 people died in or as a direct result of detention under this legislation. During the 1985 State of Emergency an estimated 11 500 people were detained without trial, amongst them more than 2 000 children under the age of 16. A further 25 000 people were arrested and charged with 'public violence', only a negligible proportion of which number ever came to trial. Even more alarming are the statistics relating to the State of Emergency imposed in June 1986, especially concerning the increasing numbers of children detained and the amendment of the Public Safety Act to include provision for an initial detention period of 180 days in contrast to the old 14 days.

Regarding militarisation, the South African defence budget has increased from R44 million in 1960/61 to an estimated R4 800 million in 1975/6, resulting in a massive military build up within the country. Apart from the extensive internal use of the armed forces in suppressing black resistance, the period since 1980 has seen the South African military machine repeatedly used, in the name of 'pre-emptive' action, to invade neighbouring territories, including major cities in Lesotho, Botswana, Mozambique, Zimbabwe, and Zambia. Indications are that South Africa has also given military support to the right-wing dissident movements of *Unita* in Angola and *Renamo* in Mozambique, further destabilising the sub-continent.

Yet perhaps the most disturbing aspect of state violence lies in the senseless killing of children.[35] For example, since the death of 13 year-old Hector Petersen in Soweto in 1976, other victims have included Bernard Fortuin (10), killed in the streets of Elsies River, Cape Town in 1980, and the three children shot in the 'trojan horse' incident in Athlone, Cape Town in 1985 when the police opened fire on a group of children from the back of a South African Transport Services truck. Many similar instances could be recounted. The Detained Persons' Support Committee estimates that between 30 and 40 percent of the approximately 30 000 persons detained between 12 June 1986, and 15 April 1987, were children under the age of eighteen.

Account could also be given of the violence of the pass laws, inferior education, influx control, and discriminatory labour legislation. In short, the magnitude of the destruction and suffering caused by the repressive violence of the state indicates where the greatest perpetration of violence lies in South African history.

History seems to suggest that 'there are more people who would use violence to protect what is already theirs than there are people who would use it to acquire new possessions'.[36] No one doubted that the South African state was prepared to violently protect its power and interests. What continues to surprise black leaders, however, is the extraordinary severity of the violence the state employs and the apparent acceptance of this violence by white South Africa in general. Let this not, however, negate the converse reality that revolutionary violence is equally inevitable in response to a repressive state. It is the state, not the masses, that creates the conditions for revolution and any consideration of revolutionary violence is ethically suspect and analytically illegitimate without prior consideration being given to the violence of oppression which gives rise to the violence of revolution. Some have criticised the ANC for not being ruthless enough in its policy of armed struggle in response to the violence of the state. A Scandinavian diplomat remarked in private conversation that he was disillusioned with the ANC's moderate approach, asserting that a truly revolutionary movement would have taken far more drastic and violent action to bring about its desired aim. On the other hand it is the ANC's commitment to the non-racial and democratic future of South Africa that has resulted in its restrained program of revolutionary violence. This limited violence actually suggests that the ANC is measurably more committed to a peaceful future than is the state with its less restrained repression. A quote from Oliver Tambo's speech on the occasion of the 75th anniversary of the ANC, later used by the

Commissioner of Police in an affidavit for a Supreme Court
hearing in April 1987 makes the point:

> The need for us to take up arms will never transform us into
> prisoners of the idea of violence, slaves to the goddess of war.
> And yet, if the opponents of democracy have their way, we will
> have to wade through rivers of blood to reach our goal of
> liberty, justice and peace.[37]

Ultimately, true revolutionaries are not characterised by the
extent of their violence, but by the determination with which they
pursue the purpose of their revolution. And clearly the more
intense the struggle, the greater the necessity for cohesion,
discipline and organisation. Equally, a protracted conflict will
necessitate more radical strategies from the revolutionary
movements.

The questions before us are: Has the armed struggle of the
liberation movements in South Africa been an inevitable response
to the violent domination and exploitation of blacks? If so in which
form has the guerilla war been most effectively waged?

These questions are answered differently by people from
different social groups in South Africa. Indications are that for the
majority of oppressed blacks the issue is not violence but
liberation. For them the debate on violence is a luxury only those
not deeply engaged in an intensive struggle for liberation can
afford. This point is well made in the essay by Frank Chikane also
included in this volume. For some oppressed people, daily
confronted by the violence of the South African state, the armed
struggle of the popular liberation movements is not an academic
option but, in addition to all else, a welcome sign of hope.

A concluding glimpse at the violence of the South African state
on the one hand and revolutionary violence on the other reveals a
stark contrast. In this regard the comment of Archbishop
Desmond Tutu on returning from consultations in Lusaka with
Oliver Tambo and other ANC leaders puts the violence debate in
its proper perspective:

> ... Mr Tambo could quote abroad the statistics that the ANC
> had caused 80 deaths from 1976 to 1984, and the security
> forces had been responsible for 2 000 deaths since 1984.[38]

## NOTES

1.   A. Luthuli, *Let my People Go*, (Johannesburg: Collins, 1962), p.235f.
2.   T. Lodge, *Black Politics in South Africa since 1945*, (Johannesburg: Ravan, 1983), p.20f.

3.   G.M. Gerhardt, *Black Power in South Africa*, (Berkeley: University of California Press, 1978).
4.   Lodge, *Black Politics in South Africa*, p.61.
5.   Luthuli, *Let my People Go*, p.126.
6.   See for example, T. Karis and G. Carter (eds.), *From Protest to Challenge, Vol.3*, (Stanford, California: Hoover Institution Publications, 1977), p.3ff.
7.   *Ibid.*, p.501.
8.   Gerhardt, *Black Power in South Africa*, p.151f.
9.   *Ibid.* p.184f. These words of Sobukwe were uttered in 1949 and expressed the essence of his basic ideology in later years.
10.  Lodge, *Black Politics in South Africa*, p.84.
11.  Gerhardt, *Black Power in South Africa*, p.232f.
12.  Lodge, *Black Politics in South Africa*, p.223.
13.  R.W. Johnson, *How Long Will South Africa Survive*, (Johannesburg: Macmillan, 1977), p.19.
14.  Lodge, *Black Politics in South Africa*, p.225f.
15.  Karis and Carter, *From Protest to Challenge*, p.740.
16.  *Ibid.*, p.777.
17.  M. Benson, *Nelson Mandela, The Man and the Movement*, (New York: W.W. Norton and Co, 1986), p.148.
18.  Karis and Carter, *From Protest to Challenge*, p.772.
19.  Benson, *Mandela*, p.106.
20.  Karis and Carter, *From Protest to Challenge*, p.717.
21.  Lodge, *Black Politics in South Africa*, p.339.
22.  In 'South Africa: The ANC' in *Africa Confidential* Vol.27, No.25, 10 December 1986, p.1.
23.  Benson, *Mandela*, p.154.
24.  Quoted by President P.W. Botha in a speech in August 1985 and in the Department of Information booklet, *Talking to the ANC*, (Johannesburg: Perskor, 1986).
25.  Benson, *Mandela*, p.155.
26.  T. Karis, 'South African Liberation: The Communist Factor', in *Foreign Affairs*, (Winter 1986/7), Vol.65(2), p.267f.
27.  Lodge, *Black Politics in South Africa*, p.241.
28.  Gerhardt, *Black Power in South Africa*, p.272.
29.  C. Bundy, *Remaking the Past, New Perspectives on South African History*, (University of Cape Town: Department of Adult Education and Extra-mural Studies, 1986), p.74.
30.  See the study on vigilante activities by N. Haysom, *Mabangalala: The Rise of Right-Wing Vigilantes in South Africa*, (Johannesburg: University of the Witwatersrand, 1986).
31.  J. Lelyveld, *Move Your Shadow*, (Johannesburg: Joseph Ball Publishers, 1986), p.328.
32.  *Ibid.*, p.328.
33.  Lodge, *Black Politics in South Africa*, p.239.
34.  Statistics on forced removals are from Lauren Platzky and Cheryl Walker, *The Surplus People*, (Johannesburg: Ravan Press, 1985), those on detentions and militarisation are in *INFO '85*, (Johannesburg: Human Awareness Programme), and in *Mission to South Africa: The Findings of the Commonwealth Eminent Persons Group on South Africa*, (London: Penguin, 1986), p.62ff.

35. See accounts of some of these killings in a soon to be published collection of Dr. Allan Boesak's speeches entitled *If this is Treason, Then I am Guilty*, (Grand Rapids: Eerdmans).

36. A.A. Mazrui, *Toward a Pax Africana*, (London: Weidenfeld and Nicholson, 1967), p.145.

37. *The Argus*, 25 April 1987.

38. *Cape Times*, 23 March 1987.

# THE CONTEXTUAL DEBATE

# Freedom Fighters or Terrorists?

## DESMOND TUTU

Violence is rampant. There have been cross-border raids which include the most recent strikes on Livingstone and Maputo, the bomb blast outside the Johannesburg Magistrate's Court, and the explosion of a South African registered kombi outside a house in Gaborone. Cosatu strikers have been shot by the police during the strike against the South African Transport Services, and the 'routine' deaths associated with repression in South Africa continue. Such events cannot be theologised about in a value-free or academic manner. Engaged theology cannot be neutral. It is one done with passion.

It is extraordinary how the subject of violence has, in South Africa, helped to further polarise an already deeply polarised society. It is a situation in which what you see and apprehend, depends on who you are and where you are. Many who benefit from an unjust and repressive dispensation want to maintain the status quo — often at any cost. They reject any attempt to challenge or destroy such structures that are to their benefit, and if force is employed to attain this goal, it is invariably regarded as totally illegitimate, being dismissed as terrorism so that it becomes justifiable to unleash any degree of repressive violence against it. Yet such violence is not seen as violence by the ruling class, it is regarded as the legitimate use of 'the sword'.

The victims of injustice and oppression, on the other hand, regard the very structures of the state as designed to repress them. And when unjust laws enable the government to perpetrate all kinds of violence against the oppressed there is hardly a squeak of protest from those who benefit from not being victims. Of course there are some whites who seek to identify with the victims of injustice and oppression, but the majority of the whites support the government in all that it does to protect white interests. The recent all-white election illustrates this clearly. The ruling party won a landslide victory because it identified the issues

71

which concern most white persons — security, safety, alleged terrorism and self-defined communism. The white community accepted the propaganda of the government that the ANC wants to overthrow a stable and civilised order to replace it with anarchy and black domination. Economic progress and social well-being, we were told, would grind to a halt and prosperity would wither away under an ANC government. Few whites stopped to acknowledge that such progress and well-being that does exist is for 'whites only' and their puppets. Even the latest constitution (the 1984 model) is designed to ensure that the small white minority continues to enjoy the lion's share of all the good things produced in this land through the exploitation of black labour.

When blacks — after many years during which their cautious protest was consistently ignored — opted in desperation for armed struggle, whites dubbed them 'terrorists', which meant they could be ruthlessly imprisoned, hanged or shot. The will to be free is not, however, defeated by even the worst kind of violence. Such repressive violence has only succeeded in throwing South Africa into a low-intensity civil war which threatens to escalate into a high-intensity war. Already South Africans are staring at fellow South Africans through gunsights.

## NON-VIOLENCE

There are some remarkable people who believe that no one is ever justified in using violence, even against the most horrendous evil. Such absolute pacifists believe that the Gospel of the Cross effectively rules out anyone taking up the sword, however just the cause. I admire such persons deeply, but sadly I confess that I am made of less noble stuff. I am a lover of peace and I try to work for justice because only thus do I believe we could ever hope to establish durable peace. It is self-defeating to justify a truce based on unstable foundations of oppression. Such a truce can only be inherently unstable, requiring that it be maintained by institutional violence.

Non-violence as a means towards ending. an unjust system, presupposes that the oppressors show a minimum level of morality. Even in such a situation the non-violence path is a hazardous one requiring considerable courage and moral fortitude. It was possible for Gandhi to arouse moral indignation and thus support for his cause against the British Raj; perhaps only because there were those in England whose sensitivities were such that they were outraged by the treatment meted out by the army to peaceful demonstrators. I doubt, however, that such a Gandhian campaign would have saved the Jews from the Nazi holocaust.

Black South Africans have tried non-violent protest. Indeed until the banning of the ANC and PAC in the sixties, conventional non-violent means such as petitions, delegations, demonstrations, protests, and boycotts, were the most drastic focus of resistance to which blacks resorted. There was even a passive resistance campaign held in an effort to bring the plight of blacks to the attention of the authorities. The commitment of the ANC to non-violence for the first fifty years of its existence was rewarded when its President General, Chief Albert Luthuli, was awarded the Nobel Peace Prize. Indeed the only South Africans to have won the Nobel Peace Prize have both been black. It was whilst blacks were protesting peacefully against the much hated pass laws that the Sharpeville massacre happened. Sixty-nine peaceful protesters were killed by the police, most of them shot in the back as they were running away. The world was shocked but, again with certain exceptions, white South Africa remained relatively unmoved. And the Sharpeville paradigm has been repeated again and again.

Only when liberation movements could no longer operate legally and openly in South Africa, did some members of these organisations believe that they were left with no option but to undertake an armed struggle to liberate the people of South Africa. The aim of this armed struggle is for a new, just, non-racial and democratic South Africa. It is enshrined in the Freedom Charter. Whether those who fight for this goal are 'terrorists' or 'freedom fighters', depends on which side of the divide you locate yourself.

It must never be forgotten that Afrikaners, who today form the bulk of the white ruling class, themselves rebelled against the British and fought what they like to call their *Vryheidsoorloe* (Wars of Liberation) at the turn of the century. And when General Jan Smuts led South Africa into the Second World War on the side of the Allies, there were those among his *volk* who opposed the war. They formed organisations such as the *Ossewabrandwag*, a pro-Nazi organisation which carried out acts of sabotage to undermine and oppose the Smuts government. Many who in time became leading Afrikaner politicians were members of the *Ossewabrandwag* and interned for their pro-Nazi sympathies and activities. A former State President and Prime Minister, Mr B.J. Vorster, was interned, and the current State President was himself a member of the *Ossewabrandwag*. Were they terrorists or were they freedom fighters? It depends on which side of the political divide you find yourself. Let it also be remembered that one of the first acts of the Nationalist government after being elected to power in 1948 was to release Robey Leibrandt who had been sentenced to death for high treason against the Smuts government.

Today we are ruled by those guilty of such behaviour who have the gall to read us lessons on patriotism while espousing the virtue of the rule of law and the rejection of all violence.

## STRUCTURAL VIOLENCE

There are different kinds and degrees of violence. White South Africa regards violence and terrorism as that which normally emanates from the oppressed black community either internally or externally. They refuse to accept that the South African situation is inherently violent, and that primary violence is the apartheid system. They are shocked, as all decent people should be, when a car bomb explodes and kills three white people. But there is hardly a word of indignation when an SADF attack on a neighbouring country leaves several innocent non-South Africans dead. There is no outrage even when refugee camps are hit, leaving one convinced that the morality of most whites concerning violence is both selective and self-serving.

What is *legally right* is not necessarily *morally right*. It is legal in South Africa for a man to be separated from his wife if he is a migrant worker living in a single sex hostel, and therefore illegal for him to sleep with his wife in an urban area if she does not have statutory permission to be there. It is not, however, morally right for a husband to be separated from his wife in this way. It contravenes God's imperative that *those whom he has joined together no one should put asunder*.

Apartheid causes untold and unnecessary suffering 'by law'. By depriving black people of their South African citizenship, the South African government has been able to uproot over three million people, disrupting stable communities, demolishing habitable dwellings, destroying schools, churches, small businesses and clinics. These people are dumped in poverty-stricken resettlement camps and their children are made to starve, not because there is no food in South Africa, but in order to satisfy government ideology. Young people are hindered in their development and old people made to suffer. This is legalised, structural violence. It is violence used to uphold an unjust and repressive system, augmented by repressive laws. Detention without trial is the order of the day, with even children being subjected to the horrendous situation where the police are able to act as both prosecutor and judge. Frequently those who are detained are held in solitary confinement and without access to a doctor of their choice, their lawyer or family. When this is the character of what is 'lawful' in a country it is necessary to obey God rather than human authority. If we are *not* prepared to do this then non-violence is necessarily ruled out as an option.

Another form of state violence requires comment, namely the death penalty. I am fundamentally opposed to capital punishment, which is why I appealed for clemency to President René on behalf of the South African mercenaries who were sentenced to death for trying to overthrow the Seychelles government. Far too many people in condemned cells in South African prisons are blacks who have fallen foul of the many laws of which they are the victims. In political trials the death sentence is often passed on people who are dedicated, idealistic and have the best intentions, while those who sit in judgement on them are as a rule totally unsympathetic to the cause of the accused. There is little doubt that the law and the judicial system are weighted against those who seek change to the existing order. When the death sentence is not passed, the sentences imposed are rarely other than viciously excessive. Young students receive twelve months or more for throwing stones. This form of legal violence merely increases their resolve with many arguing that 'they might as well be hanged for a sheep as for a lamb'.

There is, remarkably, still goodwill in the black community, but it is disappearing before the state's irresponsible intransigence and repression. Given the negative results achieved by non-violent protest and resistance it can well be asked how blacks, even at this late hour, can still talk of non-violent methods. Yet they continue to use such means in stay-aways, in consumer boycotts which have knocked some sense into the heads of white businessmen, and in the rent boycott that has been maintained in many black townships. To this the authorities responded in their usual mailed-fist way. For example, in one area of Soweto the youth erected barricades to stop the security forces from evicting those who refused to pay rent. The police went indiscriminately into homes in the area, ordered the children into the streets and beat them. When the children ran away, they shot them. I went to one such home, where a thirteen-year old boy had been shot dead. His younger brother who had been shot in the stomach was in a critical condition in hospital. The stunned mother sat silently on her chair. She kept wiping her eyes but there were no tears. I tried to talk to her about the love of God and silently asked, 'How long, oh Lord?'

## IS VIOLENCE JUSTIFIABLE TO TOPPLE AN UNJUST SYSTEM?

I am theologically conservative and traditional. I think the dominant position of my church regarding violence is this: We regard all violence as evil (the violence of an unjust system such as apartheid and the violence of those who seek to overthrow it). That is why we have condemned 'necklacing' and car bombs, as well as instances of violence perpetrated by the government and the security forces. This does not mean, however, that the mainstream tradition of the church does not reluctantly allow that violence may in certain situations be necessary. The just war theory (discussed elsewhere in this volume) makes this point clearly.

Sometimes the church is required to make a choice between what it acknowledges to be two evils. Is it better to suffer the barbarisms and horrors of Hitler's Naziism or should one go to war to put an end to the nightmare? The allies argued it was justifiable, indeed obligatory to go to war to stop Hitler's madness, and the Church concurred with that decision. Most people (apart from the purest of pacifists) knew in their bones that it was right to fight against Naziism.

This is a situation which causes much puzzlement in the black community. Not only did the allies go to war against Hitler with the approval of the church, but the church aided underground resistance movements which operated in Nazi-occupied countries. Dietrich Bonhoeffer, who plotted to murder Hitler, came to be regarded as a modern-day Christian martyr and saint. More than this, most western countries have their independence written in blood. The USA became independent after the thirteen colonies had fought the American War of Independence. But when it comes to the matter of black liberation the West and most of its church suddenly begins to show pacifist tendencies. The USA supports the Contras in Nicaragua who seek to overthrow a government elected in what independent observers regard as having been free and fair elections. The Reagan administration also supports Dr Jonas Savimbi and his Unita forces which are bent on toppling the MPLA government in Luanda. There is, however, no unequivocal Western support for black South Africans who have for decades tried to change the unjust rule in South Africa non-violently. The white minority government of South Africa cannot be called even remotely democratic when seventy-three percent of the population is constitutionally excluded from the electoral process. In this situation one can only understand why some oppressed people resort to the armed struggle. Yet the West castigates them. President Reagan calls the Contras freedom fighters, while labeling the ANC terrorists. Western governments have called on the ANC to renounce violence, while not directing similar demands to the South African government which is the cause of violence both in South Africa and in neighbouring countries. Is it because the perpetrators of such violence are white and because they contribute to the West's economic might, while the victims of injustice are black and their oppression an inherent part of the economic system of the West?

I continue to believe that we do have an outside chance that a negotiated settlement could be reached reasonably peacefully if the international community intervened decisively with effective pressure on the South African government to lift the State of Emergency, to remove the troops from the black townships, to release all detainees and political prisoners, and to unban black political organisations.

International action and international pressure are among the few non-violent options left. And yet how strident is the opposition to economic sanctions. Blacks cannot vote. We are driven therefore to invoke a non-violent method which we believe is likely to produce the desired result. If this option is denied us, what then is left? If sanctions should fail there is no other way but to fight.

Should the West fail to impose economic sanctions it would, in my view, be justifiable for blacks to try to overthrow an unjust system violently. But I must continue to work to bring an end to the present tyranny by non-violent means. Should this option fail, the low-intensity civil war I referred to at the beginning of this essay will escalate into full-scale war. When that happens, heaven help us all. The Armaggedon will have come!

## AND RECONCILIATION?

Where is the place of reconciliation and forgiveness in all this? Reconciliation is not crying 'peace, peace,' where there is no peace. It is to confront evil with its awfulness. True reconciliation is costly. It demands that we condemn evil and injustice. Forgiveness only happens when there is repentance. No person or group of people can be forgiven unless that person or group wants to be forgiven and acknowledges guilt. When this contrition manifests itself in a willingness to make amends and to make restitution where appropriate, the Gospel demands that there be forgiveness. If I have stolen your sheep no matter how eloquent my protestations of contrition and repentance may be, if I still keep what I have stolen and do not make the proper restitution then my confession can only be a sham. And you are under no obligation to forgive me.

Because I believe in the great liberator God of the Exodus and of Calvary I have no doubt at all that the oppressed will be free in South Africa, and that black and white shall live in harmony. This is God's intention and it cannot be frustrated forever. A new South Africa is in the process of emerging. It shall be democratic, genuinely non-racial and given to justice. All people are created in God's image. Black and white must strive to dwell amicably together as brothers and sisters who are members of one family, the human family, God's family. For this I am ready to die.

# Christian Soldiers

BUTI TLHAGALE

The intensity of black anger and 'violence' experienced since September 1984 is unparalleled in recent South African history. Yet it has its roots in the turmoil of the 1960s when African political leaders realised there was little hope that non-violent pressures could bring about radical change in South Africa. Apartheid had always been seen as an inherently violent system, but when the African National Congress openly resorted to violence as a means of bringing about radical political change, a new chapter in black politics began.

What is seen as violence by most whites is also experienced as violence by blacks. But blacks attach a radically different significance to it. It is a protest beyond moral indignation, beyond words. It is a direct assault on apartheid.

What the white community perceives as 'unrest', as a sheer display of savagery when persons associated with apartheid are burned to death wearing 'the necklace', the burning tyre, the black community interprets as a protest. Indeed the deaths are to be regretted. But what seems to be senseless destruction of life and property, of schools and buses and delivery vehicles, is seen by blacks, especially young people, as an aggressive statement of radical protest, of self-affirmation, a calculated tactic to compel the government to reckon with the frustrated aspirations of the black people.

For years blacks have been referred to as 'temporary sojourners' in the urban areas. The psychological impact of forced homelessness, of 'exile', has now taken its toll. The reversal of this process as a result of the Wiehahn and Riekert reports and the subsequent labour legislation of 1979 have not yet had the desired effect. Much less the inane declaration of a dual citizenship for black people. Denying blacks permanence in the urban areas has resulted in no development or improvements of township conditions.

The litany of denials: of home ownership, of industry, of business premises, of investment in cultural facilities, coupled with the iniquitous influx control system and the extremely limited availability of housing in urban areas have all created a deep sense of non-belonging. Besides, blacks have also been denied the right of participating meaningfully in the planning and management of their own local affairs. The establishment of the Community Councils was a unilateral decision by government. This explains why some councillors have been driven out of their homes, and why some councils have been dismantled. Community Councils are seen as part and parcel of apartheid.

The government insists that the 'unrest' is caused either by black political organisations (hence the treason trials in Pretoria and Pietermaritzburg) and/or by 'criminal elements' in the black community.[1] The Congress of South African Students has been banned, presumably because it is thought to be responsible for the upheavals. To blame individuals or groups of people for a situation of intense political 'unrest' ignores the widespread discontent of the people.

To blame hooligans or the ANC for the unrest is to refuse to acknowledge that apartheid is the source of the problem. Instead of taking up arms, the present generation is using boycotts, work stoppages, work stay-aways, school disruptions, protests, the destruction of selected targets, the merciless killings of 'collaborators' in an irrevocable commitment to bursting the chains of apartheid. The state has been thrown headlong into the turmoil.

Blacks do not want violence any more than whites, but this mode of resistance is highly visible. It demands immediate attention. It confuses the government, destabilises the country and solicits support from the international community. The violent upheaval therefore, far from being an accidental happening or an expression of hostility, is calculated to bring about an abrupt end to racism and political domination.

## CHRISTIAN PERSPECTIVES ON VIOLENCE
Christian discussions on violence have simply dismissed as 'terrorism', and therefore immoral, the violent struggle of oppressed people against white domination and against the ruthlessness of capitalism. 'Official' Christianity has tended to uphold 'non-violence' as a universal principle or strategy to stir the opponent's conscience and bring about reconciliation.

In South Africa the black experience denies this. For almost a century the inherently violent apartheid system has simply entrenched itself with all the viciousness imaginable. There are no signs of reconciliation on the horizon.

There is of course another option as argued by Pope John Paul II in his 1982 Day of Peace message: 'Christians have a right and even a duty to protect their existence and freedom by proportionate means against an unjust aggressor'.

Most blacks see the National Party members as having no moral legitimacy to leadership and government. They have not been elected by blacks but simply imposed themselves on the people and denied them basic human rights.

The Christian tradition recognises the legitimacy of violence to defend the rights of a state. From a township perspective the South African state is essentially a repressive state. For example, the army occupies a foreign territory, Namibia, and conducts incursions into Angola, or 'pre-emptive strikes' into Lesotho, Mozambique and Botswana — leaving in its wake death and destruction. In the townships, where the army is currently deployed under the State of Emergency it has succeeded not only in destroying life but in alienating the black community.

The 'political police' are credited with harassment and torture, and detainees have died in prisons. (Official explanations for these deaths are taken with a grain of salt by township people.) The courts mete out punishment to those who flout the apartheid laws. The different administration departments enforce apartheid either in education or in the massive forced removals. In addition, blacks are excluded from the electoral system, precluded from any access to political power and from meaningful participation in the economy.

Thus to blacks the state has no legitimacy. Can a state without any power base or even sympathy among the majority of the people have a moral right to rule over the majority or even have a moral right to use violence to preserve an intrinsically violent political system? When blacks resort to violent means to redress the wrongs of apartheid it is perceived not only as a right to resist but also as a *duty* to resist the crushing repression of the racist regime.

A Vatican document states:

> All those who enter the military service in loyalty to their country shall look upon themselves as the custodians of the security and freedom of their fellow countrymen; and when they carry out their duty properly, they are contributing to the maintenance of peace.[2]

## THE MINORITY'S ARMY

Some Christian traditions approve of investment in an army that serves not only as a deterrent but can also protect the freedom of the country's citizens. In South Africa this can only apply in its fullness to whites. Blacks have not been recruited into the army in large numbers, presumably because they are not 'real' citizens of South Africa and therefore have no stake in the country.

The freedom to be safeguarded is the freedom of whites. Blacks have not experienced the meaning of freedom in South Africa. They are denied freedom of movement, of association, of choosing their own place of residence.

The soldiers are therefore 'the custodians of the security and freedom' of the white people. In the State of Emergency, they have not contributed to the 'maintenance of peace', their callous behaviour has in fact strained race relations. To township people there is no difference between the security police and the army. Their ruthless killing of black South Africans and innocent people in neighbouring states simply puts the army in the camp of the enemy.

A significant number of young whites resist conscription. They see it as morally wrong especially because they know that they are likely to be sent into the black townships where they may have to shoot black people, fellow citizens, not so much for the maintenance of 'law and order' but rather for an ideology based on the forced segregation of races, for a status quo that seeks to retain political and economic power in white hands.

The church, through the appointment of military chaplains is seen to give direct moral support and therefore approval to the army. The army is the 'killing machine' of the state. The enemies of the state are those blacks who resist apartheid and who fight against the illegal presence of South Africa in Namibia.

An option for the poor even though it is undoubtedly a 'spiritual paternalism', would mean withdrawal from any direct or indirect involvement with the army which is clearly partisan in South Africa. Accusations levelled against the army range from harassment of innocents, searching the houses of black people, cases of rape, of beating and even shooting people as they run away. The official response is that only about one percent of the force is involved in these 'aberrations'. Such accusations cannot be so dismissed.

A church that gives moral and spiritual support to such an army cannot remain untainted; it necessarily finds itself in an ambivalent situation because both the soldiers and the people they kill belong to the same church.

The army is seen by blacks as fighting for the maintenance of white domination, while blacks see themselves as fighting for the right to be free in their own country. A choice has to be made. Racial factors play a decisive role concerning loyalties to specific racial groupings or class fractions. At times the gospel imperatives play a secondary role. The South African situation can easily be said to be a case in point.

While black people are convinced they have a right to reclaim their fatherland and uphold their dignity and freedom, they do not have the lethal instruments of war which would enable them to protect themselves. As a subjugated people, only stones and the ability to destroy and render the country 'ungovernable' remain the immediate instruments of self-assertion. The strategy of ungovernability can be dangerous and costly. But this is the price blacks will have to pay.

The church holds incompatible and contradictory positions. On the one hand it gives its blessing to the South African military service by allowing its personnel to give spiritual support to the Christian white soldiers and on the other hand preaches restraint to the black oppressed masses. It participates indirectly in the military might of the state while criticising the state's acts of repression.

## JUSTIFIED STRUGGLE

The nagging questions that still need to be answered are whether a violent struggle by black South Africans can ever be justifiable or indeed whether the violent repression by the apartheid regime is justifiable? Cast in the mould of the classical tradition of the just violent struggle, the township perspective yields the following argument.

The semblance of order and peaceful co-existence has been shattered by the spiral of violent struggle that has engulfed the black townships. The demand of the black people, especially the youth, is the abolition of the present political order and the establishment of a non-racial democratic political system on the basis of one person-one vote.

The present exploitative capitalist system ought to give way to a more equitable socialist system that will develop economic programs to amend those areas where apartheid has played havoc and left human misery in its wake.

There is no solution in sight to the present political conflict as the government stubbornly clings to its racist policies of denying blacks meaningful citizenship, of up-holding the Population Registration Act and the Group Areas Act, of refusing to release political prisoners, etc. Instead the government has responded to the black violent struggle with the might of the army and the security forces.

There is a rapidly growing belief that violence is virtually the only answer left in the face of government intransigence. The violence of blacks is in response to the violence of apartheid that has kept blacks in humiliating subjugation. The costs in terms of human suffering are incalculable. So desperate have large sections of the black community become that the present system can no longer continue without disruption. Whereas the older generation has learnt to live with injustice, not so the young people. If apartheid has to continue it will seemingly have to be over their dead bodies.

The present violence is understood as an act of self-defence against a system and a people that practices oppression and exploitation. It is hoped that through violence justice will eventually be established.

There was a time when it was thought a disinterested international authority would intervene in situations of gross injustice. But the United Nations has failed dismally to persuade South Africa to move out of Namibia, nor has it succeeded in persuading the Pretoria regime to abandon its racist ways and treat blacks as equal citizens. South Africa does not recognise the UN as a disinterested party simply because the UN condemns in unequivocable terms the intrinsically evil apartheid system. White South Africa has become a law unto itself.

The major western powers, the U.S., Britain, and West Germany, all connive with the evils of apartheid and fail to bring any measure of meaningful pressure to bear on South Africa. America's constructive engagement policy is a classic example of connivance. This leads to the belief that these powers have vested interests in this country despite their denials. The refusal to apply meaningful sanctions, claiming that blacks would suffer, is a refusal to help in the dismantling of apartheid. Against the background of the powerlessness of the United Nations and the connivance of the major western powers, black South Africans are left to fall back on their own limited resources to abolish the unjust political order. And so the violent struggle proceeds apace despite the declaration of the State of Emergency.

The complexity of the South African situation defies the neatly worked out moral principles of classical Christian tradition. The assumption is that violent struggles are waged by one state against another. The classical tradition does not envisage an unjust aggressor emerging from within the boundaries of a single state. Historically though, white South Africa could be viewed as an unjust aggressor because the indigenous black people never formed a single nation with European settlers.

In a situation of oppression, recognised leaders of the oppressed masses are the legitimate authority to lead the masses in revolt against the perpetrators of injustice. To prevent this, the government bans or imprisons the credible leadership. Consequently, the banning of the ANC and the Pan-African Movement in the early sixties, then the banning of the Black Consciousness organisations, the Christian Institute and a host of other bodies in 1977 prevented black leadership from communicating with the government.

If the present violent struggle does not seem to have any distinct leadership, it is because the leadership is not allowed to survive for long in public. Nonetheless while violence continues, spokesmen on behalf of the oppressed masses articulate their aspirations and spell out the conditions that would need to be fulfilled if the true foundations of peace were to be laid at all.

Positions expressed are generally in line with what the imprisoned leaders would themselves put forward. The conditions laid down by Archbishop Tutu or the churches and various anti-apartheid organisations reflect the aspirations of the masses. If the present violent struggle appears to be leaderless and thus failing to satisfy the moral principles of the classical tradition, it is simply because the traditional forms of leadership are interfered with by government but do not lose their identity and competence.

The apartheid machine has forcibly relocated more than 500 000 people in an attempt to streamline the apartheid policy. Thousands have been charged with pass law offences. Thousands of blacks are in exile. The influx control system has destroyed family life for those denied freedom of movement and prevented them from selling their labour in lucrative markets. Imprisonment, torture and death in detention because of skin colour still continues. The list of the crimes of the apartheid system is endless. That is why this political system is considered to be the most vicious since Nazism.

The violence conducted by the ANC in blowing up installations or government buildings can hardly be compared to the human suffering caused by apartheid. Lives have indeed been lost in the struggle for liberation. But the South African Defence Force has been swift to retaliate, destroying more lives, destabilising neighbouring countries and holding them to ransom.

Since September 1984 violent struggle has claimed more than 950 lives. More than 500 of these victims have been reportedly shot by the security forces while protecting lives and property. The loss of lives would undoubtedly have been much lower if the troops had been kept out of the townships. While any loss of life and property is to be regretted, there is hardly any comparison between the damage caused by the repressive apartheid system and the damage incurred in the present political upheaval. Today's violence may ebb, but the conviction that violence is the last resort has taken root. This conviction has come to manifest itself in the following way.

The current cycle of political upheaval is simply an intense moment in the process of resistance since the ANC was formed in 1912. This violent struggle has demanded and continues to demand a costly sacrifice in lives and possessions. But its outcome, hardly measurable in terms of immediate gains, has altered the course of history for the oppressive classes and the masses of oppressed people. While it appears to have had only a ripple effect on apartheid itself, it has produced a serious crack in the granite edifice of apartheid.

The government has responded to both internal and external pressure. It has extended citizenship to all black people — citizenship without political rights. There is a possibility of creating a 'fourth chamber' for blacks in Parliament. There is also a promise to relax the much-hated influx control system. So far there are only promises. But even so the government can no longer go back on its word.

It has been said that 'reforms' predate the events of September 1984. For example, discriminatory labour legislation was changed in 1979. But this change was partly the result of the 1976 upheavals. The inescapable conclusion is that limited violence, costly though it might have been, has undoubtedly attracted the attention of the world community and the local conservative business community. Pressure has been exerted on government.

Shifts in the apartheid policy have been made and there is no going back.

## VIOLENCE AS A LAST RESORT

From a township perspective the logic does seem to support the just violent struggle as a last resort at a rational level. The gospel imperatives on the other hand seem to challenge the moral principles of a just violent struggle.

— 'You have heard that it was said, 'An eye for an eye, a tooth for a tooth'. But now I tell you: Do not take revenge on someone who wrongs you.' (Mt. 5:38-39)
— 'Father forgive them . . . ' (Lk. 23:24)
— 'Love your enemies and pray for your persecutors.' (Mt. 5:44)
— 'Blessed are the peacemakers, for they shall be called the children of God.' (Mt. 5:9)

These citations and the entire Sermon on the Mount do not make sense in the face of continuing repression and the barbarous behaviour of the servants of the state and also tend to cultivate fatalistic attitudes among the oppressed.

For more than two centuries large sections of the white Christian community have treated blacks as 'kaffirs' and as servants. Christians have been commanded in the gospels to 'love one another as I love you'. In a South Africa where the Group Areas Act, the Separate Amenities Act, the Population Registration Act, and concepts of 'own affairs' and ethnic identity reign supreme, trust and friendship remain foreign and indeed inimical to the official policy of the repressive state.

Black history throughout the centuries is an experience of the wilderness. Thus South Africa under white domination continues to be an unending ordeal by fire for no 'apparent reason' while racists and capitalists thrive and continue to deal treacherously. So shattering is the experience of oppression, deprivation and humiliation that the experience of godlessness among sections of the black population is here to stay. And so too the growing convictions of atheism and communism are nurtured by the devastating scourge of apartheid Christianity.

This form of Christianity sees God at the service of *some* people, not *all* people. The belief held by the universal church that all men are created in the likeness of God and the implications of such a belief are completely ignored by the apartheid system of racial segregation and the myth of racial superiority.

Such beliefs and perceptions, rightly or wrongly, propel sections of the black people headlong against the wall. Opting for violence as a strategy to end apartheid therefore derives from a complex set of intermeshing factors, namely: the legacy of pain and bitterness, of repression and alienation, from empty promises of radical political reform and the continuation of racism, of those who claim to hold to the tenets of Christian faith and yet deny them in practice, of the ever-increasing cost of living, and growing unemployment — all these factors coalesce and create a desperate situation that cries to heaven for justice.

Such a desperate situation, far from crushing the burning desire to be free, has unleashed new energies especially among the young black people who have sprung forward to resist injustice. Hundreds of young people have experienced detention without trial. Some of the young people have laid down their lives for the sake of justice — as did Christ.

The desire for freedom has been rekindled, hence the relentless effort to subvert the inherently violent socio-political order. That the gospel or the life-history of Christ makes no room for the use of violence to right the wrongs of society remains a massive scandal among the oppressed. And yet the story of this Christ is a story of a series of subversions. He was continually in conflict with the socio-religious and political order of his day.

The desire to be free and the intensive assault on the apartheid institutions is not incompatible with the tradition of subversion modelled on Christ. In fact Christian discipleship demands the subversion of the oppressive socio-political order to establish justice and consequently peace.

Unless genuine radical socio-political change comes about, violence is bound to break out intermittently. Meaningful participation in politics and the economy is imperative.

If violence is to be avoided and peace to be established then apartheid must be uprooted completely. Nothing less than the fulfilment of this simple demand will do. If that change takes place then South Africa can begin to talk about 'the things that make for peace'.

## NOTES

1.   *Indicator S.A.* Vol.3, No.2, 1985, p.9.
2.   *Gaudium et Spes* in Michael Walsh and Brian Davies (eds.), *Proclaiming Justice and Peace*, (London: Collins, 1984), pp.81-140.

# Legitimacy and Struggle

MALUSI MPUMLWANA

The question of violence/non-violence as an issue for the church in South Africa cannot be addressed without reference to the social context which occasions the debate. If we take the context of the confrontation between government forces and the national resistance movement seriously we will realise that violence/non-violence is not the primary question for the church to look into. Violence is a subsidiary question of method and tactics in dealing with a problem. Methods can best be addressed by people who, at the very least, have a common diagnosis of the problem. This paper is an attempt to establish a common diagnosis. That should hopefully afford us the basis on which we can consider the most effective and acceptable methods to be used in resolving the problem. Before we explore our situation however, it will help to recall the standard position of the church on violence.

Over the ages the church has developed both a normative and a pragmatic position on violence. It opposes violence in favour of non-violent solutions to conflicts. Pragmatically, however, it accepts the use of violence on the premise of at least two presuppositions:
— A people has a right and duty to engage in the violence of national defence;
— A legitimate government has the licence of potential or actual violence for effective government.

Because of this the church has for generations blessed structures of violence in different ways, including the services of chaplains in the armed forces. It has also accommodated war through the just war theory. In South Africa as elsewhere in the world, plaques and memorials on walls and windows of cathedrals and white suburban churches stand witness to the church's sentiment over 'good violence'.

The picture alters when we consider that the South African nation as represented by the present government has no foreign enemies. Instead it is the people of South Africa and their children who, in the last few months, necessitated the largest military mobilisation yet in the country's 'peace-time' history. Who is the aggressor and who is the defender? These questions are answered differently in South Africa depending on who you are or where you place yourself in the country's legally-determined social stratification. I suggest that the real point of dissension is here rather than concerning the traditional attitudes to violence.

Black South Africans see themselves as politically emasculated and economically dispossessed. The government of this country has never acknowledged their grievances. That is basically what the cause of violent confrontation in South Africa is about. In the course of this conflict, one of the tactics used by blacks is the refusal to be governed. At least they have made it as difficult as they possibly can for effective government to take place in their townships. The extended State of Emergency is, amongst other things, intended to restore a modicum of government control over the rebellious townships. This raises the question of the legitimacy of the government in the eyes of the governed.

Many in this country believe that the government is the aggressor, and the resistance movement defensive. If this is so, then the question is whether blacks have a right and duty to engage in the violence of national resistance and defence. On the other hand there are those who believe that the resistance movement is the aggressor, and the government the defender. If that is so then it can be argued that the South African army is doing the job of defence and the government is rightfully exercising its licence of law-and-order violence. I discuss these issues in the following paragraphs, drawing on arguments that present a black viewpoint.

## LEGITIMACY OF AUTHORITY

Historically this country's government was established through the violent conquer of the black people. Albert Luthuli was to say of the undemocratic government established:

> The Act of Union (of South Africa) virtually handed the whole of South Africa over to a minority of whites, lock, stock and barrel... As far as the whites were concerned the matter was settled: They had become the owners of the new state. The members of other races who found themselves handed over officially, entirely without their consent, were the livestock which went with the estate, objects rather than subjects.[1]

Against this background the *Kairos Document* questions the churches' endorsement of the government. The document points out that this government's mandate is a mandate to protect and serve minority interests. 'Such a mandate ... is by definition hostile to the common good of all people'.[2] In terms of this position, the government's use of law-and-order violence maintains and perpetuates tyranny. It represents a continued refusal on the part of the government to recognise that all of South Africa's people have a right and duty to participate in the political process. The government runs a country of 30 million people on behalf of a privileged 5 million. Hence it has to crush those who threaten the privileges it is elected to preserve.

The dilemma of the church is that its policy of dealing with the state is to act as if the government was in fact a government of national interest, whose legitimacy is not questioned. Where a government, by law and might, hijacks the country and its national resources for minority purposes, the church's standard policy falls short.

## NATIONAL DEFENCE

Elsewhere in this volume Buti Tlhagale deals with the right of a people to national defence, on the basis of the traditional just war theory of the church. From the onset he declares that his subject is a 'Black theology of self-defence'. Tlhagale's argument is that in as much as the church has always acknowledged the right of peoples to national defence, black South Africans are entitled to the same understanding.

The situation as far as blacks see it, is as follows: They were conquered by force and have never willingly consented to any of the actions of the state since then. In every way they have tried to make their voice of appeal and protest heard, first to Britain (which was one of the primary purposes of founding the African National Congress in 1912), and later to successive South African governments. They see the present government and its predecessors as having no democratic mandate from them, and they believe they have a right to defend their destiny at all costs. What should the church's response be to this argument?

## THE CHALLENGE FACING THE CHURCH

The membership of the church is 80 percent black. But traditionally, the church has an institutional relationship with the state. Although it has often served as a voice of conscience against state injustices, or excesses thereof, it is basically supportive of the government. With the rise of black resistance the church has experienced a crisis of identity. The presence of Archbishop Desmond Tutu's cathedral next door to President Botha's throne dramatises the tension of the crisis. The two structures were built for mutual support, which explains the controversy that resulted when Tutu decided to break the tradition of having government guests invited to his 'enthronement' as the Archbishop of Cape Town. This crisis calls on the church to accept that black people want a different South Africa; a South Africa that reflects the love of God in human relations.

The church's identity crisis represents the crossroads that most liberal Christians, (particularly whites), are facing at this point. Many realise that the foundation of our national life is false. What the last couple of years have unveiled is a 'new factor' (to borrow a phrase from Robert McAfee Brown); 'The realisation by the powerless that they need no longer remain powerless'.[3]

That realisation has led thousands of young people in the past decade to flee South Africa and return as targets of 'our boys on the border'. That realisation has given rise in our people, to an unquenchable thirst for freedom. They demand the right to shape the destiny of their country as responsible stewards of its God-given resources. This explains why thousands upon thousands throughout the country have risen in a sustained rebellion against the government and its structures. By so doing they have dared to confront the 'crushing might' of the most powerful military machinery in Africa. The continued military presence in the townships is an acknowledgement, however negative, that the black demand for freedom and justice remains irrevocably on the table. Will the church endorse this demand as just and fair, or will it continue to support repressive forces by claiming that the army represents a structure of 'national defence'?

It is this kind of question, I believe, that must be addressed before we deal with the matter of the ethics of violence. It must be addressed in earnest, for our positive position on it will give integrity to our voice on violence/non-violence. That is why I say the latter is a matter of tactics best handled by those with a shared perpsective on the South African problem.

The controversy over 'the prayer to end unjust rule' revealed that the church is ideologically committed to the long life of this government, however unconsciously. Prayer is not *overtly* violent. The church has solemnly declared apartheid a heresy. What could be more faithfully Christian than to pray just as solemnly for a

speedy and happy end to such an affront to the gospel? Charles
Villa-Vicencio sums up the challenge to the church in this way:

> The burning question facing the English-speaking churches is
> whether they have fully faced the consequences of their call for
> the destruction of apartheid. This cannot be done without
> striking at the heart of the capitalist system, which in this
> country is built and maintained by racist legislation.[4]

The message for the church in South Africa is clear. We are
called upon to be partisans of human liberation in our country.
We are called upon, in God's name, to be a leaven of social
salvation. Social salvation as the church's agenda in South Africa
involves meaningful acts of protest against the evil of apartheid. It
also involves helping the victims of apartheid to emerge from
oppression. Only a church that is committed to the social
revolution can heal the scars of hatred that mar the humanity of
the oppressed. It is our urgent task to help lay foundations for
new social relations; new life in a new South Africa for all. As
Steve Biko pointed out, 'The revolutionary seeks *to restore faith in
life* amongst all citizens of his country, to remove imaginary fears
and to heighten concern for the plight of the people' (my
emphasis).[5] That is the revolutionary path of reconciliation I
believe we should embrace.

## POLITICAL VIOLENCE IN SOUTH AFRICA

Where does all this leave us as regards the question of violence?
Political violence in South Africa has many dimensions. There is
the violence of the state: structural violence, repressive violence,
military raids on and occupation of neighbouring countries. Allied
with state violence is the state-sponsored violence of the
vigilantes. From the resistance movement there are guerilla
operations, armed propaganda and anti-collaborationist assaults.
This complexity of violence needs to be analysed carefully.

Identifying with liberation efforts does not mean a non-critical
commitment. It is a call to prophetic theology, whose task goes
beyond the future celebrations of national reconciliation. Prophetic
theology should be a persisting critique of the best of human
efforts in the light of the greater call of God's 'kingdom' which,
this side of eternity, can only be approximated. In South Africa, a
non-racial democracy, as opposed to the racist oligarchy that now
rules, should be the social foundation for that approximation.
Such a democracy, however, could only be a human
approximation of the right relations God desires for us. That is

why prophetic theology will always have the role of being a
'gadfly' vis-à-vis social structures viewed in the light of the
eschatological vision.

Tutu emphasises this point when he says to the oppressed:
'God is on your side, not as some jingoistic national deity who
says 'my people right or wrong', but as one who saves and yet
also judges those whom he saves'.[6] The church's ministry of
*social discernment*, with the tool of *social analysis* is to share in
the judgement of the saving God. Therefore, whatever the church
has to say about social relations must be said after a careful
exercise of the ministry of discernment. The same is true as
regards the question of violence in our situation today.

The following discussion of categories of violence will hopefully
broaden our understanding of political violence in order to
strengthen our powers of discernment. On this subject I will be
drawing from the insights of Rollo May in particular.

In *Power and Innocence*, May devotes a chapter to an 'Anatomy
of Violence'. He takes the first violence of oppression as self-
evident and deals with reactions to it. He points out that violence
is a reaction of desperation in response to the threat to one's self-
esteem:

> When a person (or group of people) has been denied over a
> period of time what he feels are his legitimate rights, when he
> is continuously burdened with feelings of impotence which
> corrode any remaining self-esteem, violence is the predictable
> end result.[7]

In the language of Paul Tillich, substituting 'force' in place of
violence, we could say that the latter is a means whereby 'being
actualises itself over against the threat of non-being'.[8] Anyone who
has seen young people at a funeral throw stones at an armoured
vehicle spitting live bullets will understand this description of
defensive violence as an act of desperation.

In his five varieties of violence, May calls the initial eruption
simple violence. This is sporadic and often spontaneous violence;
a fit of anger. It soon leads to the second type; calculated
violence, as leadership begins to emerge and channels the energy
of anger more purposefully. In South Africa, the detention without
trial of thousands of people, including children, should be seen as
an attempt to get rid of this naturally-emerging leadership.

The government does this in the hope of containing the
violence. What happens instead is that the sense of threat to the
community is heightened, and the people keep reproducing the

sometimes directionless simple violence. It is rather like chopping off the spout of a kettle because boiling water overflows through it. That does not relieve the pressure of heat which causes the boiling. Instead it makes it more difficult to deal with the water! It is not surprising that some of the township anger has led to the emergence of units of 'necklace activists'. This is part of the concern behind the call for the recognition of the accepted leaders of the people, their release from prison or return from exile and for unhindered political organisation.

The third variety in May's schema is fomented violence. This, he says, is what a Himmler or any rabble-rouser 'of the extreme right or left in any country', would occasion. The townships may have their share of this, but it arises from the desperation of impotence and political hurt.

I find the fourth type of violence described by May very instructive for the church. It is 'absentee violence (or instrumental violence)'. This is the indirect violence of those who claim innocence despite the fact that they live in and benefit from a system that perpetrates violence. To illustrate the point, May cites the many United States citizens who thought they had no part in the war even though their taxes indirectly financed human destruction in Vietnam.

Who is to blame for the numerous deaths in detention? The deaths of Biko, Timol, Mdluli, Aggett? Nobody's to blame. Who is to blame for the orphaned children of Nyami and Mlungisi Mxenge? Nobody's to blame. Who is responsible for the deaths of the Cradock leaders? Nobody knows. How many of us are conscious of our share in the routine killings in the townships or the malnutrition and infant mortality in the bantustans? How many consider our national guilt in the destruction of families, as migrant-labour laws enforce life under animal-like conditions in the single-sex hostels? How many experience the shame of their indirect contribution to the Namibian occupation, the Angolan invasion, or the military raids on neighbouring countries?

We are involved in this violence as acquiescent tax-payers, employers, pastors and congregations, or any other category of spectators to the struggle, *Izethameli,* T.V. viewers, as such people are commonly known in the township.

The last of Rollo May's varieties is violence from above; what Helder Camara terms repressive violence. This transforms the police, agents of social protection, into terrorists. Citing experts in the field, May says this violence is 'regularly more destructive than other violence — partly because the police have clubs and guns, and partly because they have *a large reservoir of inner individual resentment* on which they can draw in their rage' (my emphasis).

## IS THERE A WAY OUT?

I have argued that the question of violence is subsidiary to the question of social transformation and radical (reaching to the roots) political change in this country. I have supported that view by showing that South African Christians are not absolute pacifists. They are ready to accommodate war and violence in accordance with church tradition. I have argued that the violence of resistance becomes an issue for the institutional church really because it deviates from the normal pattern of accommodating state violence. The liberal English-speaking church is caught up in an awkward church-state alliance with the government, although many of its members would deny this, in that the same liberal church is known to verbally support the cause of justice. Has it not roundly condemned the apartheid system as evil and contrary to the will of God?

I have argued in this essay that black political opinion recognises the resistance movement as doing a necessary duty of national defence against the self-imposed total onslaught of government machinery, and I have called on the church to judge the South African problem in the light of the black grievances of economic dispossession and political robbery. Hence I have called for the church to be a partisan of national liberation.

Through an overview of categories of violence I have tried to demonstrate the complexity of the violence in our context. I have recommended that we use the tool of social analysis in the ministry of social discernment, for the sake of social salvation. For the complex violence that is consuming our country is indicative of the prevailing *social cancer of wrong relationships.*

Relationships as a theological concept opens the way for the orthodox church to move towards orthopraxis. That, in a nutshell, is the way out for us all as Christians. Contemporary theology has recovered the patristic (especially Eastern) idea of the mystery of the God as Trinity-in-relationship. God's self-revelation is revelation of right relationship. God's self-communication is a revelation and an extension of the relationality in love, which is within the Godhead. Through Christ, in the Holy Spirit, we are enabled to partake of that relationship. Hence we call ourselves children of God and fellow-heirs with Christ, of the kingdom (kin-dom) of God; a kingdom of right relationships.

The Christian faith proclaims that the God who is Right-Relationship is not to be known in the blissful pleasure of right relationship within Godself, but that this God is known as creator and source of the right relations of human beings who are made in God's relational image. Human fulfilment, the realisation of what we are meant to be, is an acknowledgement of our call to right relationships. That is the only way to be holy, to be Godly, to be Christlike. To occasion or entertain wrong relationships is the recipe for sin. The story of sin is the story of broken relationships and the need for healing, 'from the blood of Abel' to the saving blood of Jesus. For the God who is Right-Relationship emptied Godself and took human form in order to establish right human relations. Jesus thus became both the embodiment and the model of right relations.

The church, the community of Christ's disciples, is left with both the task and example of Christ in the world of sin and violence. Violence is the result of wrong relations, and often results in a worsening of those relations. This is why the church normatively opposes violent solutions to problems. Yet the church exists in an inescapably violent world and has a mission to that world. Its mission is to witness to and struggle for right relations in the world, as a pointer to the eschatological manifestation of the God who is Right-Relation.

It would therefore seem to me that the most important thing in the Christian mission, indeed in all of human life from time immemorial, is right relationship. The laws of all societies, from the most primitive to the most advanced are established to preserve right relations. Thus they are said to be just. The law of Christ is the fulfilment of all laws, for Christ is Right-Relation in the flesh. Hence his church can have no greater commitment than the cause of right relations.

What do we learn from Christ's approach to the righting of relations? We may have little access to the 'biography' of the historical Jesus. But by all accounts it is clear that he made a point of identifying with those who were the victims of wrong relationships. He engaged in constant disputes with and castigation of those responsible for wrong relationships. The second and most important feature of Jesus' method was his violent death at the hands of the violators of relationships.

The cry of the oppressed in South Africa is a cry against a state of wrong relationships. These wrong political and economic relationships are maintained violently, with a complete denial of even the most non-violent protests. What is the church doing about this?

To follow Christ we have to be fully incarnated in the situation. We cannot sit at the pinnacle of the church tower and condemn people's responses to a violent system which we are ourselves not lifting a finger to undo. In the example of Christ we have at least two levels of operation; firstly, to identify with the victims of wrong relationships, the oppressed, and to take on their flesh as in the theological sense of incarnation. Secondly, we have to follow Christ on behalf of others suffering the violent blows of evil oppression. We have to resist evil to the bitter end. In principle, the church is expected to follow the example of Christ on both these points.

To begin with, the church must ceaselessly campaign for a radical righting of relationships in our society. This is the character of Jesus' ministry that led so many needy outcasts and marginalised of society to follow him. He emptied himself and took the form of the lowliest in society, a slave. Is it too hard for church members to leave their elevated sanctuaries and take on the form of the despised? Christ clearly and unequivocally identified with the oppressed.

It is a striking observation that while blacks are by law and tradition barred from property ownership in South Africa, the church, which is 80 per cent black, owns vast amounts of property because it 'passes for white'. Meanwhile the same church keeps quiet about black rights to land ownership in the country. It is remarkable further to observe that a church so propertied in its white identity in greater South Africa does not mind not holding full property rights for its black congregations in the townships. Township churches exist at the mercy of government officials. Clergy often report how such officials take pleasure in calling this restriction to mind in respect of churches that frequently open their buildings to be used in the cause of the oppressed.

I am alluding to structural factors that militate against the church's identifying with the oppressed but even if ties to the system could be overcome without structural changes, we have yet to follow Christ in opposing evil to the very face of death. The non-violent Christ did not shun the duty of facing the violent enemy of right relations. In doing so he himself became the victim of violence. Hence we are able to look upon Christ as the hero of the human cause of right relationships. 'No one can have greater love than to lay down his life for his friends' (Jn.15:13). The church must take the lead and demonstrate the power of non-violence in South Africa. The oppressed must be left with no doubt as to where the church stands. Such witness may occasion the violent death of the church as we have come to know it. But:

> Who shall separate us from the love of Christ? Shall tribulation, or distress, or persecution, or famine, or nakedness, or peril, or sword? . . . No, in all these things we are more than conquerors through him who loved us. For I am sure that neither death, nor life, nor angels, nor principalities, nor things present, nor things to come, nor powers, nor height, nor depth, nor anything else in all creation, will be able to separate us from the love of God in Christ Jesus our Lord. (Romans 8:35,37-39)

Is there a way out? It is then not violence with which we have to deal, but social injustice. It is for us to follow Christ outside the city gates of security; even to the repelling nakedness of the cross. Many Christians in the prime of their lives have already taken that path. Through these martyrs the church lives, and from their witness we derive hope that right human relations shall yet be established.

## NOTES

1.  A. Luthuli, *Let My People Go*, (New York: McGraw-Hill, 1962), p.88.
2.  The Kairos theologians: *The Kairos Document* (2nd ed.), (Johannesburg: Skotaville, 1986), p.23.
3.  R. McAfee Brown, *Religion and Violence*, (Philadelphia: Westminster, 1973), p.32.
4.  C. Villa-Vicencio, 'A Reluctant Response: Has the Challenge been Heard', in *Journal of Theology for Southern Africa*, 55, June 1986, p.57.
5.  S. Biko, *I Write What I Like*, (London: Bowerdeen Press, 1978), p.213.
6.  D. Tutu, 'The Theology of Liberation in Africa', in K. Appiah-Kuloi and S. Torres, (eds.), *African Theology En Route*, (New York: Orbis, 1979), p.166.
7.  Rollo May, *Power and Innocence: A Search for the Sources of Violence*, (New York: W.W. Norton, 1972), p.182.
8.  P. Tillich, *Love, Power and Justice*, (New York: OUP, 1962), p.47.

# CLASSICAL
# TRADITIONS

# Violence and the Prophets

ITUMELENG MOSALA

This study will confine itself to the descriptions of 'violence' that occur in the biblical traditions. Where, however, the prophetic traditions re-use other traditions, these will be examined for their relevance to violence in the prophetic texts. Further, this study will attempt to do more than *re-describe* violence as found in the prophetic traditions. It will try to *explain* each description of violence in terms of its historical context, class character and ideological functions. A fundamental presupposition of the analysis undertaken here is that the biblical texts are more than records or repositories of information; they are signified, discursive practices, discourses of struggle.

The texts of the Bible arise out of contexts of struggle and encode those contexts and their struggles in particular ways. The nature of the descriptions in the Bible, therefore, are colored by the interests and agendas of the struggles of which they are products as well as signified practices. Eagleton makes this point succinctly when he writes:

> The text takes as its object, not the real, but certain significations by which the real lives itself — significations which are themselves the product of its partial abolition. Within the text itself, then, ideology becomes a dominant structure, determining the character and disposition of certain 'pseudo-real' constituents. This inversion, as it were, of the real historical process, whereby in the text itself ideology seems to determine the historically real rather than *vice versa,* is itself naturally determined in the last instance by history itself. History one might say, is the *ultimate* signifier of literature, as it is the ultimate signified.[1]

Clearing the ground methodologically in this way is crucial for the debate on violence in the Bible. This is so because, traditionally, proponents of violence as well as those of non-violence/pacificism have further clouded and mystified the issue by the way they have used the Bible. Consequently their own intentions have been ill-served by their appropriation of texts that ironically subverted their purposes while on the surface seeming supportive. This essay, therefore, will argue that not all the texts

103

that speak of violence can be used to support 'revolutionary violence',[2] and *vice versa*. In other words, the progressive character of the texts must be judged independently of their description of violence.

The subject of violence in the Bible is complicated by a further methodological problem. I refer to the semantic difficulty of squeezing concepts out of lexemes.[3] Barr, in *The Semantics of Biblical Language*, demonstrates beyond doubt that attempts to equate words with concepts are fraught with enormous methodological dangers. He therefore advises that 'the linguistic bearer of the theological statement is usually the sentence and the still larger literary complex and not the word or morphological and syntactical mechanisms'.[4]

Aware of the problems which Barr refers to, this study must nevertheless enter the debate on violence by first doing concordance work on the words for violence. This is necessary in order to get at the specific places in the biblical text where violence is discussed. The danger of trying to draw meanings out of individual words, however, will be avoided.

## VIOLENCE IN THE PROPHETIC TRADITION

The biblical traditions generally use different terms to denote different forms of violence. This is notwithstanding the fact that in many poetic texts Hebrew parallelism requires the use of varying terms to convey the same meaning. It should be remembered, however, that in any of these uses it is not the terms themselves that signify but the syntactic contexts in which they occur.

In the prophetic texts, the terms *gazal, ratsats, nagas, 'anah,* and *'ashaq,* represent the most dramatic, repugnant and graphic forms of violence. This kind of violence is perpetrated by the few powerful, rich, dominant members of the society against the many weak, poor, dispossessed members of the same society. About this situation Chaney writes:

> A ruling élite of two percent or less of the population enjoyed the privilege of controlling half or more of the total goods and services produced in the society. This élite, in turn, had every incentive and more than sufficient means to extract the largest possible 'surplus' from the peasant majority, leaving it only the barest subsistence necessary to remain productive. As a result, life for the majority was brutish and short, with peasant families decimated by hunger and disease.[5]

This form of socio-economic and political violence is

graphically described in Micah 2:2 in terms of the action of people who expropriate poor peasants' fields and poor families' houses. In Malachi 1:13 this violence is described as a form of theft, legalised official theft. Isaiah 10:2 interprets this violence as the repugnant brutality of the powerful against the harmless, desperate widows and orphans. It is a violence that is committed without a conscience; it is merciless plunder against the weak (Ez. 22:1-31). This violence, according to Jeremiah 22:17, is murder; it is murderous oppression (Hos. 5:11). Gottwald grasps the essence of this violence and its institutional location, when he describes the situation in this way:

> The ruling class in monarchic Israel extracted surplus in two ways that were systematically connected: a state tax-rent, compounded by foreign tribute, was the initial and dominant method of extraction, which in turn spawned a credit/debt system that was formally outside the state administration, but that was necessitated by the peasant hardship that the state generated via the tax-rent. The class fraction that lived off the tax-rent was made up of state-functionaries and the class fraction that lived off the debt payments was made up of latifundaries, who probably for the most part had a base in state administration which gave them command of resources enabling them to extend credit to peasants. At the same time ... the state legitimated the tax-rent as payment due to Yahweh's servants who protected the patrimonies of the free agragarians, and the latifundaries explained their taking possession of indebted lands as the work of 'custodians' or 'keepers' of the patrimonial shares of those who fell hopelessly into debt.[6]

It is this structural violence that the prophetic traditions do not tire of condemning. Care must be exercised, however, not to speak monolithically about the prophetic traditions. Coote's study of the book of Amos has shown that the history of the text itself militates against any monolithic conceptions. It is a historical fact that the prophetic texts represent at least a *three-stage process* of composition.[7] The stages through which the materials have emerged are not simply temporal shifts, they are also indicative of social class and ideological reactualisations of the traditions.

The violence discussed above, therefore, relates to what Coote calls the A-stage prophetic descriptions. It goes back to the historical situation addressed by the prophet in the eighth century B.C.E. The context is one of social class, gender, and cultural violence against the weaker members of ancient Israelite society.

The A-stage theological judgement on this violence and especially
its beneficiaries is succinctly stated in relation to the book of
Amos by Coote:

> These oracles announce an *inevitable catastrophe*. They leave
> no way to squirm out of it. Their forms insist on it. Yahweh has
> passed judgment and imposed the sentence: war, exile, and
> death. Yahweh has published his war orders: *de guello*, no
> quarter. He has taken a solemn oath to carry them out. Amos
> chants a dirge, 'Woe to those at ease in Samaria': you are as
> good as dead. Your obituary has just come out.[8]

*Gazal, ratsats, nagas, 'anah,* and *'ashaq,* appear also in what
Coote calls the B-stage prophetic texts. The historical conjunctural
context of these passages is the national crisis occasioned by the
threats or reality of invasion by other nations like Assyria or
Babylon.

The B-stage appearance of the above violence texts retains the
notions of oppression and exploitation as basic elements. Micah
3:2, for instance, is still as graphic as its A-stage counterpart: 'You
skin my people alive and tear the flesh off their bones'. Jeremiah
21:12 and 22:3 describe violence as a form of cheating and
counsel the royal house and the state functionaries to practise
justice. Isaiah 42:3-4 brings out the notion of the unequal
relations between the powerful and the weak and envisions a
situation when this will be corrected. The agent of the new
relations whose specific task will be to prevent the *breaking off* of
a bent reed is the Lord's servant. In Isaiah 36:6 this violence is
described as one that is symbolised by belief : You are expecting
Egypt to help you, but that would be like using a reed as a
walking stick — it would *break* and jab your hand'. A similar
notion is expressed in Ezekiel 29:7 'The Lord says, 'The Israelites
relied on you Egyptians for support, but you were not better than
a weak stick. When they leaned on you, you broke, pierced their
armpits, and made them wrench their backs". Isaiah 58:3 relates
this form of violence to the way in which it makes religious
practice and faith hypocritical: 'The truth is that at the same time
as you fast, you pursue your own interests and oppress your
workers'. In Zechariah 10:4 Yahweh promises that the people of
Israel will regain a situation where their rulers will be able to mete
out violence against their enemies. The national character of the
violence suffered by Israel in the B-stage texts is unmistakable:
Isaiah 52:21; 54:11; Ezekiel 22:10; 16:48-50. Occasionally the A-
stage venom, directness and specificity of this kind of violence

reappear, as in Jeremiah 22:17: 'But you can only see your selfish interests; you kill the innocent and violently oppress your people'.

The logical national counter-violence that follows the national oppression of Israel is also unmistakable. Jeremiah 50:33 is clear on this: "The Lord Almighty says, 'The people of Israel and of Judah are oppressed. All who captured them are guarding them closely and will not let them go'".

For all their poignancy and retention of the basic elements of violence as described in the A-stage, these texts are cast in a different mould. Coote lists a number of distinctive features of B-stage prophetic material. The most important of these are the following. Firstly, that the B-stage material tends to address general rather than specific audiences. Secondly, the B-discourses of the prophetic tradition have an indirect basic message which is characterised by various elaborations such as the exhortation 'perform justice or else'. Thirdly, the material is marked by a great deal of prose and prosifying of poetry. The B-stage prophetic oracles are further characterised by an ideological open-endedness which is a characteristic feature of the class character of its tradents. As Coote aptly states 'in contrast to the A-stage, the B-stage offers an open future, a new possibility, and, ironically, a virtually perpetual crisis'.[9]

When the violence which is described in the B-stage texts takes place against the poor and oppressed inside Israelite society, the rich and the powerful are *exhorted* to do justice and abstain from evil. They are promised that they will regain favour from Yahweh if they repent. When the violence of these texts is directed at the Israelite ruling classes who *universalise* their condition in national terms, Yahweh promises counter-violence against Israel's enemies. In certain circumstances the prophetic tradition *reverses* the earlier prophetic discourses of struggle. A classical example in this case is the *reversal* of the pro-oppressed and exploited people's A-text in Micah 4:3(b)-4 to a blatantly ruling class B-text in Joel 3:10. It is strenuously maintained in this study that the call to arms in Joel 3:10 is a reactionary, militaristic imperialist call which can only be heeded at the expense of the oppressed and exploited majority. It smacks of the contemporary Reaganite-cum-Thatcherite romanticisation of war. It is certainly not a call to revolutionary violence.

The B-stage texts on violence, like other B-stage texts, are cast in what Hall calls a negotiated code.[10] They represent a mixture of adaptive and oppositional elements. In line with the social class

practices of its proponents, the material cast in a negotiated code
is shot through with contradictions. It reflects the differential and
unequal relation to power of its agents. It is for this reason that
violence in these texts retains the element of oppression and
exploitation even though the bearers of these texts were
themselves agents of oppression and exploitation.

The use of the term *ra'shah* in the prophetic tradition denotes
yet another understanding of violence. It refers to military
destruction especially between nations or whole groups of people.
Jeremiah 49:21 describes the fall of Edom: 'when Edom falls,
there will be such a noise that the entire earth will shake, and the
cries of alarm will be heard as far as the Gulf of Aqaba'. A similar
perspective is expressed in Jer.8:16 '... Our enemies have come
to destroy our land and everything in it, our city and all its people'.

The term *parats* denotes wanton violence whose subjects are
non-specific. This violence comes neither from the powerful
groups nor from Yahweh, and of course not from the oppressed.
Nehemiah 3:35; 2:13; 4:11; Isaiah 54:3; 30:13; Hosea 4:10,
among others, refer to this form.

In another set of prophetic texts, however, this violence is
attributed to non-identifiable groups known simply as robbers and
violent men (Jer.7:11; Ezek.7:22, Dan.11:14).

The word *'atsab* describes yet another form of violence. This
form is defined variously as sadness, grief, miserable fate. It is
closely related to violent action against religious idols, symbols
and discourses and it is very priestly in its context (Jer.44:19;
22:28; Hos.4:17; 8:4; Is.46:1; Micah 1:7). Occasionally this violence
displays A-stage tendencies as in Isaiah 58:3 where it refers to the
oppression of workers.

On the whole the terms *ra'shah, parats* and *'atsab* are used in
what Coote calls C-stage texts. The basic philosophy underlying
these traditions is captured by Coote when he says of their
bearers:

> It was not the challenge to do justice that spoke most directly
> to this new generation, but the challenge to claim justice on
> their own behalf and to have faith that Yahweh would rescue
> the relatively powerless from death and restore them to life as
> he had in the past.[11]

The social class base of the bearers of the C-stage prophetic
texts is the former ruling classes of Zion from Jerusalem and
Samaria. Violence for them is what happened to their wealth, their
palaces, their prestigious building projects and Temple

paraphenalia when the foreigners invaded Samaria and Jerusalem. Violence is their continued captivity in a foreign land. Coote poignantly concludes of this tradition:

> It is useful to look at the C-stage in terms of *reversal*. If the exile represented the A-stage fulfilled a second time, the C-stage represents the A-stage on its head.[12]

The Bible, including the prophetic traditions, is of course silent about the responses or perspectives of the oppressed and exploited on violence. The reason is simple. The oppressed did not write the Bible. It was the oppressors or their ideologists who wrote the Bible. The biblical text as a discursive practice is a ruling class document.

## NOTES

1. T. Eagleton, *Criticism and Ideology*, (London: Verso, 1976), p.72.
2. For a distinction between revolutionary and reactionary violence see H. Marcuse's article in which he argues, inter alia, that 'in terms of historical function, there is a difference between revolutionary and reactionary violence, between violence practised by the oppressed and by the oppressors. In terms of ethics, both forms of violence are inhuman and evil — but since when is history made in accordance with ethical standards? To start applying them at the point where the oppressed rebel against the oppressors, the have-nots with the haves, is serving the cause of actual violence by weakening the protest against it', in 'Repressive Tolerance', *Critical Sociology*, (Harmondsworth: Penguin, 1976), pp.315ff.
3. For a linguistic definition of lexemes see J. Lyons, *Semantics,* 1, (Cambridge: C.U.P., 1977), p.18.
4. J. Barr, *The Semantics of Biblical Language*, (Oxford: Oxford University Press, 1961), p.269.
5. M. Chaney, 'Systemic Study of the Israelite Monarchy', Sociology of the Monarchy SBL Seminar Paper, Dec. 1981, p.14.
6. N.K. Gottwald, 'Contemporary Studies of social class and social stratification and a hypothesis about social class in Monarchic Israel', Seminar Paper on Sociology of the Monarchy, (*ASDR-SBL,* 1985), p.20.
7. R.B. Coote, *Amos Among The Prophets — Composition and Theology*, (Philadelphia: Fortress, 1981), p.3.
8. *Ibid.*, p.19.
9. *Ibid.*, pp.62ff.
10. Stuart Hall, *Encoding and Decoding in Television Discourse*, Centre for Contemporary Cultural Studies, (Birmingham: Birmingham University, 1973), p.23.
11. R.B. Coote, *Amos among the Prophets*, p.111.
12. *Ibid.*

# Violence in the Gospel Tradition

EPHRAIM K. MOSOTHOANE

That violence, more than anything else, characterises life in southern Africa generally, and in South Africa in particular can hardly be gainsaid. That violence characterised life in the Roman empire during the New Testament period can also hardly be gainsaid. The much vaunted *Pax Romana* was in reality far more a matter of brutal repression than peace.[1]

If this were true of the vast Roman empire, it was particularly true of life in Roman Palestine during the first century C.E. The administration of Pontius Pilate was, according to Philo of Alexandria, characterised by 'corruption, violence, robbery, brutality, extortion, and execution without trial'.[2] Jesus, his disciples, his contemporaries, and the early Christian movement lived in a world of 'religio-political unrest, violent rebellion, and its even more violent repression'.[3] Innumerable human lives were summarily and brutally brought to a premature end by sword, stoning, or crucifixion. The New Testament shows us Christians suffering at the hands of mobs (Jewish and Gentile alike) as well as state and religious authorities (again both Jewish and Roman).

The debate among Christians today concerns the appropriate or most appropriate Christian response to the violences *we* encounter in *our* world and *our* society. This paper addresses itself to the New Testament response to violence.

Before going further the question must be asked as to whether the New Testament does, in fact, address itself to the matter of violence and the appropriate Christian response. The question becomes even more important when we realise that the Greek for *violence* (namely the verb *biazomai,* the noun *bia,* and the adjectival forms *biaios* and *biastès*) occurs very rarely in the New Testament. Notwithstanding this, the fact remains that the problem of violence is fully addressed in the New Testament. Over against the rarity of *biazomai* and its cognates, *thlipsis* (tribulation, affliction, distress), *diòkò* (to put to flight, to pursue, hence to persecute), and *anagkazò* (to force, to compel), together with their cognates, all occur much more frequently.

Far more significant than lexical statistics, however, is the fact that New Testament documents deal very specifically with problems raised by suffering and persecution for Christian communities. Pre-eminent among these, in our view, are I Peter, Hebrews, the Book of Revelation, and Mark's gospel. It is also not uncommon, for example, to find Paul in his letters encouraging and strengthening Christian communities facing persecution. Incidents of Christian persecution are found throughout the Acts of the Apostles while both Matthew and John warn, in their gospels, of the inevitability of suffering and persecution for Christians.

The basic argument advanced here is that the gospels display subtle variations that indicate reasonably clearly that there is no one uniform response of the gospels to the experience of violence. Instead of that, we find a number of different responses which are not dogmatically but rather historically and circumstantially determined. There is, in our view, a close correlation between the variations in language and behaviour related to situations of violence, on the one hand, and to the most probable *Sitze in Leben* behind the various traditions, on the other.

Broadly speaking, there seems to be two basic types or categories of material relevant to our subject. There are, firstly, those that seem to represent a *negative* response or attitude towards violence; secondly, those that seem to be or may be interpreted as representing a *positive* response or attitude.

## NEGATIVE RESPONSES

The following are perhaps the major passages where the response to violence is a negative one: Mt.5:21-26; 5:38-42 (para. Lk.6:20-30); 5:43-48 (para. Lk.6:27-28, 32-36); 18:21-22 (para. Lk.17:3-4); 26:47-56 (para. Mk.14:43-50; Lk.22:47-53; Jn.18:2-11). All the passages consist almost entirely of the sayings of Jesus, the exception, viz. Mt.26:47-56 and parallels consisting of both narrative and sayings of Jesus. These sayings of Jesus are of the *legal type*, providing directive for, *inter alia,* the ethical life of the church and of individual members of the Christian community.

We shall confine ourselves to a brief consideration of three only: Mt.5:38-42 and parallel, Mt.5:43-48 and parallel, and Mt.26:47-56 and its parallels. The first two of our passages, viz.

Mt.5:38-42 and Mt.5:43-48 are part of a group of six antitheses in Matthew's gospel.

For purposes of this study we consider first Mt.5:38-42 and the Lucan parallel, Lk.6:20-30,34. Even a cursory glance at these two passages seems to come up with an interesting suggestion. The two passages certainly share the same basic elements: the sayings concerning striking the cheek, taking a coat, begging, and borrowing ('lending' in Luke). However, there are differences as well. To begin with, Luke's version is not only somewhat shorter, it is also without the antithetical form we find in Matthew. Much more interesting, if not significant, is the difference in language between the two versions. Where Matthew has *rhapizein* (Mt.5:39) Luke uses *tuptein* (Lk.6:29); where in Matthew we read *strephein* (Mt.5:39) in Luke we have *parechein* (Lk.6:29); Matthew's *krithenai kai . . . labein* (Mt.5:40) is quite simply *airein* in Luke (Lk.6:29); and where Matthew has *apheinai* (Mt.5:40) Luke has *mè kòluein* (Lk.6:29).

Now, whereas there is very little if anything at all, to choose, both in terms of meaning and force, between Matthew's *rhapizein* and Luke's *tuptein,* the same cannot necessarily be said of the rest of the language used in these two parallel passages. Both seem to have referred originally to striking with some instrument, such as a stick, a rod, or a whip than with the hand or fist. The context in both gospels makes it abundantly clear, though, that the reference here is to striking with the hand. In both instances the focus is not so much on physical pain as it is on the insult and humiliation that the striking is intended to represent. The violence involved is thus more psychological than it is physical.

The moment we move beyond Matthew's *rhapizein* and Luke's *tuptein* the choice, or apparent choice, of language between the two gospels becomes interesting, if not significant. In both gospels Jesus not only counsels but requires that the other cheek be turned. Whereas in Matthew this other cheek has to be turned *(strephein)* in Luke it has to be *offered (parechein).* Whereas, Matthew's *strephein* has the connotation of 'twisting', suggesting a degree of 'force' (perhaps because it is an unnatural thing to do), Luke's *parechein,* in contrast, has connotations of *providing, holding in readiness, making available.* It is tempting to suggest that in Luke's version the language describing the response Jesus requires to a specific act of violence is softer in comparison to the language in Matthew's version.

No less interesting is the difference between Mt.5:40 and

Lk.6:29b. To begin with Mt.5:40 states that if the 'coat' (the *chitòn* or inner garment) be taken, the disciple should be prepared to let the 'cloak' (the *himation* or outer garment) be taken as well, whereas in Lk.6:29b it is the other way round: if the 'cloak' be taken, the disciple should be prepared to part with the 'coat' as well. Furthermore, the victim in Mt.5:40 is first subjected to a trial (cf. *krithetai*), but seemingly not so in Lk.6:29b. Then there is the choice of language. Mt.5:40, on the one hand, uses the verb *lambanein* for 'taking' the garment where Lk.6:29b, on the other hand, uses *airein*. In Matthew the response should be that of 'handing over' *(apheinai)* the remaining garment, whereas in Luke it is expressed in terms of 'not preventing' *(mè kòluein)* it being taken.

Any attempt at explaining the difference between Mt.5:40 and Lk.6:29b must start with a recognition of the different *situations* envisaged in the two texts: in Matthew a calculated law-suit, in Luke a robbery. This would, in the first place, explain the difference in the order in which the garments are taken. It would also, in the second instance, account for some of the variation in language. The 'handing over' in Matthew, for example, is appropriate to a court verdict on the basis of which the first garment has been taken, and the 'not preventing' in Luke is appropriate to a robbery in which the robber has helped himself. And yet, either in spite of this or precisely because of this, Luke's language remains more refined, less harsh, than that of Matthew: *airein*, 'to take away' (without necessarily implying physical violence); *lambanein,* 'to take' (with or without violence), 'to grasp', 'to seize'.

No less interesting is a comparison of Mt.5:43-48 and Lk.6:27-28, 32-36. Where in Matthew Jesus follows the commandment 'love your enemies' with 'pray for those who *persecute* you', in Luke he follows with 'do good to those who *hate* you, bless those who *curse* you, pray for those who *abuse* you'. In Matthew *persecution* defines who the *enemies* are, whereas in Luke *hatred, curses,* and *reviling (espēreazein)* define who they are. Where Luke keeps on repeating the one word 'sinners' Matthew has 'the evil', 'the unjust', and 'the tax collectors'. Here again we seem to be encountering a degree of refinement in Luke not found in Matthew.

The next passage, reported by all four evangelists (Mk.14:43-50; Mt.26:47-56; Lk.22:47-53; Jn.18:2-11), concerns the arrest of Jesus. Our brief comparison of the four accounts will take into consideration *content, sequence,* and *language.*

Firstly, all four gospels set the scene for the arrest of Jesus. Mark, Matthew, and John set the scene for a *potentially-violent confrontation* between Jesus and his followers, on the one hand, and his captors on the other. The scene consists of 'a crowd with swords and clubs' (Mk.14:43); more specifically 'a band of soldiers and some officers from the chief priests and the Pharisees, armed with weapons', (Jn.18:3). In Luke's gospel this hint of a potentially-violent confrontation is made somewhat earlier, and in a pericope that deserves to be looked at in its own right since it raises its own, unique problems (Lk.22:35-38). Otherwise, Luke's setting of the scene immediately prior to the arrest seems to be much less menacing, compared to the other three.

Then there is the plan agreed upon between Judas and the Jewish authorities. This is recorded by two of the evangelists, Mark and Matthew. In both gospels the plan would make it possible for Jesus to be seized *(kratein)* by his opponents, a plan not mentioned in Luke and John. The plan is followed by a report of its execution. All four gospels report that Jesus was seized, and had hands laid on him. The language through which this execution of the plan is expressed varies, however, from gospel to gospel, and the variations are not without significance. Mark, followed quite closely by Matthew, says *hoi de epebalon tas cheiras autò ekratesan auton* (Mk.14:46). In Luke it is Jesus who, reacting to his captors having come armed, refers to the violent handling. In the place of Mark's and Matthew's *epebalon tas cheiras,* however, Luke has *exeteinate tas cheiras* (Lk.22:53), and for the execution he has *sullabontes de auton* (Lk.22:54). In John the captors *sunelabon ton lèsoun kai edèsan auton* (Jn.18:12). Luke's *ekteinein* (to stretch out) with the preposition *epi* (towards) followed by the accusative case is clearly a refinement and softening of Mark's and Matthew's *epibalein* (to throw or cast upon) which has a stronger connotation of violence. Indeed, behind Mark's and Matthew's *epibalein tas cheiras* may be the Septuagint's *epibalein tèn cheira.* There is, in other words, a greater suggestion of violence in the arrest of Jesus in Mark and Matthew than there is in Luke. Again Luke's and John's *sullabein* (to take, to receive, to seize, to apprehend) seems to be a refinement of Mark's and Matthew's *kratein* (to vanquish, to subdue, to arrest, to seize, to overpower). In all four gospels the response to Jesus' arrest is the striking of the high-priest's servant's ear with the sword by one of Jesus' disciples (Mk.14:47 and parallels). Brandon's observation and comment that

> the disciples in Gethsemane were armed, [that] the Roman or Jewish officials sent to effect the arrest were heavily armed, obviously in anticipation of violent resistance, and [that] armed resistance was offered by the disciples, even if only to the extent of wounding one of the police officers[4]

would be particularly applicable to Mark's and Matthew's language which can be understood as suggesting that Jesus had to be *overpowered*.

Jesus' response to the disciple's striking the high-priest's servant is also worth noting. Mark's gospel has no reference whatsoever to Jesus responding to this particular action. He responds rather to the fact that those who have come to arrest him are armed (Mk.14:48-49). In Matthew's gospel Jesus responds as follows: 'Put your sword back into its place; for all who take the sword will perish by the sword. Do you think that I cannot appeal to my Father, and he will at once send me more than twelve legions of angels? But how then should the scriptures be fulfilled, that it must be so?' (Mt.26:52-54).

How do we explain this response of Jesus? In the first place, Mt.26:52-54 is *peculiar* to Matthew, and any interpretation of this text must take this fact into consideration. Its origin and/or background may not be easy to determine.

Perhaps the most promising approach to Mt.26:52-54 is to take as our point of departure Kosmala's suggestion that the source of the saying 'for all who take the sword will perish by the sword' (v.52) is the Targum on (Is.50:11, which reads: 'All you ... who take a sword, go, fall ... on the sword which you have taken ... you will return to your destruction'.[5] The particular value of this suggestion is that it helps us make sense of this saying within its specific context. We do not have here a general principle regarding violence. The Targum referred to is on a verse that comes at the end of one of the so-called 'Suffering Servant Songs' in Deutero-Isaiah. The Targum is thus given direct relevance to an incident within the Passion narrative.

Now, Is.50:10 is concerned with fearing the Lord, obeying the voice of his servant, trusting in the name of the Lord, and relying upon God. The servant whose voice should be obeyed himself states that

> The Lord God has opened my ear,
> and I was not rebellious,
> I turned not backward.

> I gave my back to the smiters,
> and my cheeks to those who
> pulled out the beard;
> I hid not my face
> from shame and spitting. (Is.50:5-6)

Scripture has shown clearly what is to be the lot of the servant-messiah, who is, for Matthew, the Son of God. With the 'great crowd with swords and clubs' laying their 'violent hands' on Jesus, a disciple shows readiness to resist violently. Jesus, using the most appropriate words available, declares that that which Scripture has decreed must be fulfilled and therefore not opposed. Thus, Hengel's view that Jesus' response 'indicates ... the senselessness of the undertaking ...' misses the point.[6] What we have here then, instead of a general principle regarding violence, is Matthew's account of Jesus' response in scriptural terms (via the Targums) to a specific act of violence which, if successful, would have negated the accomplishment of his divine mission. What ethical significance, if any, this may have had for Matthew's church we shall consider shortly.

The results of our study thus far seem to have come up with a consistent pattern in the *language* used by our New Testament gospels in respect of violence: Mark (where applicable) has the harshest, roughest, most violent language compared to the others; Matthew is more harsh than Luke and John, but to a degree less so than Mark; John is, at times, less harsh than Matthew and Mark, but certainly more than Luke; and Luke is the most refined of all. How are we to account for this variation?

In endeavouring to answer this question we need to refer firstly to the historical contexts to which our gospels addressed themselves. Notwithstanding the views of some recent scholars, it is likely that Mark's gospel was addressed to the needs of the Roman church under Nero's persecution.[7] Conflict and persecution seem to provide the setting for the gospels of Matthew and John as well. Matthew's church seems to have been a Syrian Jewish-Christian community in conflict with and suffering persecution from non-Christian Jews because of its confession of Jesus as messiah and its openness to Gentiles.[8] The purpose for which the fourth gospel was written is stated, though ambiguously, in Jn.20:31. If we accept the present subjunctive *pisteuète* as the original reading, then the gospel was written in order to *confirm* faith. That confirmation, we believe, was of Jewish-Christians who were subjected both to expulsion from the synagogue and 'to severe discipline and indeed to persecution which goes as far as death'.[9] As with Matthew's church, the persecutors were non-Christian Jews. Finally, the historical context for Luke's gospel is that of a Gentile-Christian community to which the evangelist sought to demonstrate the universality, and therefore the relevance of the gospel to them and to all Gentiles. How does all this relate to the question we are endeavouring to answer?

Such evidence as we have thus far looked at seems to point inevitably in one direction: namely this, that the New Testament does not have one single consistent attitude and response to violence.

Nowhere in the New Testament is the language as violent as in the book of Revelation. Not only do we find in the latter scorpion-locusts that are allowed to torture human beings to such an extent that they long to die (Rev.9:1ff) but also a God whose wrath is

> poured unmixed into the cup of his anger, and he [the beast] shall be tormented with fire and brimstone in the presence of the holy angels and in the presence of the Lamb. And the smoke of their torment goes up for ever and ever; and they have no rest, day or night . . . . (Rev.14:9ff)

In I Peter on the other hand God is 'the God of all grace' (I Pet.5:10) and Christ 'the Shepherd and Guardian of your souls' (I Pet.2:25).

So also with our New Testament gospels. Mark's gospel was written for the purpose of encouraging and exhorting a suffering Christian community. Towards this end the evangelist presented the church with the portrait of a Christ who was 'himself rejected, betrayed, denied, deserted, condemned, handed over, crucified, and mocked, but also chosen and vindicated by God'.[10] They are exhorted to follow this Christ with courage and patient endurance (cf. Mk.8:34-38; ch.13), and given the encouraging promise that they too would be vindicated and share in his victory (cf. Mk.13:27). For Christ this vindication and victory (and this is the point) followed a confrontation and an end that were truly violent. His arrest was nothing less than an act of 'laying violent hands' on him (Mk.14:46) while his 'trial' was accompanied by acts of psychological, if not physical, violence (Mk.14:65). Similarly, their share in his victory would follow their faithful discipleship to the point of death (cf. Mk.8:34-38; 13:13,27). The dramatically violent language in which it is all stated expresses something of this community's experience and feelings. Being seized, mocked, beaten, and violently killed had all been among the experiences of members of this church. Like Jesus they too may have felt forsaken by man as well as God (cf. Mk.15:6-15,32,34).

In the light of all that has been noted thus far: Why then does Jesus in Mark's gospel not respond at all (at the point of his arrest) to the striking of the high priest's servant's ear with the 'sword' or 'dagger'? In Matthew, Luke and John he responds negatively. Could it be that Mark's silence in itself indicates a response? Could it represent an inclination or tendency (at least on the part of Mark and his church) to approve of the violent reaction by Jesus' followers to the violence they have experienced and therefore suffered? Such an inclination or tendency would, if it were true, be expressed in negative rather than positive terms. Nevertheless, it would show that the depth and intensity of the violence experienced could lead to a understanding inclined towards the approval of a violent response. Such an inclination, it must be stressed though, would be seen as *implicit* rather than *explicit.*

We have already suggested that Matthew's church seems to have been a Syrian Jewish-Christian community in conflict with and suffering persecution from non-Christian Jews. These Christians were clearly persecuted because what they stood for was, in orthodox Jewish terms, a serious and dangerous corruption of the faith of Israel, particularly by confessing as messiah that Jesus who had been declared a blasphemous heretic by the Jewish religious leaders. In view of this we agree with Robinson's statement of the purpose of Matthew's gospel:

> [it] shows all the signs of being produced for a community [and by a community] that needed to formulate over against the main body of Pharisaic and Sadducaic Judaism, its own line on such issues as the interpretation of scripture and the place of the law, its attitude toward the temple and its sacrifices, the sabbath, fasting, prayer, food laws and purification rites, its rules for admission to the community and the discipline of offenders, for marriage, divorce and celibacy, its policy toward Samaritans and Gentiles in a predominantly Jewish milieu . . . . [11]

The writer of Matthew sought to equip this Jewish-Christian community 'to define and defend' itself and its position over against 'orthodox Judaism'.[12] Matthew clearly hoped his defence would be so effective as to lead to the conversion of these Jews to Christianity (Mt.28:16-20; 13-52).

What Christianity represents for Matthew has been described as 'a surpassing righteousness'.[13] 'For I tell you, unless your righteousness exceeds that of the scribes and Pharisees, you will never enter the kingdom of heaven' (Mt.5:20). If this be the case, it would then follow that Christian ethics, and therefore the proper Christian response to violence, can best be summarised in terms of 'a surpassing righteousness'. What does this mean, though?

There can be no denying that Jesus in Matthew's gospel requires of his followers unexpected, unconventional, moral responses to situations. Being able to say 'I have not killed, or committed adultery, or divorced, or sworn falsely' is not good enough. Reconciliation, inner personal purity, faithfulness and truthfulness should characterise his followers (Mt.5:21-37). This would apply even when confronted with situations of violence: over against the *lex talionis* principle enunciated in Exod.21:24; Lev.24:20; and Deut.19:21 the principle enunciated by Jesus is *mè antistènai tò ponèrò* (Mt.5:39); and over against the principle that limits love to the neighbour, Jesus enunciates the principle of a love that is not limited but extends even to the enemy (Mt.5:43f).

Now, it may be true that the *lex talionis* was, as Jeremias remarks, 'no longer literally applied at the time of Christ, but rather it formed the foundation of the whole civil law'. That means, of course, to quote Jeremias again 'the principle that the degree of punishment should correspond to the extent of the offence'.[14] If, on the one hand, it aimed at controlling revenge and retaliation, it also, on the other hand, aimed at ensuring that strict justice be done. It follows, therefore, that the degree of violence suffered calls for the same degree of violence to be meted out to the offender. Over against this principle Jesus enunciates the *mè antistènai tò ponèrò* princicple in Mt.5:39. The translation 'do not resist one who is evil' seems to be somewhat inadequate. The Greek *anthistemi* can mean 'stand' and 'take action against' as well as 'resist'; and if *hò ponèros* means 'one who *is* evil' it is because such a one actually *does* evil by, among other things, causing injury and pain. If so, then a more accurate translation would be 'do not take revenge on one who harms you'. In other words, 'do not return violence for violence'. That much seems to be clear. What is not provided is the rationale. Perhaps for Jesus, seen within the context of his proclamation of the reign of God, it was the inevitable ethical implication of the Old Testament teaching that vengeance belongs to God. For Matthew it was an important element in that 'surpassing righteousness' that firstly, constituted the self-definition and self-defence of his church over against 'orthodox Judaism' and, secondly, would lead to winning these antagonistic Jews over to the church.

Not less unexpected and unconventional is the idea, let alone moral principle, of loving the enemy (Mt.5:44). The Torah was quite specific about loving the neighbour:

> You shall not hate your brother in your heart, but you shall reason with your neighbour, lest you bear sin because of him. You shall not take vengeance or bear any grudge against the sons of your own people, but you shall love your neighbour as yourself: I am the LORD. (Lev.19:17-18)

It is this Leviticus text that is cited in Mt.5:43b, 'You shall love your neighbour'. This full Leviticus text (Lev.19:17-18) leaves us in no doubt as to who the 'neighbour' who is to be loved is. The phrases 'your brother' and 'the sons of your own people' show quite clearly that 'neighbour' refers to members of the community of Israel, members of the covenant community. They are to be loved. About those who fall outside this community Lev.19:17-18 is silent. Mt.5:43c, 'and hate your enemy' does not come from Leviticus; indeed, 'one will search the Old Testament in vain for an explicit order to "hate your enemy"'.[15]

Now, if 'neighbour' refers here to a member of the community of Israel, 'enemy' refers to non-Israelites who were hostile opponents to the covenant community — in terms of ancient Israel's history: Canaanites, Assyrians, Babylonians; and in terms of the Greco-Roman period: Ptolemies, Seleucids, and Romans. The love originally applicable to and required of members of the covenant community alone is, in Mt.5:43f, extended to those who fall outside and are in fact in hostile opposition to that community — a community now defined in relation to Jesus. The enemies' 'hostile opposition' is clearly stated in terms of persecution (Mt.5:44). While examples of rabbinic extension of the love principle in Lev.19:17-18 to all humanity may be found we are not aware of any exhortations in which loving one's enemies is *specifically enjoined*. Jesus' ethical requirement here is therefore unexpected and unconventional and unparalleled.

Once again the rationale for such a fundamental departure from conventional Jewish ethics is to be found in Jesus' proclamation of the reign of God. John Riches has argued convincingly that Jesus reworked the concept of the Kingdom of God, removing from it not only ritualistic but also exclusivist,

nationalistic, vengeful, and militaristic associations, replacing them
with associations of mercy, love, service and forgiveness. Central
to this re-working was Jesus' understanding of God as a God of
mercy, love, and forgiveness.[16] It is indeed this nature of God that
Mt.5:43ff uses as the reason why enemies are to be loved rather
than hated. And, for Matthew, of course, loving enemies and
persecutors was an important element in his church's self-
definition and self-defence and would contribute significantly in
seeking to win antagonistic Jews over to the church.

We have already suggested that Luke's handling of the same
saying compared to Matthew, represents a degree of refinement
and softening of language. Matthew defines 'enemies' as
'persecutors'. Enemies do not just hate and curse and revile (*pace*
Luke), *they actually persecute;* that is, they cause suffering, pain
and even death. Precisely because of this Matthew expresses his
and his community's feelings towards persecutors as well as his
and his community's ethical assessment of them. Using the
common Hebrew parallelism, here in chiastic form, he states that
they are 'evil' and 'unjust'. Behind the Greek *ponèros* and *adikos,*
we suggest is the Hebrew *ra'* and *rasā',* viz. 'evil' and 'wickedness'
respectively. The root from which *ra'* comes means, among other
things, 'to break in pieces', and of *rasā'* it has been said that 'it
refers more specifically to evil, not in its moral or judicial sense,
but in its active form ....'[17] That 'active form' is, moreover,
essentially *destructive.* This is language unquestionably stronger
and the feelings rather more negatively inclined than anything we
encounter in Luke whose term 'sinners' both in Greek and in
Hebrew has the basic meaning of 'missing the mark'. If Matthew
and his community are inclined to react negatively towards their
antagonists, the ethical demand made upon them by Jesus is that
they love with a love that acknowledges no boundaries and no
enemies.

In the gospel of John we encounter both language and a mood
that reflect something of the evangelist's as well as his
community's attitude towards their expulsion from the synagogue
and the persecution they were experiencing (Jn.18:2-11). This
gospel's account contains both points of resemblance with and
significant points of difference from the three synoptic gospels.
Like Mark, for example, it uses the verb *paió* for striking with the
sword or dagger. That John's account has its own characteristic
features is widely recognised, though. One such feature, for
example, is the way Jesus is presented as being in control both in

the arrest and in the trial. Alongside this, however, is the unquestionable defiance and ridicule that characterises the accounts. Both 'the Jews' and Pilate, the representative of Rome, are objects of this defiance and ridicule. It is in John alone that the arresting party consists of both a Roman cohort as well as members of the temple police (Jn.18:3). This formidable company significantly draws back and falls to the ground when confronted by Jesus (Jn.18:6). The arrest can only be carried out after he has given the order that his disciples be allowed to go (Jn.18:8). This defiant attitude of Jesus is even more pronounced in the trial: he defiantly refuses to answer the high priest (Jn.18:20-21), he responds defiantly to being struck by a member of the temple police (Jn.18:23), and behaves defiantly towards Pilate (Jn.18:33-38; 19:11).

David Rensberger has argued convincingly for a fourth gospel portrait of Pilate as a strong and cruel character as opposed to the commonly accepted one of him being a rather weak character. This leads him to the conclusion that the fourth gospel confronts both Rome and 'the Jews'.[18] It seems to us, however, that the strength and cruelty of Pilate in this gospel serves the purpose of ridiculing 'the Jews' who reckon that by persecuting and killing those among their fellow Jews who acknowledge and confess the messiahship of Jesus they offer service to God (cf. Jn.16:2). They, who have or should have no king but God, give in to this man who spurns Israel's sovereignty and ridicules the one from above by declaring that 'We have no King but Caesar' (Jn.19:15).

We suggest, then, that we have here John's (perhaps the so-called Johannine school's) response to violence: the violence of persecution. Perhaps many responded, naturally, by abandoning their new-found faith due to fear and so, in the language of the fourth gospel, were 'lost'. Others, responded by trying to strike back as Peter did (Jn.18:10). The attempt to take Jesus 'by force to make him King' (Jn.6:15) would, presumably, belong to this kind of response.

For the fourth gospel both these responses are inappropriate for Christians. The persecutors as killers and murderers are in fact neither sons of God nor sons of Abraham but sons of the devil who 'was a murderer from the beginning' (Jn.8, see v.44). To those who would respond by abandoning the faith due to fear the fourth gospel presents a Christ who is 'the good shepherd' who lays down his life for the sheep in his determination to protect

them from 'the wolf' and let them 'have life, and have it
abundantly' (Jn.10, esp. vv.1-18). They should, in fact, 'be of good
cheer' because he has 'overcome the world' (see Jn.16:33). To
those who would respond violently the answer is: 'Put your sword
into its sheath; shall I not drink the cup which the Father has
given me?' (Jn.18:11). The cup is, following Old Testament
symbolism and in keeping with John's tendency to exploit the
double meaning of certain words, not only the cup of suffering
but also of victory. Perhaps what Jesus is saying is that the only
decisive victory *over* suffering is victory *through* suffering.

The appropriate response to persecution and violence,
according to the fourth gospel, is to defy and ridicule it for what it
is, the work of those who are powerful, cruel, brutal, but
vanquished sons of the devil and savage wolves that have,
nevertheless, been defeated already. Defying and ridiculing are a
demonstration of a victory won; they effectively take the sting out
of and disarm violence by demoralising those who perpetrate it.
Even prior to the resurrection that disarming and demoralising
victory is uttered, most significantly, on the cross as the ultimate
cry: *tetelestai*, not '*It is finished*' but rather '*It is accomplished*' or
'*It is completed*'; i.e. victory won! This victory is thus moral rather
than military, or better still, over against a military one. That
means it is constructive rather than destructive; it is only to the
murderous devil (cf. Jn.8:44), 'the prince of this world' (Jn.12:31;
14:39; 16:11), that it is destructive.

As regards Luke's gospel, we have already suggested that the
language is, at significant points to this study, both refined and
softened when compared to that of the other evangelists. While
this phenomenon is to a considerable extent due to the fact that
he was clearly an educated Gentile, this is not the whole story. For
example, his addition of 'daily' to the saying concerning taking up
the cross and following Jesus can hardly be attributed to the
evangelist's greater proficiency in Greek, and yet the addition
significantly alters the tone as well as meaning of the saying; from
a violent death to self-denial in an ethico-spiritual sense. Luke's
gospel does not emerge from a context of persecution, but rather
(as we have already observed) out of that of a Gentile-Christian
community to which the evangelist sought to demonstrate the
universality of the gospel. This evangelist does not have to
highlight the violence involved in, for example, the arrest of Jesus.
Indeed he does not. No careful analysis of the four evangelists'
accounts of the arrest of Jesus can afford to overlook the

solemnity that characterises Luke's account over against the dramatic character of the accounts given by the other three. Is it pure coincidence that all three dramatic accounts which give so much prominence to elements of violence in the arrest of Jesus are also directly related to persecution?

Luke's account shows an entirely different concern. Kee has made the interesting suggestion that Jesus' healing of the high-priest's slave's ear in Luke's account of the arrest (Lk.22:51) shows an 'outsider' or marginal person benefiting 'from God's power at work in Jesus'.[19] Similarly and significantly, it is in Luke's gospel alone that Jesus, hanging on the cross, prays for those crucifying him ('Father forgive them; for they know not what they do', Lk.23:34) and promises the 'penitent criminal', 'Truly, I say to you, today you will be with me in Paradise' (Lk.23:43). In other words, Luke's account of the arrest of Jesus differs from the others because instead of representing a response to the violence of persecution it is rather an integral part of Luke's universalist theme.

Perhaps this observation that neither Luke nor his church are confronted with the violence of persecution also goes a long way towards explaining why it is that the Jesus of the third gospel seems to be a great deal more ready than the Jesus of the other gospels to accept suffering for himself, and to do so with solemnity. Indeed, this seems to be nothing less than a solemn embracing of suffering, persecution, and violence.

This examination of the gospels has suggested that, while maintaining the negative response, the greater the intensity of the violence a Christian community suffered the more inclined it was to wish its persecutors at least a taste of what it suffered. Suffering violent persecution seems to have been responsible for feelings of hostility in varying degrees towards those who had caused the suffering.

## POSITIVE RESPONSES TO VIOLENCE

Jesus taught about a loving and merciful God. And yet, as Kummel has so accurately observed, 'according to Jesus' utterances God can mercilessly punish, if man is not ready to repent.... '[20] This merciless punishment of God is, naturally, expressed in language that is unquestionably violent. Lk.13:1ff gives an account of Jesus being given a report of a particularly violent incident: Pilate mixing the blood of Galileans with their sacrifices. Jesus' response is 'unless you repent you will perish in

the same manner' (Lk.13:3,5). Now, while *homoiòs apoleisthe*
(Lk.13:3) and *hōsautōs apoleisthe* (Lk.13:5) do not necessarily
imply perishing in an identical manner they certainly imply
perishing in no less a violent and gruesome fashion. The parable
in Lk.13:6-9 suggests that Jesus implied more than just an
inevitable disaster, an impersonal fate, but rather God's actual and
positive judgement over non-repentance.

'Divine violence' is almost a characteristic feature of Matthew's
gospel. The words 'so also my heavenly Father will do to every
one of you, if you do not forgive your brother from your heart'
(Mt.18:35) refer to torture. The preceding verse states that 'in
anger his Lord delivered him to the torturers' (Greek *basanistais*),
not 'jailers'. God will deliver those who do not love their brothers
up to torture. Particularly characteristic of the God proclaimed by
Jesus in Matthew's gospel is the way he threatens to throw those
whom he condemns 'into the furnace of fire; there men will weep
and gnash their teeth'.

Not only is God portrayed in a violent light in the gospel
tradition, but also Jesus, who declares that he has not come to
bring peace on earth, 'but a sword' (Mt.10:34ff). Having violently
'cleansed' the temple (Mk.11:15ff; Mt.21:12f; Lk.19:45f; Jn.2:13ff)
he proceeds, on the very evening of his arrest, to order his
disciples to purchase swords (Lk.22:36).

What are we to make of all this? Does it indicate that the
gospel tradition does contain the advocacy of violence even if
only under certain circumstances? If the answer to this question
be positive, what are the circumstances under which violence may
be condoned if not actually advocated? If it be negative, how do
we explain the kind of language to which we have just drawn
attention?

Traditional apocalyptic language can go a long way towards
accounting for the violent kind of language we encounter in our
gospels. Not only is this true of such patently apocalyptic sections
as Mk.13 and parallels; in addition, the one christological title
most frequently found on Jesus' lips in the synoptic tradition, viz.
the Son of Man, has undoubted apocalyptic associations; so also
has the idea of the opening of heaven at Jesus' baptism (Mk.1:10
and parallels) and the oft encountered theme of divine judgement,
to mention but a few. Appealing to apocalyptic alone would not,
however, account for the differences between Mark's
*schizomenous* (tearing), on the one hand, and Matthew's
*èneòchthèsan* and Luke's *aneòchthènai* (opening), on the other,

in the account of Jesus' baptism (Mk.1:10; Mt.3:16; Lk.3:21). Nor can Mark's *ekballei eis* (being thrown out into), on the one hand, and Matthew's *anechthe eis* and Luke's *ēgeto en* (being led into), on the other, be explained in terms of apocalyptic (Mk.1:12; Mt.3:1; Lk.3:1).

Violent language may also represent the response of Mark and his community to the savagery of Nero's persecution. In response to this, and drawing on apocalyptic imagery and language, God, in and through Jesus his chosen and appointed agent, intervenes dramatically and decisively (the language suggests 'violently') on behalf of his chosen ones. God meets the savagery of Nero's persecution with his greater might: the answer to the destructive violence of Satan is the might (violent might?) of God. The only appropriate human response to this divine might, ultimately demonstrated in the awesome and astonishing Resurrection-victory, is *ephobounto gar* ('for they were afraid', or better still, 'for they were awestruck', Mk.16:8).

In brief, the use of violent language and features in relation to both God and Jesus is, we suggest, related to the response of the evangelist in question and his community and to their experience of suffering and persecution.

This brings us to the three passages that more than any other, within this category, call for our attention, viz. Mt.10:34ff and parallel, and Mk.11:15ff and parallels, and Lk.22:36ff. To these we now turn our attention.

### (a) *Mt.10:34ff and Lk.12:51ff*

The Matthean version reads: 'Do not think that I have come to bring peace on earth; I have not come to bring peace, but a sword' (Mt.10:34), while the Lucan one reads: 'Do you think that I have come to give peace on earth? No, I tell you, but rather division' (Lk.12:51). For Matthew Jesus has brought a sword *(machaira)* while for Luke he has brought division *(diamerismos)*. The questions to which we must address ourselves concern, firstly, the meaning of these texts, and, secondly, their implications for our study.

It is the view of most scholars that 'sword' is used figuratively or symbolically by Matthew. What is meant by such figurative or symbolic usage is perhaps well expressed by David Hill who comments that 'The Lucan version (12:51) has "division instead of sword" and this correctly represents the thought'.[21] What both Mt.10:34 and Lk.12:51 refer to, according to this view, is 'the divisive result of Jesus' coming'.[22] It is a 'divisive result' that will not respect family unity and harmony. One member of a family will embrace and submit to the reign of God when another will resist it.

The question must be asked, however, as to the depth and significance of this division. Will some members of a family, for example, be content with resisting the reign of God or will they actively oppose it? The context provides the answer. The disciples are to expect total opposition to their mission: so total that 'Brother will deliver up brother to death, and the father his child, and children will rise against parents and have them put to death...' (Mt.10:21). This context clearly refers to persecution, the threat of which can easily lead to denying Christ instead of confessing him (Mt.10:32f). Such persecution is inevitable and therefore to be expected (Mt.10:34ff). It follows, therefore, that 'sword' in Mt.10:34 is more than just a figure or symbol of 'division'; it means 'sword'; it means violence; it means death.

The 'sword' in Mt.10:34 is, therefore, no figurative or symbolic word for 'division'. It refers instead to persecution and violent death. Luke, whose background is not one of persecution, has weakened the language. Matthew, on the other hand, faced with persecution, retains the violence in the language to do more than warn. It is retained for purposes of exhortation and strengthening. What we have here is no positive response to violence in the sense of embracing and advocating it. Instead we have the warning that violence is the inevitable response of the forces of evil to the rightful claims of God. Mt.10:34 may not be cited as a text in favour of violence. It speaks rather of the inevitability of violence; the construction 'Think not that I have come...I have come that...' represents rather the biblical way of expressing consequences as though they were intentions.[23] Nor does Mt.10:34 reject violence; violence is instead seen as inevitable.

(b) *Mk.11:15ff and parallels*
The account of the cleansing of the temple features in all four gospels, the parallels to Mark being Mt.21:12ff; Lk.19:45ff; and Jn.2:13ff. What portrait of Jesus emerges from this account? Scholarly opinion varies widely. On the one hand we have that expressed by Richardson:

> The incident, misinterpreted by those who search for evidence for their picture of Jesus the nationalist revolutionary, could have been nothing more than a gesture, an enacted parable:

the money-changers would return as soon as Jesus and his
followers had departed.[24]

Together with a number of other scholars, Richardson contends
that the Roman cohort stationed in the fortress of Antonia
overlooking the temple would have intervened promptly and firmly
as they did in the incident concerning Paul in Acts 21:27ff.

On the other hand Verhey asserts that 'The attempts to portray
Jesus as a programmatic pacifist have always stumbled and fallen
at the temple-cleansing'.[25] Hence Brandon's view that the
cleansing or 'expulsion', as he prefers to call it, was accomplished
'under the leadership of the Prophet of Nazareth, by the violent
action of his followers and the crowd, stirred as they were to a
high pitch of revolutionary fervour by the excitation of their
Messianic hopes by the triumphal entry into the city'.[26]

The most common interpretation of this incident is that it was
intended by Jesus himself as a prophetic symbolic action, and
according to Jeremias, it was clearly 'understood to be such'.[27] In
true prophetic style, and citing Is.56:7 and Jer.7:11, he not only
pronounces but enacts God's judgement not on the temple itself
but on those who abuse it. 'Control of the temple was the basis of
both economic and religious power in Judea'.[28] The Sadducean
priestly aristocracy who had control over the temple abused it by
enriching themselves at the expense of both the poor and
pilgrims. In the light of this Jesus symbolically but authoritatively
'seized that control'.[29] In view of the fact that the priestly
aristocracy behaved like 'robbers' (Mk.11:17), Jesus as God's
agent authoritatively seized control of the temple using force. He
has come 'in the name of the Lord' (Mk.11:9) and so acts with
the *exousia* (authority, power) from heaven (cf. Mk.11:30).

What seems to be significant for purposes of this study are the
detailed and intense accounts of Mark, Matthew and John, on the
one hand, and the considerably shorter, much less dramatic and
much less intense account of Luke, on the other. While using the
same verb as is used by Mark, Matthew and John, namely
*ekballein* for 'throwing them out', to give but one example, Luke's
account leaves out altogether the drama of overturning tables and
seats and the accompanying tense atmosphere. Is it purely
coincidental that it is precisely those gospel accounts that have a
direct connection with violent persecution that are more intense
and more dramatic? The overturning of tables and seats
represents, in these gospels, the most appropriate response to the

'violence' of injustice and exploitation practised within the temple premises.

(c) *Lk.22:35-38*
This is the only text which reports that Jesus instructed his disciples to obtain swords and to do so at all costs. Where did Luke obtain this material? For Trocmé, for example, the passage demonstrates that 'the temptations to use violence accompanied Jesus until His death',[30] while for Carmichael it suggests rather strongly that Jesus was a violent, revolutionary rebel.[31]

There seem to be two possibilities worth consideration as to what Jesus meant. The first is the *self-defence interpretation*. In the words of Martin Hengel:

> The dagger or short sword belongs to the equipment of the Jewish traveller as protection against robbers and wild animals. Even the peace-loving Essenes took along nothing on their trips 'except weapons on account of robbers'.[32]

In short, violence can be used justifiably against those who employ violence against the gospel of the Kingdom.

The second possibility is *the ultimate self-sacrifice interpretation*. Hahn has the following to say on this pericope:

> If we recollect that the cloak served several men conjointly as a covering for the night and must on no account be taken from them as a pawn, for example, the saying must signify that for the disciple of Jesus a situation much more severe than extremest poverty will arise, a situation, namely, in which his life itself is threatened. Hence the disciple is called upon to surrender what is left to the poorest, and to be ready to stake his life ... For as the possession of a cloak merely is the sign of direct poverty, so the sword signifies an extreme threat to life.[33]

This interpretation would give the 'two swords' saying the same meaning and significance as the saying which, in its Marcan version reads: 'If any man would come after me, let him deny himself and take up his cross and follow me' (Mk.8:34). In terms of the latter saying, the cross would signify 'an extreme threat to life'. It should be noted, however, that to take up the cross implies, or could imply, being the victim of violence whereas taking the sword does not necessarily have that implication.

In terms of the first interpretation Jesus warned his disciples to be prepared to use violence in self-defence; in terms of the second he warned (indeed prepared) them to be ready to suffer violence. The question still remains, though, as to how Luke understood and used this saying. Here too scholarly opinion varies widely. One of the most popular theories is the 'transition to a new epoch' view. This new epoch, for the church and its mission, is to hold dangers sufficiently grave for the apostles that the instructions of Lk.9:3 and 10:4 are explicitly cancelled. If they then needed no equipment, they are now to be well-equipped with purse, bag and sword.

What, in the light of all this, does Lk.22:35-38 mean? It means that earlier missions such as those described in Lk.9:1ff and 10:1ff, were without the testing that would now be encountered by the disciples. A time of want *(husteresis)* can be a trying and testing time. For the disciples to say they did not lack anything during the previous missions (Lk.22:35), is to say that they were not tested. Jesus' 'But now' *(alla nun)* makes it clear to them that that which they did not encounter then they would encounter now. The citation of Is.53 in Lk.22:37 itself seems to suggest extreme testing, but for Jesus in this case. Finally, it should be noted that Jesus' response to the disciples' producing of two swords is in the singular. What he is saying is neither that two swords are enough (that would be ridiculous in the light of Lk.22:36) nor that the conversation must now be terminated. He is saying that his attempt to explain and their failure to grasp the severe nature of the testing they are about to encounter is enough; the testing itself would now begin.

## CONCLUSION

Our study of the most prominent passages in the New Testament gospels has suggested that there is no *one* Christian response to violence in our gospels. Responses seem in fact to vary in relation to the extent to which a writer and/or his community is exposed to and victim of violence. While the responses of evangelists may vary, a careful examination of relevant gospel passages suggests that Jesus himself never advocated, endorsed, nor condoned violence. At least that seems to be how the evangelists presented him. How accurate this portrayal of Jesus is we have no way of establishing beyond reasonable doubt.

## NOTES

1.   M. Grant, *The World of Rome,* (London: Cardinal, 1974), ch.1.
2.   Philo: *Legatio ad Gaium* in S. Benko and J. O'Rourke (eds.), *Early Church History,* (London: SPCK, 1974), pp.299-305.
3.   H-R. Weber, *The Cross,* (London: SPCK, 1979), p.8.
4.   S.G.F. Brandon, *The Fall of Jerusalem and the Christian Church,* (London: SPCK, 1957), p.103.

132                                                                         *Theology and Violence*

5. Cited by M.D. Goulder, *Midrash and Lection in Matthew*, (London: SPCK, 1974), p.127.
6. Martin Hengel, *Was Jesus a Revolutionist?*, (Philadelphia: Fortress, 1971), p.18, n.57.
7. John A.T. Robinson, *Redating the New Testament*, (London: SCM, 1976), p.115.
8. D. Hare, *The Theme of Jewish Persecution of Christians in the Gospel According to St Matthew*, (London: CUP, 1967).
9. J. Louis Martyn, *The Gospel of John in Christian History*, (New York: Paulist Press, 1979), p.56.
10. A. Verney, *The Great Reversal*, (Grand Rapids: Eerdmans, 1984), p.75.
11. Robinson, *Redating the New Testament*, p.103.
12. Robinson, *Ibid.*, p.101; C.F.D. Moule, *The Birth of the New Testament*, (London: A & C Black, 1962), ch.V.
13. Verney, *The Great Reversal*, pp.82-92.
14. J. Jeremias, *The Sermon on the Mount*, (London: Athlone, 1961), p.27.
15. David Hill, *The Gospel of Matthew*, (London: Olifants, 1972), p.129. Not only does the Old Testament contain no 'explicit order'; 'there is no precise Old Testament parallel to the command or permission, "You shall hate your enemy"'.
16. John Riches, *Jesus and the Transformation of Judaism*, (London: DLT, 1980).
17. *The New Bible Dictionary*, (London: IVP, 1962), art. 'Wicked'.
18. David Rensberger, 'The Politics of John: The Trial of Jesus in the Fourth Gospel', *Journal of Biblical Literature*, Vol.103 (1984), pp.395-411.
19. H.C. Kee, *Community of the New Age*, (London: SCM, 1977), p.206. Kee attaches the same significance to the raising of the widow's son (Lk.7:11-17) and to the grateful leper healed by Jesus (Lk.17:11-19).
20. W.G. Kummel, *The Theology of the New Testament*, (London: SCM, 1974), pp.42-43, italics mine.
21. Hill, *Gospel of Matthew*, p.194.
22. R.V.G. Tasker, *Matthew*, (London: Tyndale, 1961), p.108.
23. *Ibid.*, p.108.
24. Alan Richardson, *The Political Christ*, (London: SCM, 1973), p.51.
25. Verney, *The Great Reversal*, p.210, n.131.
26. Brandon, *The Fall of Jerusalem and the Christian Church*, p.103f.
27. J. Jeremias, (ed.), *New Testament Theology*, (London: IVP, 1962), Vol.I, p.145.
28. S.C. Mott, *Biblical Ethics and Social Change*, (New York/Oxford: OUP, 1982), p.98.
29. *Ibid.*
30. Andre Trocmé, *Jesus and the Nonviolent Revolution*, (Scottdale, Pennsylvania: Herald Press, 1973), p.132.
31. Joel Carmichael, *The Death of Jesus*, pp.117ff.
32. Hengel, *Was Jesus a Revolutionist?*
33. F. Hahn, *The Titles of Jesus in Christology*, (London: Lutterworth, 1969), p.155.

# Early Christians and the Problem of War

SEQIBO DWANE

There were two key factors which contributed towards the formation of the early Christians' ambivalent attitude towards the state and the world in general. The first was the fact that they took the reality of this world seriously. Its shortcomings they readily admitted, but nonetheless acknowledged that it was God's creation and that his love and concern for it had been shown through the Incarnation. They were helped by the teaching of the New Testament, as interpreted and re-affirmed by the church Fathers, to resist the gnostic tendency to spiritualise what God had expressed visibly and concretely. Christ had indeed come in the flesh, and dwelt among humanity. He had identified with creation in order to bring wholeness to it because the 'unassumed is the unhealed'. And on account of Christ's incarnate life, his death and resurrection, Christians felt called to play their part in the human striving for justice, peace and stability. The Lord's command to render to Caesar the things that are Caesar's and Paul's teaching in Romans 13 helped to entrench in Christian thought the idea that civil authority was ordained by God for the well-being of society. Insofar as they were concerned with the peace and welfare of all people, Christians were 'helpers and allies' of the state. To them belonged the responsibility to offer prayers to God for those in authority, that by and through them God's will might be done. Early Christians seem to have exercised diligence in praying for their rulers. J.M. Hornus refers to a letter written by Clement of Rome, at a time when memories of Nero's persecution were still fresh, as a symptom of the early church's frame of mind.[1] In it Clement offers the following prayer:

> Grant that we may be obedient
> To your almighty and glorious name
> And to our rulers and governors on earth.
>
> You, Master gave them imperial power
> Through your majestic and indescribable might . . .

Grant them, Lord, health, peace, harmony
and stability
so that they may give no offence in
administering the government you have
given them . . .

Polycarp exhorts the Philippians to 'pray also for emperors and authorities and rulers, and for those who persecute you and hate you and for these enemies of the Cross'.[2] These prayers for the welfare of the state included the army, in spite of its notoriously barbaric methods of persecution. In his *Apology*, Tertullian maintains that 'We are ever making intercession for all the emperors. We pray for them a long life, a secure rule, a safe home, brave armies, a faithful senate, an honest people, a quiet world . . .'.[3] Arnobius asks why Christian meetings were being cruelly broken up 'seeing that in them the Supreme God is prayed to, peace and pardon asked for all — magistrates, armies, kings, friends, enemies?'.[4] Christians in the early period therefore acknowledged that they were part of creation, and had a contribution to make towards its transformation.

Secondly, however, they were acutely aware of this world's imperfections and the provisional nature of its ordinances. While accepting the reality of this world, Christians nevertheless were conscious of the fact that they were pilgrims in it, and that 'here there is no abiding city'. They were prepared to honour the monarch or the emperor, and to render appropriate loyalty and service to the state, but their obedience could never be a total submission to secular authority for they acknowledged God as the highest authority, to whom all people including rulers had to bow. Commenting on Romans 13, Tertullian maintains that secular rulers are to be obeyed not in order to avoid martyrdom, but insofar as they are 'handmaids of the divine court of justice'. He understands Paul to be saying that Christians have to pay 'tribute to whom tribute is due, custom to whom custom is due', that is, the things which are Caesar's to Caesar, and the things which are God's to God; *"but man is the property of God alone"*.[5] Irenaeus' interpretation of Romans 13 is that insofar as magistrates act in a just and legitimate manner, they are not to be called into question. When however they subvert justice and act in a tyrannical fashion, then the judgement of God falls upon them as upon everyone else.[6]

There was another reason for the ambivalence of early Christians with regard to the state. It was a fact that secular rulers were pagans, who often persecuted the church. For Tertullian the persecution of Christians by secular rulers was not accidental, but a revelation of the metaphysical combat between God and the powers of darkness. He maintained that 'devils are rulers of this world'. Therefore 'all the powers and dignities of the world are not only foreign, but likewise hostile to God, because through these are punishments devised against the servants of God . . . '.[7] Hippolytus in his commentary on Daniel contrasts the Christian church with the Roman empire. The Lord through his apostles, he says, summons all nations and tongues into a 'faithful nation of Christians, who bear in their hearts the new and sovereign name'. By contrast, the empire, 'in accordance with Satan's activity', collects the nobility of all nations, arms them for war, and calls them Romans.[8] It is against this background that one should view the urge felt strongly by the early Christian community to renounce the world. The world in which they lived was one contaminated by idolatry, and characterised by crude amusements, violence and brutality. It is therefore not surprising that they felt uncomfortable in this environment, and often turned their backs on it in order to contemplate the joy of heavenly things. Early Christians then saw themselves as people *in* the world, but not *of* it. Theirs was a new life occasioned by a birth 'from above'. That new life had to be lived out within the ambiguities of the present age as a sign of the new age, a kind of leaven in the dough. This called for a realistic appraisal of the world, which at times resulted in a vigorous participation in society, and at other times a consequent turning away from its contagion of sin.

The attitude of early Christians towards violence needs to be considered within this ambiguity.

## ATTITUDES TO VIOLENCE

In the Old Testament, war is one of the facts of life, and an acceptable means of settling disputes. Israel, the people of God, went to war against the inhabitants of Canaan with God's approval. In the period of the Judges, God was believed to have raised up charismatic leaders to lead the armies of Israel against the enemy. It would appear from the writings of the early Fathers that the Christian community found the straightforward literal meaning of this material difficult to handle. As part of the Old Testament tradition it had to be appropriated, and so a new meaning in it had to be found. Irenaeus assumes that the real

meaning of these wars in the flesh is to be found in the image of
spiritual wars which they pre-figure. If this were not the case, he
says, 'I do not think the apostles would ever have transmitted, for
reading in the churches, the historical books of the Hebrews to
the disciples of Christ who came to bring peace'.[9] In a significant
passage in his treatise against the Jews, Tertullian makes two
points about violence in the Old Testament. The first point is that
whereas the custom of the Old Testament law was to inflict
retaliatory revenge for injury suffered, the new law is to point to
clemency, and to convert to tranquility the pristine ferocity of
swords and lances ... The second point is that within the Old
Testament tradition itself there are those prophecies which point
ahead to the advent of the Messiah. These prophecies reveal that
the coming of the Messiah would 'remodel the pristine execution
of "war" upon rivals ... into the pacific actions of "ploughing and
tilling" the land'.[10]

For Christians, Christ is the Prince of Peace as demonstrated in
the garden of Gethsemane on the night of his arrest. The use of
the sword is sharply rebuked: 'No more of this!' (Luke 22:51).
Tertullian captures the moment in his famous phrase '... the Lord
afterward in disarming Peter, unbelted every soldier'.[11] For
Christians therefore, the law of love is clearly revealed in the
gospel. That being the case, early Christians could

> use military narratives and bellicose expressions while at the
> same time disarming them of their brutal character. They knew
> that their battle was a real one. But it took place on a different
> plane, and with quite different weapons, from the battles of the
> world.[12]

Because Christ had suffered and died on the cross, early
Christians felt called on to suffer violence, but not to inflict it. And
the temptation must have been great for them to resort to
violence when outraged by persecutions. For example, Cyprian
comments: 'I know beloved brethren, that very many, either
because of the weight of their pressing injuries, or because of
resentment toward those who attack them and rage against them,
wish to be revenged quickly without waiting for the day of
judgement ... '.[13] But theirs was a spiritual warfare, the arm of
their conflict was prayer, and martyrdom their battle. The church,
according to John Chrysostom, was the 'army which becomes
glorious in proportion to the number of its people who are
destroyed by their adversaries'.[14]

The environment in which early Christians lived was one in

which brutality was the order of the day. This feature of their society they found horrific and hard to swallow. 'Among us' says Tertullian, 'nothing is ever said, or seen, or heard, which has anything in common with the madness of the circus, the immodesty of the theatre, the atrocities of the arena, the useless exercises of the wrestling ground'.[15] For a Christian to attend these public entertainments was to expose oneself to the devil.

'May God avert from his people' noted Tertullian, 'any such passionate eagerness after a cruel enjoyment! For how monstrous it is to go from God's church to the devil's . . .'.[16] The world is God's, he says, but the worldly is of the devil.[17] And here, if one may digress a little, is to be found a lesson for many people to whom the violence of the so-called 'necklace' as well as various other atrocities attributed to the police, the military and vigilantes have become commonplace. Where violence has become routine, human life is bound to be cheap.

This brutalising effect of violence on people's sensitivity is probably what horrified Tertullian and others about the so-called 'public entertainments'. In the same way, because of the contagion of violence, the church in this country may soon find itself compelled, not only to acquiesce to the violence of the state or the counter-violence of the oppressed, but to advocate certain forms of violence in defence of certain causes. Indeed, history is full of examples of situations in which the church has had recourse to violence and to the doctrine of just war, a reluctant but honorable symbol of the church's engagement in society. It is important, however, that Christians should ponder deeply Christ's own response of love and non-violence to conflict and hatred, as well as the witness of those saints and martyrs of the early period, before resorting to 'defensive violence' as a last resort. We need to remind ourselves that their strategy was not one of expediency, but costly obedience to the demands of the gospel.

It is important for modern Christians to come face to face with the stark realisation that early Christians found violence and bloodshed shocking and disconcerting. This reality should challenge Christians who serve in either conventional or revolutionary armies. Because this point is played down by some modern theologians it is worth spending time looking at what some early Fathers have to say on the subject. For Athenagoras the thought of anyone being put to death, even justly, is hard to bear.[18] Athanasius in handling this issue comes to the crux of the matter. Any human being is one's brother, sister, neighbour, and ultimately God indwelling in that person. Each human life is precious because God has redeemed it with the precious blood of his Son.[19] For Basil of Caesarea, murder could never be justified even in a situation of legitimate self-defence. For Tertullian the human person was the centre of creation, and human life was therefore the most precious thing in the world. Consequently, to kill another person would be a crime against God and an act of the devil.[20] Lactantius has this to say:

> For when God forbids us to kill, he not only prohibits us from violence, which is not even allowed by public laws, but He warns us against the commission of those things which are esteemed lawful among men. Thus it will be neither lawful for a just man to engage in warfare since his warfare is justice itself, nor to accuse anyone of a capital charge, because it makes no difference whether you put a man to death by word, or rather by the sword, since it is the act of putting to death itself which is prohibited. Therefore, with regard to this precept of God, there ought to be no exception at all; but that it is always unlawful to put to death a man whom God willed to be a sacred animal.[21]

Elsewhere he writes:

> If God were worshipped, there would be no dissensions and wars; for men would know that they are sons of the one God, and so joined together by the sacred and inviolable bond of divine Kinship; there would be no plots, for they would know what sort of punishment God has prepared for those who kill living beings.[22]

It is quite clear from these references that amongst many other reasons for reluctance to serve in the army, early Christians considered the value of human life ' a strong enough objection to their participating in military forces and in other institutional forms of violence.

## THE EARLY CHRISTIANS' ATTITUDE TO THE MILITARY

Before the signing by Constantine of the Edict of Milan (312 C.E.) which granted legal status to the Christian church, there were at least five reasons which accounted for Christians' apparent lack of enthusiasm for the military.

The first has to do with the obvious fact that the army represented a hostile empire and was regularly involved in attempts to root out Christianity. Soldiers were notorious for their 'savage and vicious spirit' towards Christians and other groups seen as a threat to the empire, and their methods of torture were brutal and ferocious. It was difficult therefore for Christians to identify with an institution so overtly hostile to their own values and existence.

The second reason had to do with the morals and identity of the army. Christians found this atmosphere uncongenial and tended to avoid the army for fear of moral contamination.

Thirdly, a fundamental ideological difference separated Christians from persons loyal to the Roman army. Christians considered themselves to be soldiers of Christ, and perceived martyrdom as their battle. By contrast, soldiers of this world were instruments of persecution, and therefore the 'devil's army'. To join the army would be seen as crossing the floor from the 'camp of light to the camp of darkness'.

The fourth reason relates to the third; it concerns the army's official practice of the cult of the emperor and various other ceremonies of a patriotic nature, considered by the Christian community to be idolatrous. Christians perceived the army as a representative symbol of the secular realm in its total opposition to the lordship of Christ.

The fifth reason has been a matter for considerable debate between two schools of thought. On the one hand there are scholars who maintain that the main reason for Christian reluctance to join the army in the pre-Constantinian period was the fact that the military was given over to idolatry, and that respect for human life did not play a significant role in their decision. It is important not to gloss over the fact that emperor-worship in the army played an equally significant role. The Roman empire was a variety of nationalities and cultures, and the emperor cult therefore 'Romanised' soldiers and gave them a sense of common identity. Religion held the army together, and gave soldiers a feeling of security. Because religious observance was kept uniform throughout the sprawling, cross-cultural empire, centurions could be moved from one legion to the next without having their basic allegiance or identity threatened. Religion created a sacred world, and inculcated in the minds of people how to be good soldiers and how to show respect to the gods and the emperor as their representative.[23] It is against this background that the writings of the early church Fathers are to be read. Tertullian was well-informed about the ceremonies and rituals observed in army camps. The argument in question, focusing upon the two treatises on idolatry and on the monarchy, is that there can be 'no compatibility between the divine and the human sacrament (military oath), the standard of Christ and the standard of the devil, the camp of light and the camp of darkness. One soul cannot serve two masters — God and Caesar . . .'. This quotation will be used in the subsequent discussion to show that the argument above is only one side of the coin. With regard to the *Treatise on the Crown,* the argument is further developed. Tertullian, apart from making a few statements regretting killing in connection with the army, does not say that soldiers should not enlist because killing in combat is wrong. It can be concluded that military service itself was offensive to Tertullian and indeed to the early Christian community as a whole, not on the grounds of respect for human life and property, but on account of the link between the military and state religion.[24]

On the other hand there are scholars who, while admitting that idolatry influenced Christians to keep away from the military, nevertheless would say that the question of bloodshed and of respect for human life loomed large in determining the Christian attitude to war and the military. Hornus refers to the Christian affirmation that human life is sacred as being an essential element of the Christian attitude to war and one which is 'all too often passed over in silence'.[25] He readily admits that Tertullian 'laid great stress on the idolatrous nature of the obligations — which a believer could not accept — which were imposed on the soldier'.[26] But he goes on to say that for Tertullian, 'war in the strict sense of the term produced a proliferation of the evils which were diametrical opposites of the good things which Jesus Christ had come to bring'.[27] Christ for Tertullian was not a warrior, but a 'bringer of peace'. For Christ's new law of clemency converts to tranquility the 'pristine ferocity of swords and lances'. In the *Treatise on Idolatry* there is the famous passage which, as we saw earlier, highlights the contrast between the two realms of light and darkness. The interesting thing about the passage quoted is that it goes on to refer to the incident at Gethsemane, when Peter was disarmed by Christ: 'the Lord in disarming Peter, thenceforth disarmed every soldier. No dress is lawful for us which is assigned to an unlawful action'. Clearly, Tertullian is saying that violence is not appropriate conduct for Christians because Christ forbids it. Tertullian heightens the dilemma in which a Christian is bound to find himself when the same weapon which pierced the side of Christ has to be used as a weapon of destruction.[28] There is no question of idolatry at all in the 'rhetorical questions' which he raises:

> Shall it be lawful for him to deal with the sword, when the Lord declareth that he that useth the sword shall perish by the sword? And shall the son of peace act in battle, whom it will not befit even to go to law? Shall he administer bonds and imprisonment, and tortures, and punishments, who may not avenge his own injuries . . .

In subsequent questions, Tertullian mentions temples and alludes to demons, but in the earlier section quoted above his focus is on violence as inappropriate for a Christian. In this Tertullian is not alone. Lactantius states:

> If God alone were worshipped there would be no dissensions and wars; for men would know that they are sons of the one God, and so joined together by the sacred and inviolable bond of divine kinship; there would be no plots, for they would know what sort of punishment waits for those who kill living beings.[29]

Athanasius says that when idolatrous and warlike barbarians turn to Christ, they 'turn from fighting to farming, and instead of arming themselves with swords extend their hands in prayer . . .'.[30] Marcellus argues that a soldier has to fight 'according to the brutalities of this world'.[31] He brutalises others and is himself not left unscathed by the process.

From these comments, it is clear that for early Christians a horror of violence and bloodshed played a very significant part in influencing their decision not to enlist in the army. Cadoux's comment on this subject is perhaps an apt summary of this discussion:

> . . . the objection to being implicated in idolatry was not the only difficulty that faced the Christian in connection with military service. There can be no doubt that the humanitarian objection to bloodshed played a very large part in Christian thought and feeling on the matter. While for many minds it doubtless constituted no difficulty, it was yet for many others a weighty consideration.[32]

## CHRISTIANS AND THE MILITARY DURING THE TIME OF CONSTANTINE

That there were Christians in the army before Constantine is indisputable. Between 298 and 302 C.E., the Emperor Diocletian began a systematic purge of Christians in the army in preparation for the great persecution on which he was about to embark. From this one can conjecture that if the numbers of Christians were small, they were nonetheless noticeable. Tertullian in his lifetime (c.160-246) wrote in his *Apology* that Christians had penetrated every aspect of society — cities, islands, fortresses, towns, market places, even 'the very camp'. 'We have left nothing to you', he boasts, 'but the temples of your gods'.[33] Later on he goes on to say that Christians fight side by side with unbelievers.[34] In his *Treatise on the Crown,* he refers to Christians in the army as 'laurel-crowned Christians': from him this is not a compliment, but a statement of disapproval. Early Christians could and did enlist in the army, but could not expect much encouragement from the church. This situation remained unaltered until some time in the 4th century. The change came shortly before the Council of Arles in 314. Constantine won his battle at the Milvian Bridge and proclaimed the Edict of Milan which ended the persecution of Christians. Christianity was by this edict allowed extensive privileges, not as a state religion, but simply as a permitted religion. But because the Emperor himself professed to be a Christian — even though he remained unbaptised until he lay on his deathbed — this reprieve brought much relief to the Christian community. Lactantius writes in the opening section of his *Institutes:*

> And we now commence this work under the auspices of your name, O mighty emperor Constantine, who were the first of the Roman princes to repudiate errors, and to acknowledge and honour the majesty of the one and only true God. For when that most happy day had shone upon the world, in which the most high God raised you to the prosperous height of power, you entered upon a dominion which was salutary and desirable for all . . .[35].

Later he goes on:

> For they who wished to take away the worship of the heavenly and matchless God, that they might defend impious superstitions, lie in ruin. But thou, who defendest and lovest His name, excelling in virtue and prosperity, enjoyest thy immortal glories with the greatest happiness. They suffer and have suffered the punishment of their guilt. The powerful right hand of God protects thee from all dangers; he bestows on thee a quiet and tranquil reign, with the highest congratulations of all men.[36]

One can feel the sense of relief, jubilation, and celebration in these words, and the euphoria in many Christian homes which they must have echoed. For although Christianity was not yet promulgated as the religion of the empire, its new status was privileged to have the personal backing of the Emperor. It was amidst this new atmosphere that the Council of Arles met in 314. Canon 3 of the Council which concerns Christians in the army reads as follows: 'Concerning those who throw away their arms in times of peace, it is fitting that they should not be admitted to communion'. This canon, not surprisingly, has been the subject of much discussion. Hornus interprets it in a literal sense to mean that Christians could now remain in the army even in peacetime, and in fact urges them to stay in the army in order to avoid scandal! The church, he says, had struck a bargain with the Emperor in exchange for his protection.[37] Cadoux's interpretation is much more complex and revolves round the expression 'in peace'. He says that this could mean that the church should punish army deserters in times of peace, while in times of war they would of course come under the strict discipline of the military. Or it could mean 'when there is no need to use weapons', thus declaring a ban on gladiatorial games. The difficulty with both interpretations is their assumption that Christians could now join the army with the church's blessing. Both are therefore begging the very question under consideration. Furthermore, that assumption is made questionable by historical evidence that in later years several highly reputable saints such as Martin of Tours did give up military service.[38] Ultimately one feels that the literal interpretation is not the only one.

There appears to be no satisfactory interpretation of this canon, and therefore no way of knowing quite what Arles said about Christians and the military. But what is more certain is that Christians under the 'new' Constantinian dispensation found it awkward to be as uncompromising towards the military as Tertullian and others had been in view of the favours bestowed upon them by the Emperor. Christians were now favoured by the Emperor, included in the revised Roman identity, and an implicit *quid pro quo* was beginning to emerge. To paraphrase Bainton: The empire had pacified the world and set up a communication network which made it possible for the gospel to spread rapidly. On the other hand Christianity had 'tamed belligerent people'. In this way the two spheres had contributed towards the *Pax Romana*. Those under the religion of the one God, and the empire of one ruler, had beaten their swords into ploughshares and were in happy embrace.[39] Eighty years after Arles, the marriage between church and state was consummated. The first barbarian invasion took place. Christians tended to identify with and support the official opinion that the barbarians were enemies of peace and progress; they did so because they had now moved to the nerve center of public life, and therefore the cause of the empire was their own cause. Christian theologians such as Augustine began to justify the use of violence under certain conditions:

> If to kill a man is murder, this may happen sometimes without any sin. When a soldier kills the enemy, when a judge or an executioner kills the criminal . . . I do not think they sin by killing a man . . . When a soldier kills the enemy he is enforcing the law, and so has no difficulty in carrying out his duty without passion.[40]

Once the step of accepting and of justifying violence under certain circumstances had been taken, however special those circumstances, the church lost its pristine innocence, and Christian identity would never be the same again. In 416 Emperor Theodosius issued a decree whereby Christians only could enlist in the army, and the synthesis of church with state, nationalism with Christian faith was completed.

We live in an age in which violence no longer horrifies many people. It is a regular feature of daily news and conversation. In this milieu it is a spiritually sobering experience to endeavour to step back into the distant past and hear the voices of those members of the early church and to realise that though they suffered much on account of their faith, they sought to convey to us something of Christ's attitude to violence, and of his love for his enemies.

## CONCLUSION

The fundamental theological question here has to do with what constitutes the mind of Christ in a society such as South Africa, torn apart by institutional, repressive and revolutionary violence. The essays that follow in this publication focus on the question of how successive generations since the early church have sought to address violence in relation to the issues of their time and place, with a view to determining and promoting the traditional theological resources which enable us to grapple with this difficulty in South Africa. To seek to impose early Christian values on our own situation would be historically naïve. Yet so long as the person of Christ and the attitudes of those historically closest to him, namely the early church, continue to constitute the essential identity of the Christian faith, the attitude of Christ and the early church towards violence and other socio-political issues must remain a vital aspect of contemporary theological and ethical debate. One disturbing and challenging fact that needs to be taken into cognisance today by those Christians who seek to affirm the tradition of Christ and his followers is that the early church, committed as it was to pacifism, was also a church of the poor and oppressed. Until the present-day church becomes *this* kind of church it is presumptuous for it, given its implicit and at times explicit support and legitimation of the military force of the apartheid state, to believe that it has the right to instruct oppressed people how they should respond to sustained violence and tyranny. The example of Christ and his early church must, however, continue to haunt and challenge all who call on his name.

# NOTES

1.  J.M. Hornus, *It is Not Lawful for Me to Fight*, (Scottdale: Herald Press, 1980), pp.80-81.
2.  Letter to the Philippians 12:3 in Hornus *It is not Lawful for Me to Fight*, p.82.
3.  Tertullian, *Apology* 30:4 in Hornus, *It is Not Lawful for Me to Fight*, p.82.
4.  C.J. Cadoux, *The Early Church and the World*, (London: SCM, 1960), p.572.
5.  Hornus, *It is Not Lawful for Me to Fight*, p.34.
6.  *Ibid.*, p.33.
7.  Tertullian, *De Idolatria*, XVIII
8.  Hornus, *It is Not Lawful for Me to Fight*, p.93.
9.  *Ibid.*, p.56.
10.  Tertullian, Adv. Jud., 3.
11.  Tertullian, *De Idolatria*, XIX
12.  Hornus, *It is Not Lawful for Me to Fight*, p.90.
13.  *Ibid.*, p.68.
14.  *Ibid.*, p.79.
15.  Tertullian, *De Idolatria*, XXXVIII
16.  Tertullian, *De Spec.* 25, in Hornus, *It is Not Lawful for Me to Fight*, p.92.
17.  *Ibid.*, p.15.
18.  Hornus, *It is Not Lawful for Me to Fight*, p.109.
19.  *Ibid.*
20.  *Ibid.*, pp.111-113.
21.  Lacantius, *The Divine Institutes*, Book VI, Ch.XX. in Hornus, *It is Not Lawful for Me to Fight*, p.112.
22.  *Ibid.*, Book V., Ch.VIII.
23.  Tertullian, *De Apol.*, p.39.
24.  R.J. Daly (ed.), *Christians and the Military — The Early Experience*, (London: SPCK, 1972), pp.21-29.
25.  *Ibid.*, p.24.
26.  R.J. Daly, *Christians and the Military*, pp.48-9.
27.  Tertullian, *Treatise on Idolatry*, XIX.
28.  *Ibid.*, pp.23-9 and 89.

29.  *Ibid.,* p.109.
30.  *Ibid.,* p.25.
31.  *Ibid.,* pp.73-4.
32.  Tertullian, *De Corona,* XI.
33.  Lacantius, *Institutes,* Book V,. Ch.VIII.
34.  Hornus, *It is Not Lawful for Me to Fight,* pp.88-9.
35.  *Ibid.,* p.138.
36.  *Ibid.,* p.581.
37.  *Ibid.*
38.  *Ibid.,* p.582.
39.  Lactantius, *Institutes,* Book I, Ch.1.
40.  *Ibid,* Book VII, Ch.XXVI.
41.  *Ibid.,* p.177.
42.  Cadoux, *The Early Church,* p.588, n.4.
43.  Daly, *Christian Attitudes to War and Peace,* p.87.
44.  Hornus, *It is Not Lawful for Me to Fight,* p.181.

# From Constantine to Calvin: The Doctrine of the Just War

## DOUGLAS S. BAX

In 1974 the National Conference of the South African Council of Churches, meeting at Hammanskraal, passed a lengthy resolution on conscientious objection. In this it pointed out that South Africa was a fundamentally unjust and discriminatory society, and that the government was using the country's military forces to defend the status quo against radical change. It therefore called on its member churches:

> ... to challenge all their members to consider in view of the above whether Christ's call to take up the Cross and follow Him in identifying with the oppressed does not, in our situation, involve becoming conscientious objectors.

The resolution provoked a hue and cry from the Prime Minister and the government as well as a controversy in the press. A revealing leader appeared in *The Natal Mercury*. This attacked the resolution as not only 'provocative' but also 'nonsensical'. But it did so on the ground that 'What the zealous but muddleheaded clerics at Hammanskraal seem to have overlooked is that a true conscientious objector is one who refuses to take up arms for any cause whatsoever. He cannot be selective'.[1] The *Mercury* assumed that the Christian position on war and military service had always been either strictly pacifism or else willingness to fight in any national army; that is, it had never provided for what the *Mercury* called 'selective' conscientious objection. *Die Hoofstad* went even further and stated: 'Refusal to do military service is not reconcilable with the Bible'.[2]

The significance of such statements is that they showed how unaware South Africans at that time were of the long tradition of Christian thinking about war. They indicated to what extent the church in South Africa had failed to educate the public on the issue by avoiding it as too controversial. For the main tradition of Christian ethics has in fact been just that which issues in 'selective conscientious objection', namely the just war doctrine. This has

been so ever since the 4th century, and in a qualified sense even
before that.

## CONSTANTINE'S COMING TO POWER AND ITS CONSEQUENCES

The prevailing attitude of the early church to the empire and its
army was ambivalent. This ambivalence arose because on the
one hand the empire was the persecuting enemy of the people of
God. Christians therefore identified it as demonic, as a beast from
the abyss (Rev.13). On the other hand the Roman state provided
peace and the political structure of civilisation itself. Christians
therefore also accepted that it was God's servant, appointed to
maintain order and peace by means of the sword (Rom.13). This
ambivalence may be seen in early theologians of the church like
Irenaeus, Tertullian, Hippolytus, Origen and Cyprian.[3]

Correlative to this ambivalence was the attitude of the early
Christians to the use of military force. *Although, generally
opposed to bearing arms themselves, they at the same time
recognised the need of the empire for an army.* Tertullian and
Origen, for instance, conceded that while Christians were not
permitted to take lives 'even justly', pagans were permitted to take
part in just wars.[4]

The turning point in the church's thinking was the coming to
power of Constantine. In 312 C.E. Constantine won his famous
victory against Maxentius at the Milvian Bridge and began to rule
over the western Roman empire. He believed that he had won this
victory through the direct intervention of a Divine Power, who had
favoured him with a vision on the eve of it. He may even have
understood the vision in Christian terms. Perhaps for this reason,
but at least as much for politically calculated reasons, he began to
favour the Christian church. The Christian faith was spreading
rapidly and it had become clear that persecuting the church was
futile. It therefore made sense to seek to unite the empire
ideologically around a Christian emperor. By 324 Constantine was
master of the whole empire, and Christianity was well on its way
to becoming the state religion of the empire.

As a consequence of this, one side of the Christians'
ambivalence toward the state collapsed. No longer could they
view the empire as demonic. On the contrary they accepted the
claim that God himself had given Constantine military victory.
After the persecution of previous emperors they began to see

Constantine's empire as a special dispensation from God that merited preservation and defence. The Council of Arles in 314 thus formally recognised the right of the state to go to war on the ground that otherwise it would be condemned to extinction. (The Council, however, seems not yet to have granted Christians any right to serve in such a war).[5]

Moreover with Christianity now the established religion of the state, the church rapidly expanded. It was no longer a small sect which could disclaim any social responsibility or power to affect society. Christians soon made up a large section of the population from which the emperor had to recruit his army. Indeed, was the Christian emperor not himself a soldier, one who precisely by his military exploits had brought about such a change in the church's fortunes? Church and state were beginning to ally themselves as one *corpus Christianum*. Eusebius of Caesarea (c.265-339) became Constantine's own bishop and ecclesiastical adviser. He played the most important role in the theological rapprochement of the church with the empire. He marks a sharp break from the ambivalence which had previously enabled Christian thought about the state to remain dialectical.

In reaction to the changed fortunes of the church, Eusebius viewed the emperor with completely uncritical enthusiasm as God's appointee, citing Romans 13 in support of this attitude. He hailed Constantine's victory over Maxentius as a mighty work of God comparable to the liberation of Israel from Pharoah and Constantine's victory over Licinius in 324 as the triumph of God's chosen agent over the 'adversary of God' and the pagan gods. Indeed he even believed that Constantine's empire fulfilled the prophecies in Scripture of a dispensation of universal peace.

Eusebius also marks another important change. Previously the church had set Christians and pagans in contrast: Christians as people of the new age were to abstain from all violence; pagans as people of the old age remained subject to the ethos of war, which, however, they should wage justly.

Eusebius, however, drastically shifted this line of disparity. Writing in 313 C.E. he distinguished two levels of Christian life:
(a) the higher level of *the clergy,* who were obliged to remain wholly dedicated to God and therefore to abstain from all violence (as well as sex and wealth), and
(b) the more mundane level of *the laity,* who had to bear the burdens of citizenship and therefore to wage war, if it was a just war in defence of the empire.[6]

One can either denounce this shift as a fall from the idealism of
the early church or describe it as a step towards realism.
Whichever way we feel, however, we should at least recognise that
the earlier approach that just wars were to be waged only by
pagans, while Christians kept their hands clean, was inherently
anomalous and therefore could not remain stable in the new
political situation in which the church found itself.

## AMBROSE

The coming to power of Constantine thus led to a growing
acceptance in the church, typified and promoted by Eusebius,
that as citizens the Christian laity shared the duty to defend the
empire in a just war. This meant in principle that Christians could
no longer leave the criteria for a just war to pagan ethics. But now
a second historical factor began to play a fundamental role in
influencing Christian thinking: the barbarian hordes who towards
the end of the 4th century posed a growing threat to the empire.
This awakened unprecedented patriotism among Christians. It
also finally impelled Christian thinkers to work out a proper
doctrine of the just war.

Ambrose, the Bishop of Milan (c.339-397), was the theologian
who first really began to develop the Christian theory of the just
war. Ambrose was a new kind of Christian leader. He came from
the highest social class and had himself been a high official in the
imperial civil service. In his eyes the empire was an order of
justice and peace in the world that should be preserved. Therefore
all its male citizens, including Christians, should help to defend
the empire against the barbarians who were threatening it. That
was ' a just war. Ambrose therefore relegated pacifism to the
sphere of private morals and to the clergy. He also did not
hesitate to pray in the cathedral in Milan for the success of the
imperial armies.[7]

Ambrose's concept of the just war stood on two pillars: the Old
Testament and ideas from classical antiquity. The classical ideas
included the idea of a natural law of justice which was superior to
the laws and demands of any particular state. This idea went back
to Plato and the Stoics. The Stoics had also developed the idea
that all men were really brothers, because all shared in the cosmic
Logos (Reason). This implied that if people were engaged in war
they should treat their opponents, even those of different nations
or races, with justice and respect.

Besides the Greek philosophical tradition the Roman legal

tradition was basic to the development of the idea of the just war. Roman law interpreted relations between city-states of the Mediterranean area in terms of contractual obligation. It thus granted to a state in the same way as to an individual the right to seek redress or damages from a party that had caused it or its citizens injury, as though a breach of contract had taken place. This provided two basic ideas: that of a just cause for war in the prior guilt of the offending party and that of a just war as an extraordinary legal process enacted to restore justice. To accord with its legal nature the just war also had to be waged justly. And the first step to war was a formal demand to the foreign state for the redress of injuries. If no reparation was forthcoming the fetial priests would then issue a formal declaration of war.

Cicero, the famous Roman orator and statesman (d.43 B.C.E.), gave classic form to the Roman ethic of the just war, mainly in his manual on private and political morality, *De Officiis* (On Duties).[8] This work was to exercise a profound influence on Christian thinking from the 4th to the 19th centuries. Cicero was deeply influenced by Stoicism with its theories of a universal natural law of reason, the natural rights of the human person based on this and a common unity of humankind transcending individual nations. He based his concept of a just war on the Stoic principle that justice is owed to all men. Besides Stoicism, the Roman fetial code and, more fundamentally, the concept of the just war in Roman law formulated the principle, 'Justice is binding, even in war' and 'Justice must even be preserved in all dealings with enemies'.[9]

Ambrose took Cicero's *De Officiis* as a (rough) model for his own manual, *De Officiis Ministrorum* (On the Duties of the Clergy). In the process he took over (and introduced into Christian thinking) Cicero's ideas about the just war. On this basis Ambrose influenced Cicero. This can be seen in the limiting criteria or conditions he laid down for a just war. These criteria were variously to recur in Christian writers from Ambrose on.
1. The cause of the war had to be just. This was constituted by a state's right to defend itself.
2. The conduct of the war should be just in the sense that respect for the enemies' rights must be maintained.
3. The clergy should abstain.[10]

Ambrose, however, fused what he took over of Cicero's teaching about a just war with the idea of a holy war (a war fought at God's command and for a religion). Partly this derived from attitudes he had inherited from Eusebius and others. For Ambrose regarded the *Pax Romana* as God's special providence for the church: by ending the war between Roman groups that had plunged the empire into turmoil and thus establishing peace, the Emperor Augustus had actually prepared the way for the spread of Christianity.[11] Moreover, because the invading barbarians were Arian heretics, Ambrose tended to see their attacks on the empire as threats against the Christian faith itself. For him the empire and the catholic faith were joined together in 'the contest with alien unbelief',[12] and the catholic faith would stand or fall with the *Pax Romana*. Should the fusion of Rome and Christian orthodoxy disintegrate, the world would come to an end.

Ambrose therefore pointed to the Old Testament and specifically to figures like Joshua, Gideon, Jonathan and the Maccabees, as examples to inspire Christians in the defence of the empire. And he identified the invading Goths with the mythical figure of Gog, and Rome as the house of Israel which Scripture had promised over Gog (Ezek.38f.; Rev.20:18).

Ambrose, then, formulated his doctrine of war to provide Christian and moral support for the defence of the empire together with the church against the heretical barbarians. In the end, however, his formulation has to be judged an unsystematic mingling of Old Testament with classical pagan moral ideas. As such it was an unstable mixture that would not have stood the test of time. 'Still lacking was a systematic grounding of the just war on both Old and New Testament principles'.[13]

## AUGUSTINE

It was Augustine of Hippo (354-430) who grappled with the task of supplying the just war with a grounding that took account of the New Testament as well as the Old. He sought to work out a more adequate Christian basis for the just war theory, even though he followed the example of Ambrose in combining classical Greek and Roman ideas with the Bible. In broad terms his theory was to dominate Christian thinking about war from his own time until the present.

Historical circumstances confronted Augustine, like Ambrose, with the problem of war. Throughout Augustine's life the empire was on the defensive against barbarian inroads and invasions from various directions, and these became more and more critical. His thinking about war centered on four basic problems:

— Is it not right to defend with military means a relatively just society from attack?
— If so, what about the argument which pacifists adduced from the New Testament: how could one reconcile the killing and injuring that such military means entail with the commands of Christ, 'Love your enemies', 'Do not resist an evil person' and 'Turn the other cheek' (Mt.5:38-48)?
— What are the conditions or criteria for a just war?
— What is the relation between the just war and the holy war?

In answering the first of these questions Augustine accepted the classical idea of natural justice and natural rights. He argued that in order to defend what was just and good, Christians sometimes had to use violent means. He also pointed out that in the Bible God had commanded certain wars. If this was so, war could not be inherently wrong in all circumstances.[14] And even though the empire was only relatively a good thing, its citizens were right to defend it from rape and destruction by the marauding barbarian invaders.

It must be emphasised that Augustine hated war. The plunder and slaughter endemic in his time and his own experience of such things left him with a deep abhorrence of it. Even with regard to the benefits which the spread of the empire had brought he still pointed out to his readers: 'But think of the cost of this achievement ... all that slaughter of human beings, all the human blood that was shed!'.[15]

Indeed Augustine apparently felt that most wars are in no sense just. And even 'the necessity of waging just wars' was to be regretted. In spite of all this, however, Augustine saw war as sometimes necessary because of the very nature and power of sin in human life. In itself war is always evil; only because in certain extreme situations 'the injustice of the opposing side' makes it the lesser of two evils, can it ever be tolerated.[16] War is just only when waged against a state that flouts the standards of right and justice, in order, by punishing it, to re-establish these standards.

The second basic problem Augustine faced was the one posed by the pacifists. By Augustine's time, in the wake of Eusebius and Ambrose, most Christians had moved away from the earlier pacifism of the church. But Augustine sharply attacked the Manichees and those Christians who like them were still pacifist. In the situation which the empire faced he saw their attitude as politically and thus ethically irresponsible.

Nevertheless Augustine took very seriously the question that the pacifists posed: how could any violence, even the violence of a 'just war', be reconciled with the New Testament? In reply to this he argued that the Christian religion itself did not forbid 'wars of every kind'. If it did, the New Testament would have repudiated Moses, for instance, for waging war or found fault with the God of the Old Testament for commanding him to do so; but it did not.[17] And John the Baptist and Jesus would have told the soldiers who came to them to cast away their arms and withdraw from their profession, but they did not.

The question remained, however: how could the use of violent means be reconciled with loving one's enemy? Augustine's answer was to distinguish between inward attitude and outward act. 'What is the real evil in war?' he asks. Is it the death of a man (who is mortal in any case), when this takes place in order that others may live in peace? No. 'The real evils in war are love of violence, revengeful cruelty, fierce and implacable enmity, . . . lust for power, and such like.'[18] Thus in the Gospels love is essentially an inward disposition of the heart. The attitude of love *(caritas)* behind a good deed is more important than any deed or action as such. Even such texts as Mt.5:39 and Lk.6:29 really refer to 'the inward disposition of the heart' rather than the outward or public deed. They require us 'in the inmost heart, to cherish patience along with benevolence'.[19]

This means that 'in the outward action' we are required to do that which seems most likely to benefit the other person. But to do something for the benefit of the enemy may sometimes require violence. Thus when a father disciplines his son 'even with some sternness', this is an act of love. Likewise when the state punishes evildoers in order to prevent or dissuade them from doing further wrong: This too is an act of love, so long as it is carried out with no motive of revenge and no pleasure in their suffering.[20]

Thus Christ gave us the precept, 'Resist not evil, to prevent us from taking pleasure in revenge . . ., but not to make us neglect the duty of restraining men from sin'. And, on a broader scale, war may sometimes be necessary to restrain or punish the actions of an aggressive state. Therefore the soldier who strikes down the enemy from benevolence and pity is obeying Christ's teaching. This meant, however, that even in waging war one must 'cherish the spirit of a peacemaker'.[21]

Moreover love was owed to those on the other side. It was right to defend them from attack. Augustine granted that 'killing others in order to defend one's own life' was contrary to the law of love. But 'a soldier or public functionary acting, not for himself, but in defence of others' was in a different position: he might have to kill precisely for the sake of love. As a public functionary might have to kill a robber to protect his victims from theft, so soldiers might have to fight to protect their fellow-citizens against an unjust state.[22]

The third issue Augustine faced related to the specific conditions which must be met for a war to be just. Partly on the basis of Cicero, Augustine in various places set the following criteria for a just war:

1. The war must have a just cause (or at least 'the juster cause'). This is 'the injustice of the opposing side', which justifies a just war and thus imposes 'the duty' of waging it.[23] This in the first place identified as just a defensive war, one to *prevent* the unjust actions of an aggressor 'in behalf of the peace and safety of the community'.[24] But Augustine went beyond this. He did so in the first new definition of the just war since Cicero, a definition that became the most important single statement for medieval thinking about war:

> Just wars are customarily determined as those which avenge injuries, if a nation or state which is to be warred upon has neglected to punish crimes committed by its people, or to restore what has been unjustly taken away.[25]

This meant that the just war could also be an aggressive war — if it was waged against a state that refused to act justly, either by refusing to make amends when citizens of its own had wronged citizens of the injured state or by refusing to return land or property it had unjustly taken from the injured state.

2. The ruler who conducts the war must have a right disposition or 'intention'. His motive may not be a desire to inflict harm, a thirst for vengeance, a fever of revolt, a lust for power etc.; it must be to restore or vindicate justice. (This condition derived from Augustine's emphasis on the subjective motive as distinct from the outward act.)

3. The war must be declared and directed by the person who holds supreme authority in the land. God had given rulers the right to 'bear the sword' (Rom.13:4); therefore the words of Jesus, 'All who take up the sword will perish by the sword' (Matt.26:52), did not apply to taking it up at the command or with the permission of a superior, 'constituted authority'. They did, however, prohibit it in any other case, whether in a private dispute

or for a revolution. This also meant that the king above had the
right and duty to decide whether a war was just and should be
waged. The soldiers and citizens under him had to obey his
orders, whether or not they agreed with his judgement. Augustine
thus left no room for conscientious objection. He feared it could
only bring anarchy.

4. War must be resorted to 'only as a necessity'.

5. The war must be conducted justly. Following classical antiquity
Augustine meant that faith should be kept with the enemy, in the
sense that any oaths that the warring parties made should not be
violated. There should also be no atrocities, wanton violence,
massacres, looting, conflagrations or profaning of temples.[26]

The fourth basic problem Augustine faced was the relation
between the just war and the holy war. As historical circumstances
forced Augustine to wrestle with the problem of war as a whole,
so they also contributed to a basic shift in the way he thought
about this particular issue. At first, like Ambrose, he mingled the
holy war idea with that of the just war. In 410, however, after more
than 1 100 years of steady triumphant progress, Rome itself was
stormed and sacked by the Visigoths under Alaric the Bold.
Augustine was deeply shocked by this event. Disturbed by the
pagans' argument that the empire's abandonment of the pagan
gods was what had brought disaster on its capital city, he wrote
*The City of God*. In this work he turned his back on the mirage of
the 'Christian empire'.

Augustine now distanced himself from the whole popular
tendency to equate the empire with the Kingdom of Christ and its
battles with holy wars. By contrasting the enduring Kingdom or
City of God with the perishable imperial city, he broke the link that
Ambrose had made between the fortune of the faith and that of
the empire. To that extent he unravelled from the just war
doctrine the strong holy war element which Ambrose had mixed
with it. Now he was concerned only to uphold the doctrine of the
just war and its restrictions on war and its conduct at a time when
war was becoming increasingly endemic in Europe.[27]

In spite of this, however, Augustine contributed support to the
holy war doctrine in another way, through his attitude to the
persecution of heretics and schismatics. At first he opposed such
persecution, but in the church's struggle with the Donatists he
came to the view that a Christian emperor had the right to use
the sword on Christ's behalf against heretics as well as enemies of
the state. Moreover the church had the right and duty to seek

such imperial coercion. Such coercion was for the sake of the persecuted and their eternal salvation; therefore it was also motivated by love and benevolence. From Luke 14:23 he justified the persecution even of mere schismatics like the Donatists to 'compel them to come in' to the Catholic church. On this basis he wrote the only full justification in the early church of the right of the state to suppress non-Catholics.

It was particularly this element in his thinking that contributed to the theory of the holy war. 'The enemies of the Church', he wrote, 'are to be coerced even by war'.[28] Medieval legists were later eagerly to use this doctrine of religious persecution in Augustine to forge their justifications of wars and crusades.

## AFTER AUGUSTINE

After Augustine the doctrine of the just war declined and to the extent that it survived tended to be confused with holy war ideas. Factors which contributed to this were the continuing wars against the barbarians, the continuing oppression of heretics and schismatics, the increasing claims of the Pope to authority over secular rulers, the claim of the clergy to prescribe and proscribe military activity, the taking over of a military role by popes beginning with Gregory the Great (d.604), and the generally increasing theocratic view of society and the emerging threat from the Saracene. Theologians such as Bernard of Clairvaux (d.1153) even taught that the secular authority of the sword was ultimately vested in the pope, who merely delegated it to secular rulers. All this issued eventually in the glorification of Christian militarism that was associated with the Crusades.

The church, however, did seek to restrain the violence of war in various ways. Three notable ways were:
— 'the Truce of God', a largely unsuccessful attempt (initiated by Pope Urban II at the Council of Troia in 1093) to prohibit war on Sundays and the great Christian feast days;
— 'the Peace of God', a more successful prohibition of attack on certain non-combatants such as clerics, monks, friars, pilgrims, travellers, merchants and peasants; and
— the banning by the Second Lateran Council (1139) of crossbows, bows, arrows, and siege machines in wars between Christians.

All these became part of the canon law tradition of the church.

## GRATIAN

In the 12th century a revival in the study of classical Roman jurisprudence among civil lawyers in Italy and elsewhere in Europe renewed interest in the right of self-defence against violence, the conditions which justified recourse to war and the legal consequences of war. This led to a revival in the concept of licit war and so, among canon lawyers, renewed interest in the concept of the just war.[29]

In 1148 the Italian monk, Gratian, published the *Concordia Discordantium Canonum,* better known as the *Decretum.* This was a massively researched exposition of inherited canon law. It immediately became the authoritative text on canon law in western Europe. It was also a watershed in that it initiated a comprehensive inquiry into the moral and legal limits of war.

Gratian followed Augustine's method of reconciling with war such commands of Christ as those in Matthew 5:29 and Romans 12:19: they referred to a person's inward attitude more than his external acts. Love of enemies did not mean to permit sinning with impunity. Wars with a benevolent motive were justified. As it was in the best interests of a sinner to punish him, so with an aggressive state. Gratian's wholesale acceptance of Augustine's doctrine at this point convinced the canonists and theologians who followed him. They all accepted Augustine's argument that the inward 'intention' or motive was the really important thing; any hostile act was justified if motivated by love. The Sermon on the Mount was re-evaluated in the light of the principle that sometimes violence and war itself were necessary, not sinful. Love for one's neighbour in certain circumstances could actually make it right to kill him.

Gratian collected and ordered the scattered observations of Augustine and his successors. He quoted as authoritative two complementary definitions of the just war, the first taken from Isidore of Seville and ultimately from Cicero, the second from Augustine as enlarging upon the first:

— 'A war is just when, by a formal declaration, it is waged in order to regain what has been stolen or to repel the attack of enemies'.[30]
— 'Those wars are customarily called just which have for their end the revenging of injuries, when it is necessary by war to constrain a city or a nation which has not wished to punish an evil action committed by its citizens or to restore that which has been taken unjustly'.[31]

It was Gratian who introduced this definition of Augustine into medieval thinking and made it so important. On the basis of both definitions Gratian maintained in sum that the proper purpose of war was to repel and punish injuries. He followed Isidore in comparing the just war to due judicial process. Both were procedures to correct unjust situations by means of force, the one an ordinary procedure, the other an extraordinary one. Both were therefore the prerogative of the legally constituted authority.

Thus Gratian's notion of the just war had two fundamental requirements: an injury needing to be punished and the authority to do it. This yielded three conditions as follows:

1. The war must be waged to right or redress an actual wrong or injury. More specifically (following Augustine) a just war is waged to repel an enemy invasion, to recover stolen property (or protect it from being stolen), or to avenge injuries. This included punishing another state for crimes by its citizens against the aggrieved state when the other state refused to punish them itself. (All this amounted to a just cause, though Gratian did not use this term).

2. The war must be waged by legitimate authority and soldiers under his command. Those who resorted to the sword without such authority fell foul of Christ's prohibition in Matthew 26:52. This therefore also excluded clerics from the right to shed blood. They were to use only the spiritual sword of the Word of God and not even to defend themselves when attacked. They could, however, exhort the laity to fight, and bishops with secular authority could order the laity to do so.

3. The war must be declared beforehand by means of an edict proclaimed by the legitimate authority.

To these fundamental conditions, Gratian added others:

4. The intention of the war must not be vengeance, desire to harm, lust for domination etc., but the restitution of justice and peace. (Gratian also did not use the term 'right intention');

5. The war must be resorted to only in case of necessity. (On this basis Gratian held that when war was necessary to defend one's country etc., it could be waged at any time. This opposed 'the Truce of God'.

6. The war must use just means. (Gratian, however, omitted and presumably did not go along with the prohibitions of the Second Lateran Council).

7. The war must leave unharmed pilgrims, clergy, monks, women and the unarmed poor. (This upheld the Peace of God).[32]

Gratian took a somewhat different attitude to Augustine in the matter of conscientious objection. If soldiers were sure that military commands were contrary to divine precepts, they should refuse to obey them. As an example he cited the refusal of Christian soldiers under the command of Julian the Apostate to persecute fellow Christians.[33] Gratian thus revived the doctrine of the just war and gave it clear form on the basis of Isidore and especially Augustine and Roman law. That became part of his heritage not only to the church but also to European law.

On another level, however, on the basis of the Fathers and early medieval ecclesiastics, Gratian also justified the holy war. He justified the holy wars of the Old Testament on the assumption that God's commands were necessarily just and on the ground that a divine command was a special case of the authoritative edict required for a just war. This in principle fused the just war with the holy war. Moreover, Gratian explicitly accepted the church's right to initiate and direct (though not itself actually prosecute) the persecution of heretics and infidels. He even quoted with approval Augustine's statement, 'The enemies of the Church are to be coerced even by war'.[34] On this basis Gratian fatally elaborated a justification not only of the religious persecution of heretics but also of war against the infidels. He even went along with the idea that those who died in such wars merited eternal salvation.

Following the work of Gratian, four religious and secular streams of thought and practice intermingled to give final form to the just war doctrine of the Middle Ages. These were:
— the theological tradition, which went back to Augustine;
— the work of civil lawyers who sought to interpret and update Roman law;
— the canon law tradition, especially the work of commentators on the *Decretum* and also on later papal decretals; and
— the chivalric code, the inchoate but influential code of conduct for the knightly class, which included old Germanic traditions.

The theologians concentrated on the concepts of just cause and right intent. The canon lawyers concentrated on the concept of right authority. The civil lawyers and chivalry contributed to thinking about just means.

## THOMAS AQUINAS
In the century after Gratian, Thomas Aquinas (1224-1274) was the theologian who gave classic systematic formulation to Augustine's doctrine of the just war.

Aquinas, like Gratian, followed Augustine in using Romans 13 to justify war. He also gave Christ's words, 'Resist not evil' an inward, spiritual interpretation.

Aquinas' basic theological method emphasised that it was valid to distinguish between the insights of ordinary morality which can be derived from natural reason on the one hand and the insights of faith which depend on special revelation on the other. The issue of war, in his opinion, fell into the former category. It could therefore be discussed properly by people of sound mind and good will, whether Christian or not, and Christians should take seriously the insights of non-Christians in this area. Because the moral laws which natural reason discovered were also God's laws, they were binding on Christians as well as non-Christians.

This provided a clear justification for the use of such writers as Cicero in the traditional just war doctrine. Along with Aquinas' theological method this justification came to be accepted by subsequent Catholic theology. This approach also finally cut the just war theory loose from the idea of the holy war as a war that was specially commanded by God through revelation in the Old Testament.

Aquinas sought to provide a clear and systematic list of three criteria for the just war. These were derived from the traditional doctrine, especially as it had been expressed by Augustine:

1. The war must be waged for a just cause. Primarily this meant that the enemy must have committed a wrong which made it deserve to be attacked.

2. The war must be waged with a right intention. (This applied primarily to the motives of the ruler waging the war. His intention must be 'to promote good and to avoid evil'. This applied to both the end aimed at and the means used; it must not be vengeance, a lust to dominate, etc.)

3. The war must be declared and waged by the legitimate authority, not any private individual. Following Aristotle and Augustine, Aquinas saw the ruler as charged with the common good. He had to defend the common goal with the sword in war in the same way as against criminals within the state (Rom.13:4). On the other hand 'it does not belong to a private person to start a war'; he must resort to ordinary legal means for his rights.[35]

In other writings Aquinas proposed a different formula for the just war, but one that was really complementary to the above criteria. This was that:

4. A just war is a war in defence of the community and the common good.[36]

This in fact became the basic theme of all medieval writers on the subject: that a just war is a war in defence of one's own country.

Aquinas, like some other medieval theorists, did not uphold the condition that had found its way from the Roman fetial code via Cicero and Isidore into Gratian's *Decretum*: that war must be formally declared beforehand. Consistently with his whole approach that the rules for war had to be derivable from the natural law, Aquinas also opposed the principle of 'the Truce of God'. He argued that 'it is lawful to carry on a war on the holy days, provided there be need for doing so' (citing in support I Macc.2:41 and Jn.7:23).[37]

## DE VITORIA AND DE SUAREZ

Later medieval thinkers, especially the great Catholic theologians, Francisco de Vitoria (d.1546) and Francisco de Suarez (d.1617), sought to refine the medieval view and provide a comprehensive doctrine of the just war.

Both de Vitoria and de Suarez were Spaniards. De Vitoria was exercised by the moral problem of Spanish military conquest in South America. De Suarez was concerned with the wars resulting from the bitter religious rivalries in Europe. These men set their faces against the crusading tradition and sought principles based on natural law.

De Vitoria emphasised: 'There is one and only one just cause for waging war, viz., an injury received'. He pointed out: 'This is the opinion of all the doctors in the tradition'.[38] De Suarez widened this definition to include an injury 'against allies or friends'.[39]

De Suarez granted basically three kinds of injuries as causes of a just war:

— if a ruler appropriates someone else's goods and will not return them;
— if he denies 'the common rights of nations' without reasonable cause (e.g. the right to passage or trade);
— 'severe harm to reputation or honour'.[40]

Strict self-defence against attack was therefore not a necessary condition for a just war; in certain circumstances a just war could be an aggressive one.

De Vitoria also set out the legitimate goals of a just war in

terms of what those waging it might claim, viz:
— compensation for the injuries that were the *casus belli;*
— compensation for losses incurred in the course of the war; and
— punishment of the malefactors who precipitated the war. But a prince who aimed at annihilating his enemies or demanded their unconditional surrender was not engaged in a just war.

Finally we should note that the various late medieval thinkers restored or added to Aquinas' criteria further conditions for a just war, which may be listed as follows:
— War had to be a last resort. All other means to resolving the conflict must be tried or excluded before resorting to war.
— Just or proper methods of war, not extremely violent or cruel ones, must be used.
— There must be no attack on innocent non-combatants: clergymen, women, children or farmers.
— The violence used in the war must not be disproportionate to the end at which it was aimed.
— There must be a good, or at least a reasonable, prospect of victory.
— The ensuing peace must be just.

## MARTIN LUTHER

During the age of the Reformation, Anabaptists such as the Münster revolutionaries reverted to the Old Testament and medieval idea of a holy war; others like the Mennonites reverted to pacifism. The 'magisterial' Reformers, Luther, Zwingli and Calvin, however, remained in the just war tradition. (In this survey we limit ourselves to looking at Luther and Calvin).

Luther (1483-1546), like Augustine, regarded war as a great evil. For him all war is a 'great plague'. Aggressive wars are 'of the devil', and even defensive wars are 'human disasters'. Again and again he condemns those who begin wars unnecessarily. In the end they cannot escape God's judgement, he warns, and always either lose the war or come to disaster somehow. He cites various Old Testament examples to prove this. He also repeatedly quotes Psalm 68:30, 'He (God) scatters those who delight in war'.[41]

Again like Augustine, Luther regarded most wars as waged for the wrong reasons: selfish motives, covetousness, desire for glory, feelings of insulted honour, anger, lust for revenge. A Christian prince may not wage war for such reasons. When his own Elector, John Frederick, and Duke Moritz threatened to go to war with each other over an insignificant matter, Luther summoned them both and admonished them in the name of God to desist.

At the same time, however following Romans 13, Luther regarded the role and dignity of the state with the utmost seriousness. God himself had appointed it as his agent to protect the innocent and the weak against the wicked and the violent.[42]

On this ground Luther justifies wars of defence. If it is right for the ruler to punish an individual thief or murderer, then it is all the more right that he should punish 'a whole crowd of evildoers who are doing harm in proportion to the size of the crowd'. Defence is 'a proper ground for fighting' a war against an aggressive state in the same way as one individual who kills another in self-defence 'is innocent in the eyes of all men'.[43] Defence, however, is also the only valid ground for war. Unlike Augustine, Luther did not allow for an aggressive war in any circumstances.

Three aspects of Luther's doctrine of war are of special interest:
— the way in which he underpinned the doctrine with his doctrine of the two Kingdoms.
— the way in which he supported conscientious objection against unjust wars, and
— the way in which the doctrine of the two Kingdoms led him to oppose the attitude of the medieval tradition to religious or holy wars.

Again like Augustine, Luther faced the problem of pacifism. In his case it was the pacifism of the Anabaptists. He too wrestled with the question of how to relate Christ's admonitions in the Sermon on the Mount to Paul's justification of the sword in the hands of the state. How, he asks, can the soldier's deeds of 'slaying and robbing' be called 'works of love'?.

In reply Luther insists that they are works of love. He compares a soldier with a good surgeon, who in order to save a person from a terrible illness must amputate a hand, foot, ear or eye. Looked at from the point of view of the amputated organ, the surgeon appears cruel and merciless. From the point of view of the body as a whole, however, the surgeon is 'a fine and true man' doing 'a good and Christian work'. Thus the soldier's office may seem to be completely contrary to Christian love — until we look at it from the point of view of society as a whole, when we 'think of how it protects the good and keeps and preserves wife and child, house and farm, property and honor and peace. Then I see how precious and godly this work is'.[44]

Luther cites John the Baptist, who 'as a Christian

teacher . . . praised the military profession' at the same time as 'he forbade its misuse' (Lk.3:14). He also cites the words of Jesus in John 18:36 as legitimating war for secular kings.[45]

More broadly, however, Luther's answer to the problem posed by the pacifist interpretation of the New Testament is in terms of his doctrine of the two Kingdoms, or the two ways in which God reigns.

God's 'proper' Kingdom is the spiritual Kingdom of God. It is this Kingdom (not the other) over which Christ is 'king and lord'. In it God rules by means of his Word and his Spirit. This Kingdom exists for the eternal salvation of people; all true Christians belong to it, as private individuals. But God has another Kingdom, his 'strange' Kingdom. This is the worldly or political Kingdom, and it exists for the outward protection of people's lives. God rules this Kingdom not through Christ and by means of the Spirit but through the secular government and by means of the sword. In the first Kingdom, then, love for one's enemies, mercy and forgiveness are appropriate; in the second, law and compulsion. But this second Kingdom is also essential in this sinful world.

Therefore the state needs to wield the sword in order to preserve peace, both between individuals and between nations. The individual should not resist evil but 'be willing to suffer every injustice and evil without avenging himself'. Others, however, he should be willing to protect from injustice and the state was there to do the same.[46]

Unsystematically Luther emphasised certain of the medieval conditions for a war to be a just war:
1. The primary issue, as we have seen, was that it must be a war in defence of a territory against an aggressor.
2. It must also be a war in response to prior attack. 'Whoever starts a war is in the wrong', and usually in the end is defeated or punished.[47]
3. It must be waged, as we have also seen, by the lawful ruler. The idea that any revolution could be just in God's eyes Luther bitterly opposed on the basis of Scripture and because of the chaos that revolutionary mobs bring. 'It is better to suffer wrong from one tyrant, that is, from the ruler, than from unnumbered tyrants, that is from the mob'. Tyrannous rulers must be left for God to deal with.[48]
4. The war must be a last resort, a 'war of necessity' that is the 'only miserable way left of defending ourselves'. The ruler must

seek to settle the conflict by means of arbitration, waiting until the situation compels him to fight.[49]

5. The cost of the war must be carefully weighed against its aims.
6. The war must be waged by just means.
7. It must observe the traditional exemptions.
8. Luther adds a specifically Christian condition: war must 'be fought in the fear of God'. Those who go into battle, even if they are defending their country, must not be filled with pride in their own cause or trust in it to give them victory. Instead they must humble themselves before God and trust in his sheer grace and mercy to give them victory. Otherwise it is their defeat that will be just.[50]

In spite of his emphasis that only the legitimate ruler can wage just war, Luther's position on conscientious objection contrasts sharply with that of Augustine:

> It belongs to the obedience subjects owe that they do or leave undone with all diligence and attention what their rulers desire of them .... Where, however, as often happens, the secular power and authority, as it is called, would force a subject (to act) contrary to God's commandment or else hinder him (from acting in accordance with it), there obedience ends and duty is suspended. In such a case one must say as St Peter said to the rulers of the Jews: 'One must obey God rather than men' .... For example, if a prince wished to go to war and had an openly unjust cause, in such a case one should by no means follow or help (him), and this because God has commanded that we shall not kill our neighbour or do him injustice. Likewise if he were to order us to give false evidence, rob, lie or deceive and the like. In such cases one should rather give up goods, honour, body and life so that God's command may remain standing.[51]

The subject therefore should 'find out by any possible means' whether a war in which he was called to fight was just or not.[52] If, however, he could not find out whether his prince was in the right or the wrong, he should not forfeit certain obedience for the sake of uncertain justice. He should rather, out of love (I Cor.13:4-7), give his ruler the benefit of the doubt.

On the basis of his emphatic separation of church and state and their different roles in the doctrine of the two Kingdoms, Luther early in his career as a Reformer also strongly opposed any kind of crusade or religious war, as well as the persecution of heretics by the state. He even argued against resisting the emperor in defence of himself or his followers and was not happy about defending Saxony against the Catholic princes when they threatened to invade. Against the Turks the emperor had the right to wage a war if it was purely defensive and for political reasons. He had no right to do so for religious reasons, however, because spiritual battles were to be fought with spiritual weapons. War for the sake of religion was always wrong, because it confused the two Kingdoms. 'The emperor's sword has nothing to do with the faith'.[53] Thus Luther radically separated the just war from the holy war.

In the 1530s, however, Luther's thinking shifted. He adopted Melancthon's doctrine that secular rulers had a duty to do all they could to defend and promote the true religion, even if need be by force. Increasingly he came to identify all enemies of the gospel, including both the pope and the Turk, with the forces of the Antichrist. Indeed the need to resist the pope was the greater because he could not claim to be a legitimate government, which the Turk at least could! Under the impact of the Anabaptist revolution in Münster and the Peasants' Revolt, Luther also changed his mind about persecution of heretics by the state.

## JOHN CALVIN

Calvin (1509-1564), like Luther, largely accepted the traditional doctrine of war. This is shown for one thing by the comparative brevity with which he writes of war in the *Institutes*. He also specifically refers to, and substantially depends on, Augustine and Cicero. And he shows the influence of his study of Seneca's *De Clementia* when he urges that war must be humane.[54]

Calvin's whole argument starts from Paul's understanding of the state in Romans 13. Rulers are God's servants: they bear the sword as the agents of his wrath or vengeance on the wrongdoer (Rom.13:4). Thus they protect the innocent and preserve the social peace. He then develops Augustine's analogy of a robber gang. If it is appropriate for the ruler to use the sword against robbers who harm only a few, is it not even more appropriate to use it against an invader who threatens to devastate the whole country, destroy its common peace and violently oppress its people?[55]

Like Luther, Calvin here is seeking to refute the pacifist views of the Anabaptists as exemplified in articles 4 and 6 of the Schlechtheim Confession. What is interesting is that Calvin's argument starts at the same point as article 6, with Romans 13, but comes to just the opposite conclusion. This is not because

the Confession and Calvin disagree about the political
responsibility of the state: the Confession too agrees that the state
properly 'punishes and puts to death the wicked, and guards and
protects the good'. It is because Calvin refuses to grant what the
Confession goes on to assert: that the Christian must withdraw
from this political responsibility into an apolitical sphere which it
calls 'the perfection of Christ'.[56]

Calvin grants to the pacifists the point that the New Testament
does not expressly teach that Christians may engage in war. But
this is because the books in it were written 'not to fashion a civil
government, but to establish the spiritual Kingdom of Christ'.[57]
Following Augustine's example, however, Calvin points out that
the New Testament does indirectly sanction war in that the
soldiers in it who ask counsel concerning salvation are not told to
throw away their arms or withdraw from military service (e.g.
Lk.3:14).

Calvin then goes on to qualify his defence of the right of rulers
to wage war by calling on them:
—   to act without giving vent to passions of anger or hatred and
    to have pity on the enemy rather than 'burn with implacable
    severity';
—   to resort to arms only when driven 'by extreme necessity' and
    after trying every other recourse;
—   to be motivated by no private feelings but only 'by concern
    for the people'.

From all this it is clear that Calvin followed Augustine and the
medieval theologians in seeing what he called the 'lawful' war as
essentially defensive. We may set out the points he makes as
follows in terms of the traditional criteria:
1. A just war should be in defence of a country against invasion.
2. The ruler who wages war must have a right intention or motive
(concern for the public good, and not any private passion of
anger, hatred or implacability).
3. He must exercise pity rather than unnecessary cruelty.
4. War must be a last resort only.

Like Luther, Calvin abhorred the chaos that revolutions led by
private individuals incurred. But unlike Luther he did not strictly
exclude all revolution. He allowed that in certain circumstances
people appointed to a secondary rank of government might act
against a tyrant. That, however, was the only exception.

Unlike Luther, Calvin does not directly address the problem of
the individual citizen who may wish to object to conscription on

conscientious grounds. *Prima facie* he thus seems to relapse into Augustine's approach of being concerned only that rulers use the criteria he outlines to distinguish whether a war will be just or not. This, however, is qualified in principle, though without specific application to military service, at the end of his chapter on 'Civil Government'. There are found the famous words:

> But in that obedience which we have shown to be owed to the authority of rulers we must always make this exception, and indeed observe it in the first place: that such obedience is never to lead us astray from obedience to him to whose will the desires of all kings ought to be subject, to whose decrees all their commands ought to yield, to whose majesty all their sceptres ought to be submitted .... The Lord, therefore, is the King of kings; when he has opened his holy mouth, he alone must be listened to, before and above all men, After him we are subject to those men who rule over us, but subject only in the Lord. If they command anything contrary to him, let us not pay the least attention to it.[58]

## IN CONCLUSION

The term 'just war' from Aristotle onwards meant, as we have seen, a war that accorded with justice, as defined by the natural moral law, or war for a morally just end or purpose. The English term 'just war' today, however, is misleading to many people not schooled in the tradition. It obscures the fact that traditional Christian thought never identified war as a positive good but only as sometimes justifiable as the lesser of two great evils. As a result the term 'just war' seems to such people to deny the horrendous nature of all war. For this reason and because the traditional definition of just in terms of natural law has become problematic anyway, it would be better today to use the term justifiable war (or justified war).

When we seek to apply the above discussion on just war theory to our particular situation in South Africa, we must insist that ultimately Christ alone is our Lord and therefore our allegiance is ultimately to him alone in the political as well as the private sphere. We must insist on this in spite of the implicit denials of it by Prime Ministers and other politicians and even from some theologians, and in spite of the contrary claims of, say, *Die Stem van Suidafrika* or *Die Lied van Jong Suidafrika!* To Christ alone, ultimately, we must be obedient, not to the government or the country, much less to one or other population group or our own interests. If we understand his will to require disobedience to the will of the government, we must, as Luther said, let God's command remain standing. Thereby we stand or fall as God's people. 'The Lord is the King of kings; when he has opened his holy mouth, he alone must be listened to, before and above all men' (Calvin).

## NOTES

1. *Natal Mercury*, 6 August 1974, p.10.
2. *Die Hoofstad*, 1 August 1974.
3. J.M. Hornus, *It is Not Lawful for Me to Fight*, (Scottdale: Herald Press, 1980), p.32,35f.,45f.,49, together with p.258 n.87-89 and n.103.
4. J. Ferguson, *War and Peace in the World's Religions*, (London: Sheldon, 1977), p.104.
5. Hornus, *It is not Lawful for me to Fight*, pp.171-78.
6. Eusebius, *Demonstratio Evangelica*, I. viii. 29b-30b, in R. Bainton, *Christian Attitudes Toward War and Peace: A Historical Survey and Critical Reevaluation*, (Nashville: Abir.gdon, 1960), p.84.
7. Cf. Ambrose, *On the Christian Faith (De Fide Christians)*, II.16.143, in *Ibid.*
8. Cicero, *De Officiis*, I.ix,xi,xii,xiii,xxiii, II.viii, III.xi, and *De Res Publica*, II.viii,xvii, III.xi,xviii,xxiii.
9. Cicero, *On the Duties of the Clergy*, I.xxix.139f.
10. *Ibid.*, I.xxxv.76, xxix.139f., II.vii.33, III.viii.54-56, x.67-69.
11. Ambrose, *Enarratio in Psalmum 45*, 21, in F.H. Russell, *The Just War in the Middle Ages*, (Cambridge: C.U.P., 1979), p.12f.
12. Ambrose, *On the Christian Faith*, II.xvi.
13. Russell, *The Just War in the Middle Ages*.
14. Augustine, *Reply to Faustus the Manichaean*, xxii.74, in Russell, *The Just War in the Middle Ages*.
15. *Augustine, City of God*, (New York: Image Books, 1958), III.14, 17-20, 30f., xix.7.
16. *Ibid.*, XIX.7.
17. Augustine, *Reply to Faustus the Manichaean* XXII.78, in Russell, *The Just War in the Middle Ages*.
18. *Ibid.*, XXII.74.
19. Augustine, *Letter CXXXVIII*, ii.11,13f., (to Marcellinus), cf. *Reply to Faustus*, XXII.76.
20. *Ibid.*, ii.14.
21. Augustine, *Letter XLVII.* 5 (to Publicola), *Letter CLXXXIX.* 6 (to Boniface).
22. Augustine, *Letter XLVII.* 5.
23. Augustine, *City of God*, XV.4, XIX.7.
24. Augustine, *Reply to Faustus*, XXII.75.
25. Augustine, *Quaestiones et Locutiones in Heptateuchum*, VI.x, super Josue (c.419) in J. Barnes, 'The Just War' in N. Kretzmann, et al. (eds.), *The Cambridge History of Later Medieval Philosophy*, (Cambridge: C.U.P., 1982), p.777f.
26. For these criteria see *Reply to Faustus*, XXII.74f., 70, *Letter CLXXXIX*, 6, and Bainton, *Christian Attitudes*, p.97.
27. R.A. Markus, 'Saint Augustine's Views on the Just War' in W.J. Sheils, (ed.), *The Church and War*, (London: Blackwell, 1983), pp.4-14.

28. J.T. Johnson, *Ideology, Reason and the Limitation of War*, (Princeton: Princeton University Press, 1975), p.36.

29. Russell, *The Just War in the Middle Ages*, ch.2.

30. Johnson, *Ideology, Reason, and the Limitation of War*, p.36, and Russell, *The Just War In the Middle Ages*, p.62 and n.24.

31. Johnson, *Ideology, Reason and the Limitation of War*, and Russell, *The Just War in the Middle Ages*, p.63 and n.28.

32. Johnson, *Ideology, Reason and the Limitation of War*, p.37f., 73f., and Russell, *The Just War in the Middle Ages*, pp.63-71,77-83.

33. Russell, *The Just War in the Middle Ages*, p.69f.

34. Johnson, *Ideology, Reason and the Limitation of War*, p.36.

35. Thomas Aquinas, *Summa Theologica*, Part II,II, q.40., art.1.

36. Russell, *The Just War in the Middle Ages*, p.290.

37. Thomas Aquinas, *Summa*, art.4.

38. *De Indis*, q.3., par.13 in Barnes, 'The Just War', p.779.

39. *De Bello*, IV.3, in *Ibid.*, p.778.

40. *De Bello*, IV.3, in *Ibid.*, p.781.

41. M. Luther, 'Whether Soldiers, Too, Can Be Saved' (1526), in J. Pelikan, (ed.), *Luther's Works*, (American Edition) Vol.46, pp.96f., 118-122.

42. *Ibid.*, Vol.46, p.121.

43. *Ibid.*, pp.98f., 120.

44. *Ibid.*, p.96.

45. *Ibid.*

46. M. Luther, *Temporal Authority: To What Extent it Should Be Obeyed* (1523) in Pelikan, *Luther's Works*, Vol.45, p.101.

47. Luther, 'Whether Soldiers, Too, Can Be Saved', Vol.46, p.118., Cf. M. Luther, *On War Against the Turks* (1529) in J. Pelikan, *Luther's Works*, vol.46, p.165.

48. Luther, 'Whether Soldiers, Too, Can Be Saved', Vol.46, p.106f.

49. *Ibid.*, pp.118; 123-125.

50. *Ibid.*, pp.123-125.

51. 'Von den guten Werken', in O. Clemen, (ed.), *Luther's Werke in Auswahl*, (Berlin: de Gruyter, 1933), p.287.

52. Pelikan, 'Temporal Authority', in *Luther's Works*, Vol.45, p.126.

53. Luther, *On War Against the Turks* (1529), Vol.46, p.185f.

54. F.W. Battles, in endnotes to p.213f. of his translation of the 1536 ed. of Calvin's *Institutes*, (London: Collins, 1986), p.332.

55. J. Calvin, *Institutes* (1559 ed.), IV.xx.10-11.

56. J. Leith, *Creeds of the Churches*, (Richmond: John Knox, 1973), p.287.

57. Calvin, *Institutes*, (1559), IV.xx.12.

58. *Ibid.*, IV.xx.32.

# Radical Peace-Making: The Challenge of Some Anabaptists

JOHN W. DE GRUCHY

Those mainline churches in South Africa which, through the years, have formally opposed apartheid, have demonstrated a certain ambiguity in their attitude towards war and violence. This ambivalence derives firstly from the fact that while none of them is pacifist by tradition, all standing generally in the 'just war' tradition, they have all formally (that is, by the decisions of their synods, et al) committed themselves to non-violent means in the struggle for justice and social change. But, secondly, the ambivalence also derives from the fact that their constituency straddles the social spectrum, so that while white members would almost invariably reject violence as a means, this would not be true for the black membership as a whole, some of which would identify as Christians with the armed struggle of the ANC and PAC.

A third factor, however, is the emergence of a pacifist option within these non-pacifist churches, an option which has been grasped by increasing numbers of young white military conscripts who, in all Christian conscience, have decided that they cannot be part of the South African Defence Force for both religious and political reasons. In many cases this has resulted from the discovery of a radical form of Christian discipleship not normally associated with mainline Christianity. Throughout Christian history, such radical discipleship has often implied pacifism. Thus, it is not surprising that in South Africa it has likewise led to the espousal of a pacifist consistency which requires the renouncing of the use of violence in perpetuating apartheid and violence as a means to overthrow it. What is surprising is the fact that it has happened within a church context where, apart from the presence of a very small Quaker community and an equally small chapter of the Fellowship of Reconciliation, there is no significant 'peace-church' (e.g. Mennonite, Church of the Brethren) presence. Even those who are the closest heirs of the Radical Reformation, the Baptists and, to a lesser extent, the Congregationalists, have not generally espoused pacifism as part of their creed.

Indeed, as already indicated, all the major' churches in South Africa have stood firmly within the just-war tradition. Illustrative of this within the so-called English-speaking churches is the extent to which all of them (Anglicans, Baptists, Congregationalists, Methodists and Presbyterians) supported the allied forces in the South African, and the First and Second World Wars.[1] The fact that some of them have more recently begun to make what might be called quasi-pacifist statements, especially since the WCC Programme to Combat Racism's support for liberation movements began in the seventies, is more indicative of social pressure than any change in basic theological conviction.

Since the time of Gandhi and the founding of the African Nationalist Congress, there has been, of course, a significant group of South Africans, both Christian and non-Christian, who have been committed to non-violent action for social justice and change, irrespective of the stance taken by the churches. It is well known, however, that such a position came under increasing strain within the black community after the banning of the ANC and PAC in 1960, and, more recently in the years since the uprising in Soweto in 1976. Thus it has been at the same time as the ANC and an increasing number of young blacks have turned in desperation to armed struggle, that white Christians in South Africa who oppose the status quo, particularly males confronted by compulsory military service, have turned towards non-violence and pacifism. Many of them have suffered a great deal as a result of taking this stand, some spending extended periods in prison and others in community service. Their testimony has not only forced the churches to reassess their traditional position on issues such as conscientious objection and military conscription, but has also put the state under some pressure.

Those aware of church history, and especially the sixteenth-century debates between Lutheran and Reformed leaders, on the one hand, and those more radical reformers whom they called Anabaptists, on the other, and the continuing of that debate in other contexts right up to the present, will recognise a familiar pattern. The contexts and issues have changed, of course, and it would be misleading to suggest that what happened then is simply being replayed. Nevertheless there is a similarity. In the midst of the present debate on just war and just revolution, with the reluctant yet growing acceptance by some Christians of violence as a means to a more just end, it is of vital importance to remember that there is an alternative Christian approach to the struggle for a just society. Not all Anabaptists were committed to non-violence, but a significant group were, and they have left us a legacy which has not only influenced subsequent church history for good, but which may also be of timely relevance for us in South Africa.

Sixteenth-century Anabaptism has been the subject of considerable research during this century. Apart from a renewed interest more generally in Reformation historiography, scholars have shown a new interest in the Peasants' Revolt and, more particularly, in the thought and revolutionary activity of Thomas Muntzer. Some even see Muntzer as a sixteenth-century religious precursor of Karl Marx. Another reason for the exploration of Anabaptism has been a contemporary Mennonite concern to rediscover the original vision of those radical reformers who laid the foundation for their own understanding of the Christian faith, the church and its task in the world. As a result, there is a huge and growing literature on the subject and an ongoing debate on the issues, including that of the question of non-violence, reflecting the complexity of the subject.

The intention of this essay is not to enter that debate, even though some reference to it is necessary. My concern is a much more limited and basic one. It is to remind those of us engaged in the struggle for justice in South Africa of the theological vision which motivated those Anabaptists who believed that Christians could not engage in any act of violence. Perhaps the fact that the dominant theological traditions in South Africa have simply taken the just war position for granted has led us to the unwarranted assumption that there is no alternative theological position except that of a just revolution. It has also tended to reinforce the assumption that pacifism is a secular humanist stance rather than one rooted in biblical faith.

## THE MAGISTERIAL AND RADICAL REFORMERS

In his major study on *The Radical Reformation*, George H. Williams first drew the distinction between what he called the 'magisterial' and the 'radical' Reformations. The magisterial Reformers, Luther, Zwingli and Calvin, were so-called by Williams

because they sought to bring about their reforms with the help of
the secular authorities. Where this was not possible because of
religious or political opposition, their reforms nevertheless

> presupposed or proposed a truly Christian state, and always
> carried the seed of a complete Christian commonwealth within
> the temporary and protective husks of their clandestine
> conventicles.

Moreover, as Williams continues: 'They did not, on principle,
eschew fighting for the word of God, given a favourable
conjuncture of events'.[2] The radical Reformers, on the other hand,
were committed 'to clear away the old abuses root and branch
and at the same time to dispense with earthly magistrates and
prelates'.[3] And for some of them this radicalism and its rejection
of the secular powers as instruments of reformation, meant non-
resistance, non-violence, as well as non-participation in
government. It was a radicalism grounded in their reading of the
Sermon on the Mount and their conviction that they had been
called out of the world to be a holy people.

The Radical Reformation, as Williams so comprehensively
describes it, was a diverse and complex phenomenon. Heinrich
Bullinger, whose work on the origin of the Anabaptists written in
1560 has influenced opinion ever since, spoke of the 'marvellous
and manifold divisions and bands' of the Anabaptists.[4] It was also
Bullinger who first claimed that Thomas Muntzer, the ex-priest
turned visionary and revolutionary, was the father of the
Anabaptists. Ever since there has been a debate about the role of
Muntzer within Anabaptism,[5] and the relationship between the
different parts of the movement.[6]

The fact of the matter is that the origins of Anabaptism are
complex, with strong roots not only in the Swiss Reformation but
also in medieval piety, giving it an identity which separates it from
both Protestantism and Catholicism. As the movement grew and
expanded, many different groups with increasingly diverse points
of view and practices emerged. But they were generally lumped
together by their opponents as much for the sake of convenience
and control as for the fact that they 'rebaptised'. Nevertheless,
however much the more evangelical heirs of Anabaptism may
have tried, the title Anabaptist cannot entirely escape being
associated with the Peasants' Revolt or those bizarre events in
Münster in the 1530s in which the good citizens, fired by
apocalyptic expectations, sought to establish the kingdom of God
on earth. Nor can they avoid some identification with those off-

shoots of the movement in which unusual doctrines and practices flourished.

Then as now, in times of historical crisis and transition, it is impossible to maintain clean and clear lines between groups for the sake of our latter-day typologies. The breaking free from inherited traditions and institutions invariably means experimentation and fragmentation, much of it leading to dead-ends. This is compounded when those involved are hunted and hounded by both church and state authorities, as were the Anabaptists, and so forced to flee across Europe, spreading their ideas and gathering new ones. That there was a historical connection between the various parts of the radical reformation, and between them and their descendents thus cannot be denied. But historical connection does not mean theological or practical agreement on every issue. One such issue was precisely that of non-resistance and non-violence.

There can be little doubt that the Anabaptists who flourished in Switzerland, southern Germany and Austria, and who adopted the *Schleitheim Confession* (1527), as well as those in Holland who were shepherded and organised by Menno Simons (1496-1561), and who eventually formulated the *Dordrecht Confession* (1632), stand broadly within the evangelical tradition of Christian faith. This remains true of their Mennonite descendents, and of others influenced by them, notably the Baptists. For want of more precision, we could follow others and describe them as evangelical Anabaptists. These, like the saintly Swiss leader, Michael Sattler, and Conrad Grebel, were as much perturbed by the excesses of Münster and other aberrations of the evangelical faith as anyone else. And it is the 'peace-witness' of these early and largely Swiss Anabaptists who first broke with Ulrich Zwingli in Zurich that concerns us in this essay.[7]

The 'peace witness' of these Anabaptists can best be examined by comparing their position on the one hand with Zwingli, the magisterial Reformer par excellence and an exponent of the just war, and, on the other, with Thomas Muntzer, a radical Reformer and exponent of what we would now call the just revolution. Though the evangelical Anabaptists owed their existence in many respects to Zwingli, and though they had early sympathy for what Muntzer sought to do for and with the poor peasantry, they developed a different theology and social praxis. Yet it was not an easier one, a middle-of-the-road path of escape; on the contrary, like Zwingli and Muntzer, many of them died violently at the hands of their opponents. The difference was that, unlike Zwingli and Muntzer, they refused to engage in war or violence against their opponents because of their Christian confession.

## AGAINST ZWINGLI AND MUNTZER

In September 1524, shortly before the break took place between the first Anabaptists and Ulrich Zwingli in Zurich, Conrad Grebel, the Anabaptist leader, wrote two letters to Thomas Muntzer.[8] Muntzer had become a Lutheran in 1520, but by 1523 he had broken irrevocably with Luther and was poised to lead the Peasants' Revolt which erupted the following year. The Zurich Anabaptists had never met Muntzer, but from what they had heard of his struggle against Luther, they recognised a kindred spirit and a 'dearly beloved brother' who had courageously broken with the 'phony faith' not only of the papalists but also the antipapal evangelical preachers. Indeed, Grebel tells Muntzer that his booklets 'have almost immeasurably instructed and strengthened us, the poor in spirit.'[9]

In many respects, the two Grebel letters, written the same day, provide a programmatic statement of the emerging free church tradition. Following Zwingli, but going much further, Grebel insists that all doctrine and practice in the church must conform solely to the divine Word. This applied, in the first place, to the question of baptism, hence their rejection of what they regarded as the unbiblical practice of infant baptism. On this the Anabaptists and Muntzer were agreed. But it also applied to a great deal else pertaining to the life and worship of a Christian congregation, and on these points Grebel felt strongly that Muntzer was not following Scripture. 'Therefore', wrote Grebel,

> we ask and admonish you as a brother in the name, power, Word, Spirit, and salvation, which comes to all Christians through Jesus Christ our Master and Saviour, to seek earnestly to preach only God's Word unflinchingly, to establish and defend only divine practices, to esteem as good and right only what can be found in definite clear Scripture, and to reject, hate, and curse all the schemes, words, practices, and opinions of all men, even your own.[10]

This admonition relates to several issues regarding the reformation of the church, and reveals that the Swiss Anabaptists were deeply concerned that Muntzer remain on a truly evangelical and therefore biblical track.

Grebel and company make it absolutely clear that the only

weapon which the church can use in seeking the reformation of the church and in establishing the church, is the Word of God. Against Zwingli, the use of the sword by magistrates sympathetic to reformation is firmly rejected; against Muntzer, the use of the sword either in self-defence or against those in authority, is equally rejected. Grebel writes accordingly:

> the gospel and its adherents are not to be protected by the sword, nor (should) they (protect) themselves, which as we have heard from our brother is what you believe and maintain. True believing Christians are sheep among wolves, sheep for the slaughter. They must be baptized in anguish and tribulation, persecution, suffering, and death, tried in fire, and must reach the fatherland of eternal rest not by slaying the physical but the spiritual. They use neither worldly sword nor war, since killing has ceased with them entirely, unless indeed, we are still under the old law, and even there (as far as we can know) war was only a plague after they had once conquered the Promised Land.[11]

Three years later, the *Schleitheim Confession* declared:

> there will also unquestionably fall from us the unchristian, devilish weapons of force — such as sword, armour and the like, and all their use (either) for friends or against one's enemies — by virtue of the word of Christ, Resist not (him that is) evil.[12]

More than a century later, the same position was adopted by the Dutch Anabaptists at Dordrecht,

> Regarding revenge, whereby we resist our enemies, with the sword, we believe and confess that the Lord Jesus has forbidden His disciples and followers all revenge and resistance, and has thereby commanded them not to 'return evil for evil, nor railing for railing', but to 'put up the sword into the sheath', or, as the prophet foretold, 'beat them into ploughshares.' (Matt.5:39,44; Rom.12:14; I Pet.3:9; Is.2:24; Micah 4:3).[13]

As already intimated, such a confession of faith was not an easy option, nor was it an a-political action of escapist piety. It needs to be remembered that in sixteenth-century Europe issues like 'rebaptism', to say nothing of pacifism, were politically explosive because they fundamentally challenged the structures of society and the authority of both church and state, whether Catholic, Lutheran or Reformed. The question of baptism no longer has that political significance, but that of pacifism and Christian non-resistance certainly has. Throughout the period of the Reformation 'Christian Europe' felt threatened by the 'infidel Turk'

on its eastern border. This was not very different from the way in
which many South Africans today feel threatened by 'atheistic
Communists' on our northern borders. Thus war against the
Turks, like war against the Communists, was regarded as a
Christian duty, a means to defending the 'holy faith' from
destruction.

In the light of this, consider the testimony of Michael Sattler,
who drafted the *Schleitheim Confession*, at his trial prior to being
burned at the stake:

> If the Turk comes, he should not be resisted, for it stands
> written: thou shalt not kill. We should not defend ourselves
> gainst the Turks or our other persecutors, but with fervent
> prayer should implore God that he might be our defense and
> resistance.[14]

Sattler's refusal to take up arms against the Turks was, as the
prosecutor noted, 'a great offence' because, in his reckoning, it
meant taking 'the side of the greatest enemy of our holy faith
against us'.[15] Yet for Sattler it was precisely the taking up of arms
against the Turks, or, with Zwingli against the papists, which was
the enemy of faith because such action went against the divine
Word and Spirit. In the same way, there are Christians in South
Africa today who refuse to take arms against 'atheistic
Communism' in defence of 'Christian civilisation' because not
only is that seen to be a false analysis of the situation, but also
because it is regarded as an unbiblical way to defend the
Christian faith.

If it was wrong for Christians to take up the sword against the
Turks or the papists, for the Anabaptists it was equally wrong of
Muntzer to encourage the revolutionary violence of the peasants
in seeking to overthrow the power of the feudal princes. The elect
were not chosen to fight with the sword 'of the flesh', but the
'sword of the Spirit'. Thus, in taking their position to its logical
conclusion, the Anabaptists were not adopting a neutral stance,
but affirming a radically different approach to Christian
discipleship and witness. For them it was not a matter of trying to
avoid conflict, which they clearly did not, nor was it a lack of
commitment to the cause of the poor. The Anabaptists' priority
was faithfulness to the testimony of Scripture and witness to the
gospel of Jesus Christ, even if they had to suffer severely as a
result. For them, such faithfulness to the gospel was what the
reformation of the church was primarily about, and it was
precisely because Luther and Zwingli failed to take it sufficiently

seriously that they took the stand they did. For this reason, it would be totally misleading to consider their 'peace-making' testimony outside the context of their theology as a whole. They regarded themselves as called out of the world to be a holy people obedient to the Word of God along and not conforming to the values and ways of the surrounding culture of so-called Christendom.

## THE PACIFISM OF THE MESSIANIC COMMUNITY

There is an unfortunate tendency in discussions on pacifism to cloud the issues because of a failure to recognise that historically, pacifism includes a variety of positions. John Howard Yoder, one of the paramount contemporary interpreters of historic Anabaptism, has described at least fifteen variations of religious pacifism, and there are, of course, forms of pacifism which are strictly secular and humanist.[16] In our assessment of the Anabaptist contribution to Christian 'peace-making', and in our attempt to interpret its meaning for our time and situation, it is important that we do not read into it what is not there. Indeed, a major hermeneutical task faces those who wish to engage in interpreting the tradition for today. Not only are the respective historic contexts different, but the issues are by no means identical. This does not mean, however, that the Anabaptist peace-testimony does not fundamentally challenge our predeliction for just wars and just revolutions. But it does so best when it forces us to go beyond the debate on pacifism versus non-pacifism, and to explore more deeply the theological and biblical foundations upon which the Anabaptists rested their case and pursued their cause.

Few have done this better than Yoder who, in his many writings is not simply restating a historic position, but is engaging afresh in biblical, theological and ethical reflection in relation to our contemporary situation. Indeed, Yoder's *The Politics of Jesus*,[17] together with his own lectures in South Africa in 1976 and 1981, have had considerable influence upon the thinking of many South Africans in their attempt to respond as Christians to militarisation and escalating violence in our present context. Illustrative of this is not only the expressed indebtedness of some of the first conscientious objectors to Yoder's thought, but also the fact that a major critical study of Yoder's position deals in part with its significance for the issues facing Christians in South Africa today.[18] This is not the place to engage in an attempt to describe or evaluate Yoder's position in any detail, but by way of conclusion to this essay, and as a contribution to the debate it is important that the up-dating of the Anabaptist tradition be taken into serious consideration.

As already indicated, the pacifist position adopted by the evangelical Anabaptists was based on a solid theological foundation. It was not a secular-humanist position, but one which they regarded as self-evident to any person who read the Scriptures with open eyes. In particular, it arose out of a Christology and ecclesiology which took seriously the fact that the church is a community which has been called out of the world to bear witness to the gospel of Jesus Christ. Their protest, unlike that of the Protestant Reformers, was fundamentally against Constantinianism, that alliance between the church and secular authority which had become characteristic of Catholic Christianity since the fourth century and which was taken for granted by the sixteenth-century reformers. In the same way, Christians committed to the pacifism of the messianic community today reject any attempt to confuse discipleship with uncritical patriotism, a patriotism which exalts the nation and places it beyond prophetic critique.

The evangelical Anabaptists were, thus, not pacifists on pragmatic grounds; their pacifism followed on from their 'baptism into Christ' in which they renounced the ways of the world and began to live their lives in obedient discipleship. For them the charter for this discipleship was the Sermon on the Mount, and their model was none less than the suffering servant-messiah, Jesus. Hence Yoder comes closest to their position when he speaks of 'the pacifism of the messianic community'.

> To say that this is the pacifism of the *messianic* community is to affirm its dependence upon the confession that Jesus is Christ and that Jesus Christ is Lord. To say that Jesus is the Messiah is to say that in Him are fulfilled the expectations of God's people regarding the man in whom God's will would perfectly be done. It is therefore in the person and work of Jesus, in His teachings and His passion, that this kind of pacifism finds its rootage, and in His resurrection that it finds its enablement.[19]

For Yoder, as for the Anabaptists, the prime issue is not one of obedience to rules or principles, but the following of Jesus the suffering Messiah. This is why they would regard such an ethic as beyond the understanding of those who had not chosen to follow Jesus Christ in faith and obedience in the first place, even though some heroic individuals might well take a similar stance. Similarly, it would be expecting too much of secular powers, whether in government or in revolt, to follow Jesus Christ. The ethic of the Sermon on the Mount is an impossibility for any group which does not recognise the Lordship of Jesus, and is prepared to suffer the consequences of such an obedience. Moreover, it is an ethic which cannot be evaluated in terms of success, even though it may 'succeed' more than its critics allow, because it is motivated by a commitment to faithfulness, to being the people of God in the world.

The evangelical Anabaptists of the sixteenth century were not overtly engaged in any attempt to change the social order; all their energies were devoted to keeping their own fellowship intact. Their witness to the world, and therefore their testimony to God's order for the world, derived from their struggle to be the church. In our context today, this may well become a form of escapism, especially as religious tolerance and the 'freedom of religion' allows a wide divergence of religious practice. Hence criticism has been levelled against those who misuse the idea of the church as the 'alternative community' to justify a refusal to become involved in the political arena on the grounds that Christians must be 'neutral'.

The re-working of the Anabaptist vision by Yoder and others has, however, sought to overcome the false dichotomy inherent in this view. For them, a contemporary understanding of the Anabaptist vision requires socio-political engagement, but a way of engagement which derives from the gospel rather than secular norms, values and pragmatism. In particular, the Christian and the church are called to take sides with the oppressed in the struggle for justice, but in ways which are consonant with the cross of redemptive suffering. The 'enemy' is always to be regarded as a human being for whom Christ died, and therefore the goal for Christian witness is not only justice for the oppressed but also redemption for the oppressor. The Christian's position in the struggle for justice is therefore not neutral; sides have to be taken, but in taking sides Christians may well find themselves caught in the crossfire of opposing forces. It is a form of radical peacemaking through a willingness to suffer for the cause of right.

As already intimated, there are critical questions that need to be addressed to the position that Yoder articulates. But these questions cannot be raised in all honesty until the challenge of his position is taken seriously. And, for those who do adopt his position and seek to be the 'alternative community' in South Africa, it must be said that the proof of their position will not be made primarily in argument but in example and witness. Even if not all Christians are willing to espouse such pacifism, it is surely of vital importance that there be such communities of Christians in South Africa who can point to an alternative witness and way to justice in which violence is overcome not only as an end but also as a means.

Reflecting on the ethics of the radical reformation in an ecumenical perspective, Yoder suggests that there is a growing consensus amongst contemporary Christians that enables them to transcend the historic divisions which separated the Radical and the Magisterial Reformers on issues such as this. He writes:

> Whether it takes the path of a new seriousness about letting the doctrine of the just war have a critical negative impact upon the conditioned willingness of Christians to accept some violence in the civil order, or whether it takes the more radical path of vocational or personal integral pacifism, there is widespread agreement — once again joining Roman Catholic thinkers with participants in the WCC — that militarism and nationalism conceived in a military tone constitute the fundamental challenge to the unity of the church and of humankind which must be condemned and transcended in our age. A common commitment to bring to bear on the menace of war and tyranny the full critical capacity of the total Christian community would be a path to Christian unity in mission, which would probably be more promising than a resumption of the older patterns of negotiating from the fixed, correct positions of established confessions. Then the contemporary ethical consensus might be the needed 'end run' past the lines set up to defend already obsolete alternative ecclesiologies.[20]

It may well be that the time has come in South Africa for some fresh ecumenical thinking on the issues that have hitherto divided the heirs of the Magisterial and Radical Reformations so that the church's witness for justice may contribute to genuine peace and so prevent total and devastating conflict from engulfing all.

## NOTES

1.    See G.C. Cuthbertson, *The Nonconformist Conscience and the South African War: 1899-1902*, (unpublished doctoral thesis, University of South Africa, 1986).

2.  George H. Williams, *The Radical Reformation,* (Philadelphia: Westminster, 1962), p.xxiv.
3.  *Ibid.,* p.xxiv.
4.  Calus-Peter Clasen, *Anabaptism: A Social History, 1525-1618,* (Ithaca and London: Cornell University Press, 1972), p.30.
5.  On the relationship between them see James M. Stayer and Werner O. Packull, (eds.), *The Anabaptists and Thomas Muntzer,* (Toronto: Kendall/Hunt, 1980), p.82.
6.  See, for example, James M. Stayer, 'Was Dr. Kuehler's Conception of Early Dutch Anabaptism Historically Sound? The Historical Discussion of Anabaptist Munster 450 Years Later' in *The Mennonite Quarterly Review,* vol. lx, no.3, July 1986, pp.261-288.
7.  Fritz Blanke, *Brothers in Christ,* (Scottdale: Herald Press, 1961), p.31.
8.  Leland Harder, *The Sources of Swiss Anabaptism: the Grebel Letters and Related Documents,* (Scottdale, Pa.: Herald Press, 1985), pp.285-294.
9.  *Ibid.,* p.289.
10. *Ibid.,* p.286.
11. *Ibid.,* p.290.
12. John H. Leith, (ed.), *Creeds of the Churches,* (Richmond, Va.: John Knox, 1973), p.289.
13. Article XIV, published in Leith, *Creeds of the Churches,* p.304.
14. See John H. Yoder, (ed.), *The Legacy of Michael Sattler,* (Scottdale, Pa.: Herald Press, 1974), p.72.
15. *Ibid.,* p.71.
16. John H. Yoder, *Nevertheless: Varieties of Religious Pacifism,* (Scottdale: Herald Press, 1971).
17. John H. Yoder, *The Politics of Jesus,* (Grand Rapids: Eerdmans, 1972).
18. See David Russell, *A Theological Critique of the Christian Pacifist Perspective, with Special Reference to the Position of John Howard Yoder,* (unpublished Ph.D. thesis, University of Cape Town, 1984).
19. Yoder, *Nevertheless,* p.124.
20. John H. Yoder, *The Priestly Kingdom,* (South Bend: Notre Dame, 1984), p.122.

# CONTEMPORARY
# DEBATE

# Nationalism and Revolution: The Nineteenth Century and Karl Barth

ROBIN PETERSEN

In any study on violence and war, the ideas of nationalism and revolution must play a central part. As two competing, and sometimes co-operating paradigms, the 'myth of nation and the vision of revolution'[1] have been the central ideological focii for virtually all wars and violent struggles since the 19th century. Within the South African context it is the former which has been the dominant force since the turn of the century, when Boer 'nations' sought their liberation from British colonial encroachment. African nationalism in turn emerged in a formal structure with the formation of the ANC seventy-five years ago. The history of this country since then, as well as its future prognosis, has therefore often been described as a 'clash of competing nationalisms'. But nationalism is not the only political ideal at work in our context. The vision of revolution cannot be ignored. The role of the South African Communist Party and its close alliance with the ANC since the 1950s, and the more recent emergence of an ultra-left discourse which subordinates national to class struggle, or negates national struggle altogether, have ensured that the difficult question of the role and relationship of national and class struggles remain very much on the political agenda. Much of the internecine struggle in the townships these past few years has its ideological basis in this emotive question.

This paper is removed historically from this immediate context, although its current struggles remain as an undercurrent throughout. It is, rather, a study of the emergence of nationalism as the dominant political idea in the 19th and early 20th centuries, and nationalism's struggle with and ultimate victory over the vision of revolution in this period. The ultimate concern throughout this analysis is not however these crucial political questions, but lies rather at the ethical and the theological levels.

The close link between these ideas and the ethical question of war and violence has already been noted, and this will be further drawn out. But fundamentally it is the theological aspects which will be discussed; that is, how theologians of that period addressed the questions of nationalism, revolution, violence and war, and what theological insights emerge for us through these responses.

Central to this will be the theology of Karl Barth. Although a twentieth-century theologian, Barth lived through and participated in, these political struggles, and his theology was forged in this context. It is therefore necessary that this background be clarified prior to dealing with his theological and ethical views.

# THE HISTORICAL AND POLITICAL BACKGROUND

## THE BIRTH OF NATIONALISM

In the pervasiveness of the idea of nationalism, and its seemingly easy accessibility as a defining category of political thought there lies a real danger of failing to perceive its ambiguous nature. Nationalism, like most other political ideas, can mean, and has been, democratic or authoritarian, progressive or reactionary, socialist or facist. It is a term that therefore cannot be used in the abstract, as is so often done. It is not possible simply to equate one nationalism with another — it is essential to enquire what content is given to the concept in each context. (Dipping into our undercurrent, this can vividly be demonstrated in a comparison between the authoritarian, chauvinistic and reactionary 'nationalism' of the ruling party and the democratic, non-racial and 'non-*volk*' nationalism of the ANC).

The emergence and development of the myth of the nation as the dominant *idée force* [2] in Europe in the 19th century finds its roots in four streams; the Enlightenment of the 18th century, the French revolution of 1789, the development of Romanticism in the early 19th century and the political philosophy of Hegel. Politically and economically its bearers were the emerging bourgeoisie and petit-bourgeoisie, although as shall be seen, the aristocracy exploited its power and the proletariat increasingly fell sway to its charms in the latter half of the century. It reaches its first great apogee (or nadir, depending on one's perspective) in 1914, with the outbreak of the First World War, only to be reborn in a far more virulent and rampant form in post-war Germany and

Italy, triumphing in the National Socialism of Hitler and the facism of Mussolini.

## THE ENLIGHTENMENT

'The people's growth to maturity and its release from tutelage', was Kant's definition of the Enlightenment. As such, nationalism of the 19th century was part of this process, the growth of a people to political maturity, where rule was no longer by divine right, but by the will of the people; where the right of the church, the monarch and the aristocracy to claim 'natural' authority over a people was challenged and defeated. The growth of nations was therefore a release from tutelage, the tutelage of the *ancien régime* and the church.

In its Enlightenment garb, nationalism was always part of a liberal humanism. The right of the nation was limited by the rights of the individual. Nationalism was part of a broader liberal cosmopolitanism, it was a means to achieving the end of furthering the autonomy and rights of the individual and humanity. This liberal strand was to persist through the century, but not prevail.

## THE FRENCH REVOLUTION

Jean-Jacques Rousseau can rightly be called the father of the liberal, democratic and egalitarian aspects of nationalism. His ideas of liberty, fraternity and equality became the rallying cry of the revolution and the foundation of the first French Republic. The Republic thus embodied at the outset the 'cosmopolitan pathos of the Enlightenment',[3] the revolution was conducted on behalf of rational humanism. Very soon, however, with the Jacobin period which followed the revolution and the need to defend the Republic from outside attack, this revolutionary nationalistic heritage became outwardly militant and aggressive, and the rhetoric of the nation which must be defended in the name of the revolution emerged. This rhetoric was then utilised by all future leaders, from Napoleon to the Bourbon aristocracy.

This event thus introduced two important dimensions into nationalism; its link with revolution and the democratic movement, and the need to defend the nation's political gains in the name of the revolution. These two trends often stood in fatal contradiction to one another, the one leading to the progressive links between nationalism and socialism, the other eventually providing for the triumph of nationalism over socialism.

The revolution was important too in one further dimension. In

the words of Lammenais, a French nationalist and theologian
writing in 1839:

> What the people wills, God Himself wills; for what the people
> wills is justice, the essential and eternal order, the fulfilment in
> mankind of that sublime word of Christ, that they may be one,
> my Father, even as You and I are one. The cause of the people
> is therefore the sacred cause, the cause of God; it will triumph.[4]

These words, or words like it, were to echo down that century
and our own.

## ROMANTICISM

In contrast to the nationalism which emerged in Britain, America
and France, forged in the realities of political struggle, nationalism
in the fragmented and politically-divided countries of central and
eastern Europe drew its inspiration from another source, that of
anti-Enlightenment Romanticism. Not possessing the present
political reality of a nation, the myths of the past and the dreams
of an ideal future became the source of romantic nationalism.

In Germany in particular, drawing from Herder's glorification of
the pre-political and pre-rational grounds of the nation — its
language, folk traditions and common descent — the romanticists
developed the myth of the *Volk* and the ideal fatherland. In
contrast to the democratic and progressive trends of the
nationalism of the Enlightenment and the Revolution, nationalism
in this nexus was conservative, consecrating the past and glorying
in the hierarchies and structures of authority. In place of the legal
and rational concept of citizenship, German nationalism
postulated the much vaguer but more emotive and primal
concept of 'folk'. As Kohn writes, this concept

> lent itself more easily to the embroideries of imagination and
> the excitations of emotion. Its roots seemed to reach into the
> dark soil of primitive times, and to have grown through
> thousands of hidden channels of unconscious development,
> not in the bright light of rational political ends, but in the
> mysterious womb of the people, deemed to be so much nearer
> to the forces of nature.[5]

Although Herder himself located his romantic nationalism
within the humanist paradigm of the Enlightenment, those who
followed him rejected this basis. The Enlightenment and its
rationalism were discarded, the individual was subordinated to the
nation and in fact was seen to reach fulfilment only by
participation in the 'project' of the nation. For this development,
the political philosophy of Hegel was important.

## THE POLITICAL PHILOSOPHY OF HEGEL

Hegel in many ways represents both the completion and the dissolution of the Enlightenment project, as well as its fusion with Romanticism. For Hegel, history and the state were the vehicles for the Divine, and for reason as the Absolute Idea. The individual only truly shares in history and the Idea as he or she shares in the state. 'The State is the true embodiment of mind and spirit, and only as its member the individual shares in truth, real existence and ethical status'.[6]

The *libertas* of the French Revolution, which Hegel gloried in, was made the central focus of his political philosophy, but he transferred this liberty from the individual to the state. This, as Kohn points out, brought about that unity between idealism and absolutism which was to become such a dominant force under nationalism.[7]

Hegel's grand philosophical synthesis fell apart soon after his death, splitting into a right and a left wing. The right drew from his political philosophy the subordination of individual liberty to that of the state, the legitimising of the political order of the authoritarian and hierarchical Prussian state in the name of reason, and his integration of the Romantic vision of historical institution with reason. The left-wing Hegelians drew on his concept of dialectic, and inverted it, applying it to the development of successive historical stages. Marx and Engels gave this its revolutionary dynamic, thus linking it with the revolutionary ethos of 1789, but transforming it into a historical and class-based process. Whilst the bourgeois revolution of 1789 was seen as a key example of this revolutionary process, it in turn needed to be superseded by a proletarian revolution. This revolution would be the inevitable historical product of the development of capitalism.

## THE DEVELOPMENT OF THE IDEA

The revolutions which swept through Europe in 1848 precipitated a decisive shift in the development of nationalism. The revolutions had all begun in the spirit of the French Revolution and in the name of democracy, liberalism and national rights. Marx and the revolutionary socialists, then a relatively small group, both predicted these revolutions and saw in them a decisive demonstration of proletarian internationalism. A revolution in one country would, and did, precipitate similar uprisings across Europe.

With the defeat of these revolutions by the regrouped forces of the aristocracy and the ruling class, both the liberal-democratic and the socialist forms of nationalism, each of which had subordinated nationalism either to the rights of the individual in the case of liberalism, or to the internationalism of the working class in the case of socialism, were defeated.

The ruling classes were quick to exploit the nationalist sentiments that had been aroused. From this point on, nationalism became a predominantly conservative and reactionary movement, assimilating the ideas of authoritarian goverment and breaking with the camps of general revolution on the one hand, and liberal democracy on the other.

The bearers of this new, militant and reactionary nationalism were the petit-bourgeoisie. To them

> the idea of the nation appeared as a lifebelt: the rich were selfish and effete, the workers were serving alien causes, the petty bourgeoisie (sic) was the core of the nation, had no other interest than the national interest.[8]

The ideas of Darwin regarding the struggle for existence and the survival of the fittest, de Gobineau's theory about the genetic inequality of the races and the economist List's theory of economic protectionism and the 'national good' all combined to give to this reactionary nationalism the force of a scientific worldview.

By 1880 most nationalist movements had achieved their goals of national unification or independence. This had the effect of changing the way in which nationalism came to be articulated. No longer was the nationalist vision simply one of cultural renaissance or social-spiritual regeneration. It now became one of imperialism linked to a cult of vitality and power and of "'self-idolatry' disguised as integral nationalism or even incipient racism".[9]

## THE OUTBREAK OF THE FIRST WORLD WAR — THE TRIUMPH OF NATIONALISM

Benedetto Croce, the great Italian historian and philosopher, described the period from 1871-1914 in Europe as 'the Liberal Age'.[10] In light of what has been discussed until now, this seems a strange description. Croce used it, however, to describe the process whereby the anti-democratic forces of the right and the revolutionary forces of the left gradually moved towards democratic liberalism. From the right, by 1880 democratic rights had been extended to virtually all strata of the populations in almost every country in Europe (Tsarist Russia being one notable exception). From the left, the rise to respectability of the Social Democratic Party (SPD) in Germany, and its split with the Anarchists and Bakunin in 1880 served to move it away from its revolutionary and internationalist position.

But Croce's description masks the growing conflict between the extreme right-wing nationalism and the revolutionary vision of the left. Although liberal rights had been extended to all in Germany, for instance, the right-wing nationalists with their doctrine of racial superiority, of the divine mission of the German nation, (leading to anti-Semitism and a glorification of war) continued to grow in influence and power. The SPD too had not lost complete touch with their revolutionary heritage. Engels and later Luxembourg and Liebknecht kept the spirit of revolution and internationalism alive.

Prior to the outbreak of World War I, one can identify four primary forces at work in Germany. On the extreme right were the conservative nationalists, tied to the Prussian state and glorying in the cult of war. To their left were the remaining proponents of the German liberal tradition of the Enlightenment, also nationalist but less willing to subordinate the individual to the nation. The reformist wing of the SPD under Bebel and Kautsky, although paying lip-service to revolution and internationalism, influenced the SPD into voting for the Kaiser's war credits in the months preceding the war. They too succumbed to the spirit of nationalism although they attempted to justify it in terms of a war of defence. Kautsky, for instance, argued:

> Germany was waging not only a war of defence, but also a crusade on behalf of the international proletariat and for the world revolution: it was fighting the unspeakable Tsarist regime.[11]

Similarly the French socialists conjured up the spectre of Prussian aristocratic authoritarianism and called on the memories of 1789. The war was described in terms of a revolutionary war that would unseat the crowned heads of Austria and Germany and bring freedom to the world. 'The revolutionary traditions of the "nationalism of the left" were appealed to for the purpose of justifying the abandonment of attempts at international action'.[12]

Only the left wing of the SPD under Luxembourg and Liebknecht stood firm. Rosa Luxembourg especially had maintained faith in the strength of proletarian internationalism to stem the tide of rampant nationalism. Both she and Lenin had worked towards using the war and the economic and political crises created by it to rouse the masses against their own governments and thus bring about the downfall of capitalist class rule. (Ironically they were supported in this stand by the then radical Italian socialist, and later author of facism, Benito Mussolini).

As in the wake of the counter-revolution of 1848, so too did the war shatter both the optimistic humanism of the liberals and the hopeful vision of revolutionary and internationalist socialism. Throughout Europe monarchial heads, parliaments, and socialists alike rallied around their respective national causes. The only victor was, once again, nationalism. 'Nation' replaced both 'humanity' and 'class' as the central political motif.

## NATIONALISM, REVOLUTION, VIOLENCE AND WAR

This brief historical overview of the development and clash of the ideas of nationalism and revolution has already indicated their close link with violence and war. What has not been fully discussed however, is the extent to which a cult of violence and militarism emerged alongside nationalism.

Significantly, and ironically given our current debates, revolutionary socialists by-and-large avoided glorifying war. In fact the most significant anti-war groups prior to 1914 were the socialists. Even those who saw the need for revolutionary struggle to achieve the overthrow of capitalism did not, by-and-large, glory in war or the act of violence itself. It was usually seen as a means to an end, never as an end in itself, although Marx and Engels, in the wake of the 1848 revolutions came close in some of their statements, to a 'power is right' position. Engels wrote: 'You (referring to the Slavs) cannot realise such things (independence) without violence. Without force and utter ruthlessness, nothing is achieved in history'.[13] Towards the end of his life, however, he became far more wary of war, speaking of the 'horror of modern warfare', and pressing for anti-war agitation.[14] Only Georges Sorel on the left proclaimed violence in itself to be a liberating force in the hands of the proletariat. Violence, Sorel proclaimed, 'was noble and chivalrous because it was open and direct and constituted a full and unequivocal commitment'.[15]

During this period, especially in the latter half of the century, the military face of Europe was transformed under the dynamics of right-wing nationalism. Military spending, related to capitalist expansion, increased at a phenomena! rate, rising in Germany between 1858 and 1883 by 304 percent, and from 1883-1913 a further 402 percent, making Germany the most heavily-armed European nation at the outbreak of the war. Conscription was introduced in most European nations during the latter half of the century, spreading the ideas of war and militarism through the population. Engel's hope that the arming of the masses would ensure the victory of the working class in their struggle proved to be poignantly hollow.

This material and human investment in the preparation for war both arose from and produced a certain kind of discourse on violence and war. War came to be regarded as not only inevitable, but right and moral, divinely ordained and part of the incessant struggle for the survival of the fittest. Violence and militarism were seen as noble and purifying. Treitschke wrote:

> War must be taken as part of the divinely appointed order. It is both justifiable and moral, and the idea of a perpetual peace is not only impossible but immoral as well... War naturally embodies the beauty and sublimity of history.[16]

Even the poet Thomas Mann, later a staunch opponent of Hitler, was swept away in militaristic enthusiasm: 'The military spirit is akin to the "spirit of art"... How the hearts of our poets were immediately ablaze, once war was declared!... German militarism is the manifestation of German morality.'[17]

German nationalists were not alone in glorifying war, although Prussian militarism had a particularly dominant influence on the ethics of war and violence in Germany. In France, Michelet lamented that it was only in the people that he still found surviving 'the sentiment of military honour, always renewed by our heroic legend, the invisible spirit of the heroes of our war, the wind of the old flag...'.[18]

Conscription and citizen armies fed the ideology of militaristic nationalism in another important way, as Hamerow points out:

> In the era of professional armies, war had been waged without regard for ideological justification. The soldier had fought because that was his business. There was no need to vindicate a military struggle by portraying it as a contest between good and evil or between justice and lawlessness.[19]

This now became necessary, and nationalism was the ideal vehicle — 'My country, right or wrong!'.

Thus militaristic and chauvinistically nationalist sentiments won the day, and with the outbreak of the war of 1914, Croce's age of liberalism gave way to an age of violence.

# NATIONALISM, REVOLUTION, WAR, VIOLENCE . . . AND THEOLOGY

## 'THE BLACK DAY IN AUGUST'

In August 1914, 93 German intellectuals, including the great liberal theologians von Harnack and Hermann, published a proclamation in support of Kaiser Wilhelm's war policies.

> Our army, is now engaged in the struggle for Germany's freedom, and therefore, for all the benefits of peace and morality, not only in Germany. We believe that for European culture on the whole, salvation rests on the victory which German militarism; namely mainly discipline, the faithfulness, the courage to sacrifice, of the united and free German nation will achieve.[20]

This document, so indicative of the spirit of German nationalism and militarism, was seen by a young Swiss pastor and theologian, Karl Barth, as a 'terrible manifesto'. His revered teachers, whose liberal humanism he had so admired, were exposed as nationalists and militarists. All their 'religion and scholarship' had changed completely into 'intellectual 42-centimetre cannons'.[21]

This event, amongst others, caused Barth to call into question his whole theological heritage. Being so compromised, in his eyes, by their failure 'in the face of the ideology of War', the whole liberal tradition of exegesis, ethics, dogmatics and preaching was, for him, 'shaken to the foundations'. In September, Barth wrote concerning these events to his friend Thusneysen:

> The unconditional truths of the gospel are simply suspended for the time being and in the meantime a German war-theology is put to work, its Christian trimming consisting of a lot of talk about sacrifice and the like.[22]

Out of this crisis, Barth forged a new theology, which called into question the whole theological methodology of the 19th century, with its easy relation between the gospel and bourgeois culture, between the kingdom of God and the Prussian state, between the ethical individual and the will of God.

But what was this theology which Barth questioned so radically? What were the alternative visions offered? And how did they develop their position on the questions of nationalism, war and violence? To analyse this, a return to the four pre-war political positions earlier identified is necessary.

## THEOLOGY AND POLITICS IN PRE-WAR GERMANY

### Right-wing nationalism — Adolf Stoecker

In 1874, Adolf Stoecker was appointed to be court pastor to Kaiser Wilhelm I. Stoecker was an ardent nationalist, who had great visions of a Germany united not only politically but ideologically, or, as he called it, 'spiritually'. He was a fierce opponent of the Social Democrats who, along with the Jews, formed for him an 'alien element' in the glorious unity of the German nation. He was convinced that God had ordained him to persuade his fellow Germans of their racial and national superiority, and argued fervently that faith in God went hand-in-hand with patriotic nationalism. Love of God and love of the German nation was correlated.

He also advocated a form of socialism, virulently anti-internationalist and anti-Marxist. To further propogate his views, he formed the Christian Social Workers Party, in order 'to win the working man to national and Christian thought, to better the workers' position, and to conquer the Social Democrats for the spirit of nationalism'.[23]

Militarism was the inevitable bed-fellow of Stoecker's nationalism!

> One cannot think enough of the fatherland, and it is inspiring when young men give their father-land more than themselves, and give their blood and lives for the fatherland.[24]

Whilst Stoecker's position was a minority view, both within the church and certainly within the theology of the 19th century, his formula of nationalism, socialism and anti-Semitism was to become the explosive mixture upon which the ideology of Nazi Germany, and of the German Christian movement of the period would be constructed.

### Liberal theology

Whilst Barth had much to say about the appalling war-theology and nationalism of his liberal mentors, he categorically refuted the suggestion that their theology in any positive way prepared for the rampant evil of Nazi nationalism and militarism. But it certainly was powerless to prevent this evil, as had so glaringly been exposed in the 1914 war.

The great liberal theological tradition of the 19th century began with the Romantic theologian Schleiermacher. But Schleiermacher's romanticism was never anti-rationalist or anti-humanist. Although, as Barth points out, he, like his contemporary

Hegel, was a great admirer of the Prussian state, Schleiermacher was 'incomparably more liberal than Hegel'.[25] He never subordinated all to the concepts of nation, history or *Volk*.

Barth argued nevertheless that the theological methodology which Schleiermacher introduced decisively prepared the way for the war-theology of the manifesto.[26] This it did by shifting the locus of theology from God to the human being, and by positing a relationship between human beings and God independent of God's revelation of Godself in Jesus Christ. This opened the door, Barth argued, for all kinds of identities to be established between God and human beings, between Christian faith and bourgeois culture, between the kingdom of God and the Prussian state. In this theological environment it was easy for the 'unconditional truths of the gospel' to be allied or identified with a particular nationalist, or militarist cause.

Albrecht Ritschl (1822-1889), one of the greatest social theologians of the century, drew out the implications of Schleiermacher's methodology in the rapidly changing political and social arena. Although a passionate admirer of Bismarck and the united Germany which he created, Ritschl's nationalism was relativised, at least initially, by his use of the concept of the 'Kingdom of God'. Whilst the state prepared people for the kingdom, it was not itself the kingdom. The kingdom was rather 'a kind of international ethical-religious spiritual community which would express a world wide consciousness of human solidarity'.[27] The kingdom thus was a safeguard against nationalism, in that it 'transcends the view of the national state, and takes up an attitude essentially opposed to it'.[28]

And yet the practice and later theological writings of Ritschl do not demonstrate this crucial critical distance from nationalism. After German unification in 1870 he spoke of the church strengthening the state by forming a cultural community to reconcile human culture and Christian faith. He also attacked social democracy, like Stoecker seeing in it a breach of the God-given harmony of the German nation, to be overcome by consecrating the work of the labourer, thus integrating the worker into the spiritual community of the church and at the same time the moral community of the state.[29]

Adolf von Harnack stood squarely in this liberal tradition. He too sought for harmony between faith and culture, 'between the teaching of Jesus and the wisdom of Goethe and Kant, between the Kingdom of God and the policies of Kaiser Wilhelm II'.[30] In a similar vein to Ritschl and even Stoecker, he opposed the Social Democrats, although he recognised that the social problem they were articulating was of crucial concern to the church.[31]

Harnack's pro-war position has been noted. The contrast between this and his liberalism and humanism prior to the war can perhaps in some way be explained by the personal friendship and support of both Bismarck and the Kaiser which he enjoyed. When the Berlin church vetoed his appointment to teach at Berlin University, the Kaiser and Bismarck overruled the decision. He had many honours bestowed upon him by the Kaiser, and as President of the *Kaiser Wilhelm Gesellschaft* organised the research of the German universities around the German war effort.[32]

## Social Democracy — The religious-socialists

A smaller group of theologians were allied with the political aims of the Social Democrats. These religious socialists, with the exception of the Blumhardts, remained by-and-large within the liberal theological paradigm but understood the reality of the class divisions of society to need a political rather than a spiritual or religious solution. Instead of wondering how to integrate this 'alien' element into the bourgeois cultural and political community, the religious socialists sought with the Social Democrats to overthrow the class system and thus do away with class oppression. The identities which liberal theology established between the kingdom of God and the bourgeois state were transferred to the kingdom and the struggle for socialism.

These theologians were all vehemently and consistently opposed to the war, although to some extent, they supported the need for the revolutionary overthrow of capitalism. Thus the war and nationalism were opposed on primarily political grounds, although, of course, this was seen to be consistent with the message of the kingdom and the call of God.

Within this group of theologians a variety of socialist positions were adopted, from liberal reformist to radical revolutionary. Predominantly, however, they were aligned with the position espoused by the reformist wing (Bebel and Kautsky) of the SPD.

## Karl Barth — From religious-socialist to socialist theologian

Barth initially associated himself with the Swiss religious-socialists. His ministry in the industrial village of Safenwil had brought him into immediate contact with workers under capitalism, and within months of beginning his pastorate, he involved himself actively in socialist activities. He organised trade unions, he addressed various socialist groups and workers' clubs, he studied the philosophical and practical concerns of the workers' movement, he marched with the workers under the banner of the Red Flag on May Day parade, he joined the Swiss SPD in 1915 and was a delegate to many socialist congresses, including the crucial 1919 congress when the Swiss SPD voted not to join the Third Socialist International.[32]

The disillusionment with his liberal theological heritage precipitated by the outbreak of the war has been discussed. But there was a second crisis which he faced, which contributed as much to his theological formation. This crisis was, in his own words, 'the apostasy of the Party'. Barth, as a religious socialist, had identified the struggle for socialism as the struggle for the kingdom of God. With the outbreak of the war, however, the Second International collapsed as the socialist parties of each of the combatant nations rallied around their respective national causes.

These shifts made Barth realise that his easy identification of God's kingdom with socialism was parallel to and part of the liberal identification of *what we do* with *what God does*. Religious-socialism was thus exposed as a fundamentally flawed project, still part of the liberal theological heritage that had become, in his eyes, so discredited. Not only that, but the ideology of the war, its nationalistic militarism, made him realise that theology itself could become ideological, a product of the ruling class used by them for their own ends; a war-theology, or a national theology.

It was thus in the triumph of nationalism over liberal humanism, over socialism and over the established churches, that Barth's new theological program was forged.

It is, of course, impossible to spell out the details of this new program, or to chart its later course and developments from dialectical theology to the mature Christological theology of the *Church Dogmatics*. What will be undertaken, however, is to link up this new theological program with the question of nationalism, revolution, violence and war. In so doing, Barth's response to the 19th century and his own theological position will hopefully become clear.

**Nationalism and socialism**
Barth was a consistent opponent of nationalism; that is, the

elevating of the nation to a superordinate position. Right-wing nationalism was for him abhorrent, especially when linked with the label 'Christian'. His struggle against the German-Christians with the Confessing Church had its roots in his opposition to the nationalism which resulted in the 1914 war.

The particular danger of nationalism lay for Barth in the fatal temptation to make of it a form of religion, with its own sources of revelation, its moral life and claim to obedience, and its cultic worship expressed in flag, parade and patriotism. This danger he identified as early as his *Commentary on the Epistle to the Romans,* where he speaks of the 'No-God', the idols, the 'half-spiritual, half-material creations of nation, state, church, fatherland'.[34] These arise when the gap between God and creation is forgotten and God is identified with any material or historical entity. The crucial point for Barth is that there can be no hyphenation between God's work or ours, between God's world and ours, between God's kingdom and ours. All such hyphens are 'dangerous short-circuits', they produce 'idols' and 'No-Gods'.

The second danger of nationalism is its tendency to absolutism. This is a form of Titanism, where human beings stand almost in the place of God, exercising their rights, even with violence, taking the law into their own hands and making the state omnipotent. This divinity of the state is both theologically and politically dangerous.

Having said all that, Barth is at pains to affirm a limited God-affirmed national identity. One must receive as a gift of God one's national identity and learn to treat it rightly. But then he warns:

> What is meant by rightly ... will not of course (be learnt) ... from any abstract idea of blood and soil, from any *nomos* supposedly lurking in the mind of his people and his own mind, from any independent theology and ethics of place, home and motherland invented by sentimental or wicked fools. Only that which the command of God wills for him is right.[35]

One will then handle one's identity 'critically but positively, gently and in love', remembering that it has 'no religious power' over one. Neither the nation's history, nor any symbol or place or language is holy. 'God alone is holy'.[36]

The critical feature of Barth's treatment of the nation is that which is common to his theological method as a whole. Firstly there is God's **No!** to all human pretensions to be divine, to all divinised politics, holy symbols, religious-cultural or religious-political hyphenations. God alone is God.

But this **No!** is always enclosed in God's gracious **Yes!** to us in Jesus Christ. In Christ, God has bound Godself eternally and finally with humanity. God therefore affirms creation, affirms the human world and its struggles for peace, justice and freedom. But the two worlds must never become confused. In an analogy of the two natures of Christ, God and human beings are inseparable, but not confused. There is no God-human hybrid, Jesus is fully human, but also fully God. There is therefore no divinised politics, no holy way, no human Titanism or absolutism which usurps God's place. But there is much space for politics as politics, and for our human struggles as an analogy of God's commonwealth and rule.

Hence Barth's rejection of religious-socialism and his simultaneous affirmation of socialist politics. At the same time as he breaks with the religious-socialists, he joins the Swiss SPD. The struggle for socialism is not identical with the commonwealth of God, but it is an analogy of that commonwealth. Socialism is the correct direction for human political praxis, but it must not be divinised, or given a religious basis.

## Violence and war — Barth's response

Barth saw clearly the links between nationalism and war, and argued that the first task of ethics in relation to the question of war was to 'demythologise' it by breaking this link and exposing war in all its brutal and awful reality. The ideology of the nation as the justification of war was to be unmasked.

Reflecting his socialist roots, Barth writes: 'War is about material interests, power, etc, although cloaked in myths about nation, justice or freedom'.[37] These myths, and the militarist ethos of the glory, dignity, and chivalry of war must be exposed. 'War does in fact mean no more and no less than killing'.[38] Contrary to the nationalist, liberal and traditional Protestant view of the state, Barth argues that war is never 'normal' or essential to the state's function. It is in fact foreign to the task of the state under God, which is to fashion a just peace. Thus the church can never give the state *carte blanche* to grasp the *ultima ratio* of organising for or implementing the mass slaughter of war.

The second myth which Barth worked to expose was the idea that because one was a citizen of the nation and a conscripted soldier the responsibility for participating in the war was not one's own, it was the nation's. To this Barth responds that the fact of being a citizen and of being conscripted in fact heightens rather than removes the ethical burden from the individual.

> Today everyone is a military person, either directly or
> indirectly ... All nations as such and all their members, have
> long since become responsible military subjects. It would be
> ridiculous today to throw the responsibility on the collective
> body ie the fatherland which calls, the people which rallies, and
> the state which orders. Each individual must act where war is
> waged, and each has to ask whether war is just or unjust.[39]

Given this burden, the most ethically-dangerous position for a
Christian is not as a soldier but as a chaplain. Here the dangers of
confusing nationalism, participation in war and the legitimisation
of this by theology is especially real. Here is the place 'where it is
so uncannily easy to betray the cause of ethics publicly and to
promote that evil ideology instead of ethical reflection'.[40]

So strongly did Barth wish to break the cult of war and
violence, the myth of the supposed inevitability of war and the
traditional theological affirmation of the need to constantly
prepare for war, that he was often accused of pacifism. John
Howard Yoder correctly points out that Barth stands closer to
pacifism than any other mainline Christian theologian.[41] But Barth
consistently resisted the pacifist position, although asserting that it
has 'almost infinite arguments in its favour'.[42] Pacifism, as with all
'-isms,' was a moral absolute which stood as theologically
exposed as all absolutes.

> A church which knows its business well, will it is true with a
> strong hand keep itself free of militarism; but it will also with a
> friendly spoken gesture rebuff the attentions of pacifism.[43]

Barth's unmasking of militarism and the cult of violence, his
reworking of the ethics of war and of the state did not lead him to
the opposite absolutism. In his crucial essay, 'Christian
Community and the Civil Community', published first in 1946 in
the aftermath of the Second World War, he formulates his
position on the possibilities of violence and war in terms of an
analogy of God's anger and judgement:

> The Church knows God's anger and judgement, but it also
> knows that His anger lasts but for a moment, whereas His
> mercy is for eternity. The political analogy of this truth is that
> violent solutions of conflict in the political community — from
> police measures to law-court decisions, from the armed
> uprising against a regime that is no longer worthy or equal to
> its task (in the sense of a revolt undertaken not to undermine
> but restore the lawful authority of the state) to the defensive
> war against an external threat to the lawful state — must be
> approved, supported and if necessary even suggested by the

Christian community — for how could it possibly contract out
in such a situation? On the other hand, it can only regard
violent solutions of any conflict as an *ultima ratio regis*. It will
approve or support them only when they are for the moment
the ultimate and only possibility attainable.[44]

This de-absolutising of positions, this radical and critical pause
which Barth introduces into the debate is captured in his ethical
concept of the *Grenzfall,* the borderline situation, the limiting case.
The concept de-absolutises positions on two fronts. Firstly it de-
absolutises violence, by asserting the command of God not to kill,
the command of God for life and its preservation. But, secondly, it
de-absolutises pacifism. It places a limit on human aspirations to
create of God's commands an absolute. God is free, and God's
commands are free. And it is at the *Grenzfall* that God's freedom
to command killing is perhaps discovered. Here there is no
casuistic legitimising of war or violence, here the command of
God is simply obeyed.

## CONCLUSION

The danger of any war or armed struggle lies in the absolutising
of one's own position, and of allowing a cult of violence to
develop. The history of the 19th century is a warning of the easy
identifications of culture, the nation, the revolution and the will of
the people with the will and command of God. In the divinising of
any war or any struggle, no matter how serious or just, lies both a
political and a theological danger. Politically it absolutises
positions, it closes the gap needed for self-criticism and
correction, and it produces an ideology and rhetoric of violence
that tends to feed on itself. Little remains to prevent the
revolution, or the war, 'from devouring its own children' in
counter-revolution and reaction. Theologically it runs the danger
of identifying a particular cause with the cause of God. When that
cause fails, or is exposed as inadequate or even evil, (as
happened to the cause of German nationalism in both wars), then
theology stands similarly exposed and vulnerable.

This does not mean that discriminating political choices should
not be made by the church. Barth's politics, and as he claimed,
the politics of God's commonwealth, were consistently socialist in
direction. So too the possibility of revolution or of war in the
defence of the (relatively) just state must be held open. These
choices are made in the direction the Christian community
receives from its center, God's revelation of Godself in Jesus

Christ, but are never identified with that center.

Barth's theology as a critique of the theology of the 19th century and its inability to deal adequately with the crucial question of nationalism, violence and war, remains as a permanent challenge to all theological ethics forged in the hubris of struggle and war. Revolution, yes! Violence, if necessary, yes! Nationalism in the cause of humanity, yes! But never with the **Yes!** of absolutism or of divinised politics.

# NOTES

1. J.L. Talmon, *The Myth of the Nation and the Vision of Revolution*, (London: Secker and Warburg, 1980).
2. H. Kohn, *The Idea of Nationalism*, (New York: MacMillan, 1944).
3. H. Kohn, 'Nationalism' in the *Dictionary of the History of Ideas*, Vol.III, p.326.
4. H. Kohn, *Prophets and Peoples: Studies in 19th Century Nationalism*, (London: Collier Books, 1946), p.56.
5. Kohn, *The Idea of Nationalism*, p.331.
6. 'Philosophy of Right', p.240., quoted in Kohn, *Idea of Nationalism*, p.111.
7. H. Kohn, *Prophets and Peoples*, p. 16.
8. J. Talmon, *The Myth of the Nation*, p.12.
9. *Ibid.*, p.10.
10. B. Croce, *History of Europe in the 19th Century*, (London: Unwin, 1934), p.266ff.
11. Talmon, *The Myth of the Nation*, p.398.
12. E. Cahn and V.C. Fisera, (eds.), *Socialism and Nationalism*, Vol.III, (Nottingham: Russel Press, 1979), p.78.
13. Talmon, *The Myth of the Nation*, p.47.
14. *Ibid.*, p.61.
15. *Ibid.*, p.465.
16. Kohn, *Prophets and Peoples*, p.118.
17. L.L. Snyder, *German Nationalism*, (Port Washington: Kennikat Press, 1969), p.233.
18. Kohn, *Prophets and Peoples*, p.62.
19. T.S. Hamerow, *The Birth of a New Europe*, (London: University of North Carolina Press, 1983), p.368.
20. H.M. Rumscheidt, *Revelation and Theology*, (Cambridge: C.U.P., 1972), p.202.
21. E. Busch, *Karl Barth. His Life from Letters and Autobiographical Texts*, (Philadelphia: Fortress Press, 1976), p.81.
22. K. Barth, *Revolutionary Theology in the Making*, (London: Epworth, 1964), p.26.
23. Snyder, *German Nationalism*, p.187.
24. *Ibid.*, p.189.
25. K. Barth, *Protestant Theology in the Nineteenth Century*, (London: SCM, 1972), p.438.
26. Busch, *Karl Barth: His Life*, p.81.
27. J.H.S. Kent, 'Christian Theology in the Eighteenth to the Twentieth Centuries', in H. Cunliffe-Jones, (ed.), *A History of Christian Doctrine*, (Edinburgh: T. & T. Clark, 1978), p.551.

28.  A. Ritschl, *Justification and Reconciliation*, (New York, 1966), p.252, quoted in Kent, 'Christian Theology', p.551.
29.  *Ibid*, p.552.
30.  Rumscheidt, *Revelation and Theology*, p.19.
31.  A. von Harnack, 'The Social Mission of the Church of Today' in A. von Harnack and W. Hermann, *Essays on the Social Gospel*, M.A. Lanney (ed), (London: Williams & Norgate, 1907), p.79.
32.  See W. Pauck, *From Luther to Tillich*, (San Francisco: Harper & Row, 1984), p.84.
33.  See Busch, *Karl Barth: His Life*, and G. Hunsinger, (ed.), *Karl Barth and Radical Politics*, (Philadelphia: Westminster, 1976).
34.  K. Barth, *Epistle to the Romans*, (London: Oxford Press, 1933), p.50.
35.  K. Barth, *Church Dogmatics*, Vol.III, 4, (Edinburgh: T. & T. Clark, 1961), p.242.
36.  *Ibid.*, p.295.
37.  *Ibid.*, p.452.
38.  *Ibid.*, p.453.
39.  *Ibid.*, p.451.
40.  K. Barth, *Ethics*, (Edinburgh: T. & T. Clark, 1981), p.158.
41.  J.H. Yoder, *Karl Barth and the Problem of War*, (New York: Abingdon, 1970), p.37.
42.  K. Barth, *Church Dogmatics*, p.455.
43.. K. Barth, *Romans*, p.471.
44.  K. Barth, *Against the Stream*, (London: SCM, 1954), p.41.

# Armed Struggle as a Last Resort: The Roman Catholic Position

## ALBERT NOLAN AND MARY ARMOUR

In their pastoral letter on war and peace issued in 1983, the U.S. Catholic bishops point out that the Roman Catholic tradition on war and peace is a long one that 'stretches from the Sermon on the Mount to the statements of John Paul II'.[1] The just war tradition is not a single theory, but a complex and 'evolving ethical process'.[2] The Roman Catholic tradition always begins with a presumption against war and for peaceful settlement of disputes and only in exceptional cases, determined by the moral principles of the just war tradition can some use of force be permitted. This applies equally to wars between nations and civil wars. Although just war doctrine was developed largely from the perspective of the ruling authorities, its historically-conditioned and open-ended nature has allowed for developments such as the question of armed struggle and revolutionary violence against a tyrant. As pointed out in Paul Germond's paper elsewhere in this volume, it can be argued that liberation theology stands within the just war tradition.

It was Augustine who developed the theological foundations of the just war theory. He maintained that since perfection on earth was not possible, war and conflict were an inevitable part of life. War could only be waged, however, if its purpose was just, and peace was the ideal to be restored and striven for. 'Even in the course of war you should cherish the spirit of a peace-maker'.[3] This rudimentary code of war was more fully developed by Thomas Aquinas as well as by the Spanish scholastics De Vitoria and De Suarez to become a comprehensive set of guidelines for the initiation and waging of war.

Just war criteria can be divided into two major categories:
1. criteria concerning the right to make war *(jus ad bellum)*;
2. criteria affecting the conduct of war *(jus in bello)*.

## CRITERIA OF *JUS AD BELLUM*

For the recourse to war to be ethically justified, the following criteria must be applied:

1. There must be a *just cause*. A just cause according to Augustine for example would include the restoration of 'what has been taken unjustly'.[4] It is important to note that this cause should be sufficiently serious and weighty enough to overcome the presumption against killing. Childress offers three likely instances:
— protection of the innocent from unjust attack;
— restoring rights wrongly denied, and
— re-establishing a just order.[5]

2. There must be a *just intention*. This would require that those waging war should always have in mind as the ultimate object of the war a just and lasting peace.

3. There must be *proportionality of ends and means*. This requires that a serious attempt be made to weigh up the probable good against the probable evil which may result. The consideration of the probability of success would need to be considered here and this point links up with the earlier argument that the cause should be sufficiently weighty.

4. War must be a *last resort*. All other means must have been tried first before the resort to force can be regarded as justifiable. Russell points out that there would be no justification in taking up arms against prolonged oppression if democratic peaceful channels were available for the achievement of a just end.[6]

5. War must be declared by a *legitimate authority*. For Thomas Aquinas it was only the ruler who had the authority to declare war and not a 'private individual'. A major concern here would be to avoid giving any basis for an anarchist ethic which might justify any individual taking up arms in a personal and individual cause. The meaning and interpretation of this criterion is one of the most keenly debated issues in just war theory. If government were to be considered synonymous with legitimate authority, it would seem that armed resistance to tyranny could never be justified in terms of just war theory; both Augustine and Aquinas, however, raise fundamental questions about the legitimacy of the authority wielded by a tyrant. Aquinas has this to say about the right to resist tyranny:

> A tyrannical government is unjust because it is not directed to the common good, but to the private good of the ruler, as Aristotle says. Consequently, disturbing such a government has not the nature of sedition, unless perhaps the disturbance be

so excessive that the people suffer more from it than from the tyrannical regime. Indeed it is the tyrant rather that is guilty of sedition, since he fosters discord and dissension among his subjects in order to lord it over them more securely. For this is tyranny, to govern for the ruler's personal advantage to the people's harm.[7]

A further development of Catholic tradition on this point can be seen in the papal letter of 1937 to the bishops of Mexico entitled *Nos es muy conocida*:

> If a situation arises when the duly constituted authorities oppose justice and truth to the extent that their destructive acts affect the very basis of authority, one cannot see how one should condemn those citizens who unite to defend the nation and themselves, by legitimate and appropriate means, against those who take advantage of their power to lead the country into ruin.[8]

The tradition is so strong that when Pope Paul VI in *Populorum Progressio* (1967) discourages revolutionary uprisings he has to make mention of this famous exception:

> Everyone knows, however, that revolutionary uprising — except where there is manifest, longstanding tyranny which would do great damage to fundamental personal rights and dangerous harm to the common good of the country — engender new injustices, introduce new inequities and bring new disasters.[9]

The same point is made, now more directly and pertinently, in the latest Vatican *Instruction on Christian Freedom and Liberation* (1986):

> There is a morality of means. These principles must be especially applied in the extreme case where there is recourse to *armed struggle*, which the church's Magisterium admits *as a last resort* to put an end to an obvious and prolonged *tyranny* which is gravely damaging the fundamental rights of individuals and the common good. Nevertheless, the concrete application of this means cannot be contemplated until there has been a *very rigorous analysis of the situation* .... One can never approve ... crimes such as reprisals ... , torture, methods of terrorism ... smear campaigns.[10]

Tyranny then qualifies as an 'extreme case', an exception. The importance of this exception as a last resort needs to be emphasised. The 1980 *Instruction* would seem to be warning against a 'mystique of violence' when it condemns as a destructive illusion 'systematic violence put forward as the necessary path to liberation'. This warning is intended to counter the romanticisation of revolutionary force most often associated with Franz Fanon, who in *The Wretched of the Earth* (written in the context of the Algerian struggle for freedom) spoke of violence as vesting its perpetrators with positive and creative qualities as well as a cathartic cleansing power. J.G. Davies points out that this is to confuse power with violence and that 'force cannot be sanctified; its exercise may be forgiven'.[11]

Clearly the just war theory does also apply to armed struggle in a revolution and the criteria are exactly the same. However, one cannot help noticing the extreme reluctance with which the Catholic church 'admits' the application of the just war theory to a revolutionary uprising. Is that because in practice it tends to be on the side of the ruling authorities? On the question of the right to revolution, O'Brien says 'Catholic tradition recognises this thought... although often in a most reluctant and tortured fashion'. He goes on to argue that 'it will be necessary to assimilate revolutionary warfare problems into the traditional just-war categories'.[12]

## THE CRITERIA OF *JUS IN BELLO*

The criteria of just conduct in war emerged later in the development of just war doctrine, but are considered indispensable as components of a mature just war doctrine. In terms of international law, points relating to these criteria have been set out in codes 'centering around the Hague Convention of 1907, the Geneva Convention of 1949 and the two 1977 Geneva Protocols to those conventions'.[13]

1. There must be proportionality of means and ends. In the conduct of war this criteria would concern such issues as the use of weapons and methods subject to restraint and the avoidance of wanton violence or atrocities. With the development of nuclear technology this principle of proportionality is of central importance.

2. There must be discrimination in terms of targets. This would prohibit 'direct intentional attacks on non-combatants and non-military targets' and the questions that immediately come to mind are: How are non-combatants to be defined? How are non-military targets to be distinguished from military? Nevertheless, the ethical objective of this argument is clear enough, the need to avoid injury to innocent people wherever possible. It is in this context that many have argued for the banning of nuclear weapons for example, in that the principle of discrimination can never be met. Russell points out that it is possible to be a 'nuclear pacifist' while

supporting just war doctrines (see also the essay by Villa-Vicencio elsewhere in this volume).[14]

3. There are some means which are prohibited altogether. This criterion is a development of the principle of proportionality, in that it is argued that there are means which 'by definition are considered disproportionate and cannot be used even if they can be discriminatory'.[15] Under this criteria many would include the use of torture, napalm, chemical warfare and nuclear bombs.

It should be noted here that a further development of the just war tradition is emerging on nuclear war, as indicated by the US bishops' pastoral letter of 1984, *The Challenge of Peace*.[16] Stating that no use of nuclear weapons which would violate the principles of discrimination or proportionality may be intended in a strategy of deterrence, the document goes on to address individuals on matters such as refusal of military service work in armaments industries and weapons research; to governments and policy-makers it speaks on the morality of nuclear deterrence and on the aiming of weapons of mass destruction at civilian populations. Another aspect of the pastoral letter which the bishops stressed as being of equal importance to the emergency over nuclear weapons is the role of the arms race as 'an act of aggression against the poor' in that the arms traffic is seen as draining funds away from desperately needed social aid programs, so that the poorest nations are often the most victimised in the escalating militarisation of large and small states.[17] This increasingly broadbased analysis emerges in turn out of the definition of peace expressed most clearly in the *Pastoral Constitution* of Vatican II:

> Peace is not merely the absence of war. Nor can it be reduced solely to the maintenance of a balance of power between enemies. Nor is it brought about by dictatorship. Instead it is rightly and appropriately called 'an enterprise of justice' (Is.32:7). Peace results from that harmony built into human society by its divine founder and actualised by men as they search after ever greater justice.[18]

## JUST WAR CRITERIA AS APPLIED TO SOUTH AFRICA

Essays elsewhere in this volume have dealt with this topic comprehensively and a simple resumé of the relevance and applicability of certain of these criteria in South Africa will suffice.

The criteria of a *just cause* being present is not really at issue, in that ample evidence exists as regards the existence of a 'manifest longstanding tyranny'.[19] The essay by Boesak and Brews on the history of the armed struggle in this country points out the protracted failure of non-violent strategies vis-à-vis the intransigence of the state and how many of those strategies have been pre-empted by state action.

The question of the illegitimacy of the state directly relates to the question of existing tyranny and this has been raised in a particularly sharp and provocative way in the critique offered by the *Kairos Document.*

Perhaps the most pertinent issue then relates not to the *jus ad bellum* criteria but those having to do with *jus in bello,* the question of proportionality and the cost incurred to human life in a protracted guerilla struggle, bearing in mind Helder Camara's warning on the danger of a 'spiral of violence'.

## NOTES

1.  U.S. Catholic bishops, *The Challenge of Peace: God's Promise and Our Response,* (Washington: United States Catholic Conference, May 1983).
2.  David Russell, *A Theological Critique of the Christian Pacifist Perspective with Special Reference to the Position of John Howard Yoder,* (University of Cape Town Ph.D. thesis, 1984), p.232.
3.  Augustine, quoted in *Ibid.,* p.246.
4.  Augustine, quoted in *Ibid.,* p.247.
5.  James Childress, 'Just War Criteria', in T.A. Shannon (ed.), *War or Peace,* (Maryknoll, N.Y.: Orbis, 1980), p.40.
6.  David Russell, *A Theological Critique of the Christian Pacifist Perspective,* p.235.
7.  Thomas Aquinas, *Summa Theologica,* quoted in C. Villa-Vicencio (ed.), *Between Christ and Caesar,* (Grand Rapids: Eerdmans, 1986), p.217.
8.  Pope Pius, *Nos es muy conocida,* quoted in J.G. Davies, *Christians, Politics and Violent Revolution,* (Maryknoll, N.Y.: Orbis, 1976), p.164.
9.  Pope Paul VI, *Populorum Progressio,* (1967), M. Walsh and B. Davies (eds.), *Proclaiming Justice and Peace,* (London: Collins, 1984), p.141.
10. Society for the Propagation of the Faith, *Instruction on Christian Freedom and Liberation,* (Vatican City, 1986), p.15.
11. J.G. Davies, *Christians, Politics and Violent Revolution,* p.167.
12. W. O'Brien, *The Conduct of Just and Limited War,* (N.Y.: Praeger, 1981), p.14.
13. Philip J. Murnion (ed.), *Catholics and Nuclear War, (A Commentary on the Challenge of Peace),* (London: Geoffrey Chapman, 1983), p.169.
14. David Russell, *A Theological Critique of the Christian Pacifist Perspective,* p.249.
15. *Ibid.*
16. U.S. Catholic bishops, *The Challenge of Peace.*
17. Sissela Bok, 'A Practical Ethic of Non-violence' in D. Eck and D. Jain, *Speaking of Faith,* (London: The Women's Press, 1986), p.240.
18. 'The Pastoral Constitution on the Modern World', (*Gaudium et Spes*) in Walsh and Davies, *Proclaiming Justice and Peace,* p.35.
19. Paul VI, *Populorum Progressio,* p.141ff.

# Liberation Theology: Theology in the Service of Justice

## PAUL A. GERMOND

The twentieth century can properly be called the century of revolutions, a century in which no continent has remained untouched by revolution. The Christian church has had to shape its life and witness in this context of revolution. J.G. Davies observes that:

> Since revolution is indeed such a widespread contemporary phenomenon, Christians cannot simply ignore it. They may not like it; they may wish to repudiate it, but they cannot pursue their discipleship in the world and pretend that it does not exist. They have no real alternative but to seek to understand it and its relationship to the gospel and to define their own position vis-à-vis revolution in the light of this critical appraisal.[1]

Latin American liberation theology arguably provides the clearest contemporary attempt to establish a Christian praxis and theology which is fully cognisant of its context of revolution and violence. Enrique Dussel speaks of the present crisis of liberation in Latin America as 'the crisis of popular revolution'[2]: a crisis which began in the early 1960s as a revolt against the oligarchies which came to power in the national revolutions of the 19th century.[3] It is in this context that Christian communities in Latin America ask what it means to be Christian on a continent of oppression, violence and revolution. Gustavo Gutiérrez expresses it thus:

> In Latin America we are in the midst of a full-blown process of revolutionary ferment. This is a complex and changing situation which resists schematic interpretation ... the untenable circumstances of poverty, alienation, and exploitation in which the greater part of the people of Latin America live, demand that we find a path toward economic, social and political liberation.[4]

It is in the search of a path to liberation, to a just and

humanised society, that liberation theology has emerged; a theology which addresses in a systematic way the conviction that the violence which is employed in the service of the poor and the oppressed, to the ends of justice and humanisation, can be a legitimate Christian option.

To treat violence as an isolated issue, divorced from the full matrix of human relations out of which it comes, leads to a reification of violence and a distortion of the issues facing liberation theology. A significant part of this paper will therefore be devoted to setting the ecclesiastical and socio-political backdrop to liberation theology. With that done the position of liberation theology on violence will be examined by specifically treating the Medellin documents and three leading liberation theologians, namely Gustavo Gutiérrez, Jon Sobrino and Juan Luis Segundo.

## TWO DEFINITIONS

Before embarking on an examination of violence in liberation theology, two terms which require definition, namely 'liberation theology' and 'violence' will receive attention.

*Liberation theology.* We are concerned here with *Latin American* liberation theology. Like most theologies it evidences internal diversity while pursuing a common aim. Leonardo Boff thus insists:

> ... there is one, and only one theology of liberation. There is only one point of departure — a reality of social misery — and one goal — the liberation of the oppressed. In a discussion of mediations, accents can be discerned. It is on this latter level that a variety of tendencies can be discerned — which does not, however, constitute alternative liberation theologies.[5]

Liberation theology is predominantly Roman Catholic (and it is here that this essay focuses), although there are notable Protestant exponents, the foremost being José Miguèz Bonino. This Catholic-Protestant divide constitutes one element of the diversity within liberation theology.

Juan Luis Segundo has identified another point of diversity. He speaks of 'at least two theologies of liberation co-existing now in Latin America'[6] which are different in pastoral consequences'.[7] The one type *has its roots in* the ideas of university students and elements of the middle class in the 1960s. It is a theology of liberation which finds its fullest expression in the academic world, the articulation of liberation theology by scholars in debate with their European and North American peers. The second is a theology that emerges from faithful people grappling with the meaning of faith in their resistance to oppression. This theology, says Segundo, requires a conversion experience on the part of academic theologians, 'a kind of self-negation. Instead of teaching they should learn . . . from common people . . . and give up the chronic suspicion among intellectuals that common people are always wrong'.[8]

The second term requiring definition is 'violence'.[9] The *Concise Oxford Dictionary* defines violence as the 'unlawful use of force'. This perjorative understanding of violence is common. Force is regarded as morally neutral, whereas violence is morally repugnant. As Davies expresses it, 'Force is properly used only in the context of legitimate power and right. It may never be executed beyond the extent necessary to secure those ends, or else it becomes violence'.[10] Force is thus a descriptive term, while violence is a term with unequivocally negative implications. Liberation theology rejects this distinction and employs the word 'violence' to refer to the use of both illegitimate and legitimate force. Force, understood as the use of power to inhibit the freedom of an individual or collective of people, must inevitably dehumanise the people against whom it is directed. This, suggests liberation theology, is violence. In this paper, as in liberation theology, the distinction between violence and force is eschewed. Violence will be referred to as either legitimate or illegitimate violence.

## THE VATICAN AND VIOLENCE — A SHIFTING BASE

Within Catholicism two loci dominate the debate on violence: the Vatican and the Episcopal Conference of Latin America (CELAM), which provide the ecclesiastical context out of which liberation theology has emerged.

The Vatican's concern with social justice, and therefore with revolution and violence, is part of a trajectory which began with Pope Leo XIII's *Rerum Novarum* (1891), and extends through the encyclicals of John XXIII, the Second Vatican Council (1962-1965), in particular in *Gaudium et Spes*, the encyclicals of Paul VI in the late 1960s and early 1970s and those of John Paul II in the late 1970s and the 1980s.[11] Cardinal Joseph Ratzinger, Prefect of the Congregation for the Doctrine of Faith, has been the key Vatican protagonist in the debate in the 1980s.[12]

Leo XIII's *Rerum Novarum* was innovative because it displayed a genuine concern for people suffering conditions of poverty and oppression. It nevertheless rejected outright any suggestion that change by means of revolution might be legitimate.[13] It was not until John XXIII that there was a move to break out of the conservative social stance that had characterised Vatican teaching for the seventy years after Leo XIII.[14] In the words of Donal Dorr, *Mater et Magistra* (May 15, 1971) which celebrated the seventieth anniversary of Leo XIII's *Rerum Novarum*, 'began the process of breaking the long alliance between Roman Catholicism and socially conservative forces'.[15] With *Pacem in Terris* (April 11, 1963), issued during the course of the Vatican Council, Pope John XXIII stressed the need for social justice, and gave a trenchant analysis of the misuse of individual rights at the expense of social justice for all people, not only the privileged. But he spoke out clearly against revolution (which implied violence), preferring development to revolution (paragraphs 161 and 162). *Gaudium et Spes*, the Vatican II pronouncement on the church in the modern world, addressed the question of violence primarily in terms of the ethical issues raised by the two World Wars, and not in terms of the revolutionary violence of the Third World.

Pope Paul VI maintained the impetus by promulgating his encyclical *Populorum Progressio* (March 26, 1967). He displayed a keen concern for the relationships between rich and poor nations, and how the economic imbalance between them was perpetuated. In this context the question of revolutionary violence was raised.

> The injustice of certain situations cries out for God's attention. Lacking the bare necessities of life, whole nations are under the thumb of others... They are sorely tempted to redress these insults to their human nature by violent means (para.30).
>
> Everyone knows, however, that revolutionary uprisings — except where there is manifest, long-standing tyranny which would do great damage to fundamental personal rights and dangerous harm to the common good of the country — engender new injustices, introduce new inequities and bring new disasters. The evil situation that exists, and it is surely evil, may not be dealt with in such a way that even a worse situation results (para.31).

The correct interpretation of the parenthesis in paragraph 31, is a matter of some contention. Dorr maintains that it 'is clearly meant to suggest that in certain extreme situations a revolution might be justified'.[16] Walsh and Davies assert that the Pope gives 'a very slight hint that violence might, in certain circumstances, be justified — but he hurriedly backs away from saying so explicitly'.[17] Whatever the case may be, this is the first time the question of revolutionary violence is addressed in a papal document and, as we shall see, it is identified and further developed by the Latin American bishops at Medellin.

In his opening address to the Medellin conference (1968), Pope Paul said 'Violence is neither Christian nor evangelical'. As Segundo observes, 'such an assertion is new in Catholic theology. The latter canonized warrior saints and inquisitions, and for centuries it debated the conditions for a *just* war.[18] Segundo's point is important. The official position of the Catholic Church, historically, has been one of just war. Not since before Constantine has it been pacifist. It appears to be probable, in the light of this, that the Vatican pronouncements from Leo XII to Paul VI reflect a departure from mainline tradition, while liberation theology actually stands more firmly within the tradition. We shall address this question in more detail below.

Paul VI returns to the subject of violence in *Evangelii Nuntiandi* (December 8, 1975). Here the question of liberation from oppression receives close attention:

> Evangelisation involves an explicit message ... about the rights and duties of every human being, ... about life in society, about international life, peace, justice and development — a message especially energetic today about liberation (para.29).
>
> The church has the duty to proclaim the liberation of millions of human beings ... (para.30) and it touches the very concrete situations of injustice to be combatted and of justice to be restored (para.31).

In this task of combatting injustice the means by which justice may be achieved are crucial. 'Pope Paul was concerned lest there be any confusion between the Christian conception of liberation and the kind of political liberation sought by revolutionaries. He saw the danger that a certain kind of liberation theology could be used to justify violent rebellion against unjust regimes'.[19] To this end Paul VI articulates his position on violence with great clarity:

> The Church cannot accept violence, especially the force of arms — which is uncontrollable once it is set loose — and indiscriminate death as the path of liberation, because she knows that violence always provokes violence and irresistably engenders new forms of oppression and enslavement which are often harder to bear than those from which they claimed to bring freedom. We must say and reaffirm that violence is not in

accord with the gospel, that it is not Christian; and that sudden
or violent changes of structures would be deceitful, ineffective
of themselves, and certainly not in conformity with the dignity
of the people (para.37).

The Vatican next addressed the question of violence, not
through the encyclicals of John Paul II, but in two documents
issued by the Congregation for the Doctrine of the Faith, under
the prefecture of Cardinal Joseph Ratzinger, both concerned with
a critique of liberation theology. The first of these, *Instructions on
Certain Matters of the 'Theology of Liberation'* (August 6, 1984)
appears to be a categorical rejection of any use of violence, both
oppressive and revolutionary:

> The truth of mankind (sic) requires that this battle (for justice)
> be fought in ways consistent with human dignity. That is why
> the systematic and deliberate recourse to blind violence, no
> matter from which side it comes, must be condemned. To put
> one's trust in violent means in the hope of restoring more
> justice is to become the victim of a fatal illusion: violence
> begets violence and degrades man. It mocks the dignity of
> man in the person of the victim and it debases that same
> dignity among those who practise it (para. XI,7) . . . By the same
> token, the overthrow by means of revolutionary violence of
> structures which generate violence is not *ipso facto* the
> beginning of a just regime (para. XI,10).

The last statement is bolstered by reference to the millions of
people who long for liberation in countries which are the result of
violent revolution (presumably referring to socialist regimes). This
document is a strong polemic against any use of physical
violence. The second document, entitled *Instruction on Christian
Freedom and Liberation* (1986), contains a shift in position. The
expected rejection of violence as a necessary element in the
struggle for liberation is present, but a qualification is added in
which the possibility of violent revolution is more positively stated
than in any other Vatican document:

> These principles must be especially applied in the extreme
> case where there is recourse to armed struggle, which the
> *Church's Magisterium admits as a last resort* to put an end to
> an obvious and prolonged tyranny which is gravely damaging
> the fundamental rights of individuals and the common good.
> Nevertheless, the concrete application of this means cannot be
> contemplated until there has been a very rigorous analysis of
> the situation (para. 79. My italics).

In this document, the Vatican gives formal recognition to the
legitimacy of revolutionary violence under very particular

conditions. This is a conclusion clearly differing from the positions of Leo XIII and John XXIII. John XXIII was committed to non-violence (as is best seen in *Pacem in Terris*), a position that has been compared to the pacifism of Mohandas Gandhi.[20] This committed non-violence stance is unusual in Catholic theology, where the mainstream tradition has been the just war position. The tension between these two positions is seen in Paul VI who evidences an ambivalent attitude to violence. It is only with the last of the documents examined above, that there is a clear, unambivalent return to the traditional theological position, a position occupied already by liberation theology.

## THE LATIN AMERICAN CONTEXT: INSTITUTIONALISED VIOLENCE

We now turn to an examination of the Latin American context of liberation theology. The fundamental point of departure for liberation theology is the tragic condition of the Latin American continent, characterised by the domination of international capitalism, ubiquitous internal oppression and the suffering of people who live in poverty and squalor, together with the struggle for liberation and the repressive measures used to quell such attempts. The removal of these oppressive conditions is one of the central features of the program of liberation theology.

The second general conference of Latin American bishops (CELAM) met at Medellin in 1968, an event often regarded as the ecclesiastical genesis of liberation theology.[21] The Medellin conference had as its central concern the Latin American situation, which it characterised as a situation of institutionalised violence:

> In many instances Latin America finds itself faced with a situation of injustice that can be called *institutionalized violence*, when, because of structural deficiency of industry and agriculture, of national and international economy, of cultural and political life, 'whole towns lack necessities, live in such dependence as hinders all initiative and responsibility as well as every possibility for cultural promotion and participation in social and political life', thus violating fundamental rights.[22]

This was a foundational observation for liberation theology, that structural injustice and oppression ought to be understood in terms of violence. Liberation theology thus begins its evaluation of violence with the recognition that institutions and structures of society can do violence to persons. This violence is institutionalised violence; the violence which Dom Helder Camara has called violence 'number 1': 'You will find that everywhere injustices are a form of violence. One can and must say they are everywhere the basic violence, violence number 1'.[23]

Gutiérrez forcefully expresses this departure point:

> The true face of Latin America is emerging in all its naked ugliness. It is not simply or primarily a question of low educational standards, a limited economy, an unsatisfactory legal system, or inadequate legal institutions. What we are faced with is a situation that takes no account of the dignity of human beings, or their most elemental needs, that does not provide for their biological survival, or their basic right to be free and autonomous. Poverty, injustice, alienation, and the exploitation of human beings by other human beings combine to form what the Medellin conference did not hesitate to condemn as 'institutionalized violence'.
>
> It is only within this real context that one can honestly raise the complex question of the moral rightness or wrongness of putting down violence. No double standard will do. We cannot say that violence is all right when the oppressor uses it to maintain or preserve 'order', but wrong when the oppressed use it to overthrow this same 'order'.[24]

Liberation theology argues that the roots of the violence in Latin America lie in the realm of international relations and international capitalism, called 'external neo-colonialism' by the Medellin conference.[25] In this view, the violence in Latin America emerges from the economic base upon which it rests. Liberation theology employs the class analysis of society as the tool with which to understand the social dynamics of society, an analysis which sees conflict between classes as an inherent characteristic of capitalist society. Gutiérrez asserts:

> The class struggle is part of our economic, social, political, cultural, and religious reality. Its evolution, its exact extent, its nuances, and its variations are the object of analysis of the social sciences and pertain to the field of scientific rationality. Recognition of the existence of the class struggle does not depend on our religious or ethical options.[26]

According to Gutiérrez, the class struggle is a fact that has to be accepted. Liberation theology consciously chooses this analysis as the correct analysis, and understands violence in terms of the class struggle.

Central to liberation theology is the understanding that for centuries the church has abetted the oppression and domestication of the people. The church has helped to legitimate and perpetuate a situation of violence: both the naked violence of the conquistadores in the colonial period and the structural and oppressive violence of the national states. The denunciation of institutionalised violence by liberation theology 'implies the rejection of the use of Christianity to legitimise the established order'.[27] The church and its theology should now be committed to the liberation of the oppressed and exploited masses of Latin America. It must develop a praxis which takes the preferential option for the poor and powerless, in contra-distinction to its historical position on the side of the rich and the powerful.

The task which liberation theology sets itself is quite explicit. 'In Latin America, the Church must place itself squarely within the process of revolution, amid the violence which is present in different ways. The Church's *mission* is defined practically and theoretically, pastorally and theologically in relation to this revolutionary process'.[28] In this context of revolution, liberation theology works for the liberation of the oppressed, for full justice in society, and the humanising possibility of life for all persons.

# LIBERATION AND JUSTICE THROUGH VIOLENCE

Against this background we now can turn to the question at hand: liberation theology's understanding of violence.

## MEDELLIN

*The Medellin Conclusions* discuss the issue of violence under section 2, 'Peace'. The position of Medellin on violence can be summarised in nine propositions.[29]

1.  Violence is not a Christian virtue. Pacifism is regarded as the Christian ideal (2:15,17),[30] and violence, in itself, is always destructive and does not generate situations restorative of justice and human dignity.
2.  A prerequisite for peace is justice (2:16).
3.  'Violence constitutes one of the gravest problems in Latin America' (2:15) which finds itself in a situation of 'institutionalised violence' (2:16).
4.  Because of this institutionalised violence, the 'temptation to violence' for those who are oppressed is very real (2:16).
5.  The wealthy, privileged minority who 'jealously retain their privileges and defend them through violence' are responsible for 'provoking revolutions of despair' (2:17).
6.  Those who remain passive in the face of mounting injustice

are regarded as also being responsible for the situation of revolution (2:18).

7.  In many cases those who opt for revolutionary violence, do so out of 'noble impulses of justice and solidarity' (2:19).

8.  Revolutionary insurrection can be legitimate under certain specific conditions. However, it must be recognised that such armed revolutions demand a very high payment in human suffering (2:19).[31]

9.  What is more desirable therefore, is that justice and peace be achieved by means of 'a dynamic action of awakening and organisation of the popular sectors' (2:18). This action leads to the liberation of the masses from servitude.

These nine points encapsulate the essence of the Medellin position on violence. As one may expect from a document produced by CELAM, given its ecclesiastical responsibilities, it is a cautious document. Nonetheless, it provides liberation theology with a number of foundational observations with respect to violence: i) that there can be no peace without justice, ii) that the primary violence in Latin America is structural violence, and iii) that despite the obvious dangers of revolutionary violence, there are cases in which it would be legitimate. Medellin formulated in 1968 a position which the Vatican would only reach eighteen years later.

# LIBERATION THEOLOGIANS AND VIOLENCE

## 1  GUSTAVO GUTIÉRREZ

In 1971 Gustavo Gutiérrez wrote what is widely regarded as the seminal work of liberation theology, *The Theology of Liberation*.[32] In it he works from the theological base established by Medellin. Latin America exists in a situation of structural violence. This fact must inevitably affect one's assessment of oppressive violence and liberative violence. He cites with approval a document signed by over 900 Latin American priests, which states that we should 'by all means avoid equating the *unjust violence* of the oppressors (who maintain this despicable system) with the *just violence* of the oppressed (who feel obliged to use it to achieve their liberation)'.[33] In essence Gutiérrez argues that revolutionary violence in Latin America is just, for it is pitted against a violence that is truly evil, for the sake of liberation from oppression.

> Moreover, as awareness of existing legalised violence grows, the problem of counterviolence is no longer an abstract ethical

concern. It now becomes very important on the level of political efficacy.[34]

The approach to violence, it is argued, must come from 'a clear option in favour of the oppressed and their liberation' which 'leads to basic changes in outlook[35]; there emerges a new vision of the fruitfulness and originality of Christianity and the Christian communities' role in this liberation'.[36] Liberation, if it is to have any meaning at all, must be undertaken by the oppressed people themselves if it is to be authentic.[37]

Gutiérrez recognises that in the political arena different forms of confrontation and violence are inevitable. Conflict is the stuff of politics. So when the church enters this realm, by making a conscious choice to work for the liberation of the oppressed, it inevitably enters the realm of violence. 'More precisely, the building of a just society means the confrontation — in which different kinds of violence are present — between groups with different interests and opinions'.[38]

> In Latin America the world in which the Christian community must live and celebrate its eschatological hope is the world of social revolution; the Church's task must be so defined in relation to this. Its fidelity to the gospel leaves it no alternative: the Church must be the visible sign of the presence of the Lord within the aspiration for liberation and the struggle for a more human and just society.[39]

> Every attempt to evade the struggle against alienation and the violence of the powerful and for a more just and humane world is the greatest infidelity to God. To know him is to work for justice. There is no other path to reach him.[40]

## 2  JON SOBRINO

In his book, *The True Church and the Poor*, Jon Sobrino begins his discussion of violence by speaking of the violence inherent in Latin America and asserts that it is the Church's task to struggle for justice in the midst of violence and revolution:

> The most fundamental datum ... is the fact that life is threatened and is being taken from the masses, and this at elementary levels, by structural injustice and institutionalised violence. It follows that the testimony of the Church on behalf of life takes very seriously these elementary levels of life and that it promotes a 'just' life through struggle against injustice.[41]

Having made this point, Sobrino spells out his understanding of the church and violence in a section entitled 'The Subjective Testimony of the Church in Persecution and Martyrdom'.[42] Here he introduces a new element into the debate; the matter of martyrdom. To his mind morally-justified violence leads to martyrdom, for this kind of violence is always done in the service of others. Sobrino defines martyrdom as 'the most complete form of holiness, not only for general theological reasons but also for contemporary historical reasons, which make martyrdom a real and not a remote possibility and show clearly that it is the greatest proof of love'.[43]

Martyrdom is a fact of life in Latin America:

> I need not dwell on the fact that the Church, which has given its testimony on behalf of life, has been persecuted and has produced martyrs. Thousands of peasants, workers, catechists, students, and intellectuals have suffered persecution and death. There is something new and eye-catching: hundreds of priests, religious women and men, and bishops have been attacked, slandered, threatened, expelled, tortured, and murdered ... persecution and martyrdom ... are the most typical and most complete forms of holiness for the Church precisely because the Church therein gives testimony in behalf of the just life.[44]

Martyrdom, according to Sobrino, is as closely linked to the violence of the martyr as it is to the violence of the persecutor; albeit the purely moral violence of a person committed to justice:

> Objectively, every struggle generates some kind of violence. Martyrdom in our day cannot be understood without this element of violence, just as Christian life in general cannot be understood without it, although of course it is necessary to determine what kind of violence is just. Martyrdom cannot be understood without bringing in this element of violence, just as the death of Jesus cannot be understood without it, since, at least objectively, Jesus made use of moral violence.[45]

Here then is the violence of love, the violence of those who denounce the sin of this world, with its oppression, injustice and violence: it is the violence of those who oppose the proud, who humble the mighty, who do violence to the powerful in the name of life, in the name of Christ. For this violence they are martyred.

For Sobrino the violence of martyrs must be extended 'to include the case of armed popular insurrection'.[46] He provides two arguments in support of this position. Firstly, 'the ethical legitimacy of the insurrection as judged in the light of the conditions of moral theology'.[47] In certain concrete situations armed revolution may be pronounced legitimate by the church. This is the classical just war position, and, as such, it is not a unique theological exposition. On the other hand, Sobrino's second point is novel: 'holiness can be developed by means of an insurrection',[48] a point which he argues convincingly:

> An insurrection can by its very nature engender dehumanizing and sinful values such as hatred, vengeance, disproportionate violence, and outright terrorism. However, if the passions that logically accompany a struggle are overcome, then the struggle can engender a number of Christian values such as fortitude, forgiveness, generosity and magnanimity in victory. All this means that it is very possible for even an armed struggle, if it is inevitable and just, to be the means of holiness, and that the life given in such a struggle can be regarded as a testimony of the greatest possible love. Saint Thomas saw no difficulty in regarding the death of a soldier as a martyrdom, since 'the good of the community is the highest of human goods' and 'any human good can become reason for martyrdom insofar as it is referred to God'.[49]

Sobrino does not hold this position simplistically, for he recognises the inherent problems of personal motivation and human selfishness in such situations. For this reason he does not attempt an idealisation of the individuals who are martyred in such a struggle. Yet he does insist that they are martyrs. Violence in this case, is, for Sobrino, *an opportunity for holiness*, for discovering the possibility of Christ's love in concrete action, the love that lays down its life for its friends.

## 3. JUAN LUIS SEGUNDO

Segundo provides a more theoretically searching treatment of violence than either the works of Gutiérrez or Sobrino we have addressed.[50] In the first of his works which we will examine, *The Liberation of Theology*, Segundo, in what is essentially a treatise on ethics, treats violence merely as an illustration of the fact that there are no concrete absolute ethical positions, and that the problem of ethical relativism is acute and needs to be faced courageously. He does not therefore pursue his discussion of violence in order to treat the question of revolutionary violence as a legitimate means to achieve the end of justice in Latin America. It is, however, clear that Segundo would argue that, given the historical exigencies of the moment, violent revolution might well be the legitimate means to the end of justice and humanisation in Latin America.

In this discussion, Segundo does make one point which is worth noting here. He is concerned to explode the definition of violence which locates violence purely within the realm of revolution. 'I do think that it is sociologically relevant that all the talk about violence comes in connection with the subject of revolution, but not in connection with such subjects as the police or army, for example'.[51] Violence for him (as for liberation theology as a whole), includes a wide range of activities: revolutionary as well as police and army activity, a punch, an insult, a prejudice and a pervasive social structure. All these are acts of violence.

In a later work, *Faith and Ideologies*,[52] Segundo returns to the question of violence. The significant difference between this discussion and his earlier position, is that here Segundo is concerned to address the concrete experience of violence in Latin America. This discussion 'is offered as an explanation of a historical phenomenon which became general on our continent',[53] the phenomenon of revolution. He poses two problems that confront anyone attempting such a task from the outset, if (s)he works from the assumption that violence is a recent phenomenon to be associated with revolution:

> The *first* problem is that our starting point seems to disregard the *cause* of the subversive or revolutionary violence; i.e. the violence that had already been institutionalised for years or for centuries.
>
> The *second* problem in associating the start of the violent stage with 'subversion' is that we may lose sight of the fact that the violence subsequently practised to repress subversion, the violence of repression, was immensely greater in physical terms, more thoroughgoing in its disturbing effects on the social ecology, and more inhuman in its use of the 'reasons of reason' at the expense of the 'reasons of the heart'.[54]

In the light of this persisting calculus of violence, Segundo finds the response of the institutional church to the crisis inadequate, for it has failed to engender a creative praxis which liberates people from the terror of this violence. 'The inefficacy of the social encyclicals, their lack of historical realisation, is due at bottom to the fact that Christians put their trust in a faith which will be without works. They work up a model of social duty, of what ought to be, without simultaneously working out an effective methodology for implementing it'.[55]

The pernicious danger of structural violence is that its longevity creates what Segundo terms 'a certain *social* ecology'.[56] In many Latin American countries the foundations of the social ecology rest on injustice and must be changed 'even if we have to *do violence to it*'. And so, Segundo observes, we have witnessed the rise of sustained guerilla warfare in an attempt to modify particular social ecologies.

Segundo then embarks on a detailed discussion of the destructive nature of sustained guerilla war. For him, such a war undermines many basic relations that sustain human co-operation in society, precisely because the identity of people is no longer certain;[57] the ordinary citizen may be a clandestine guerilla or an informer of the security forces. In this way the enemy is unidentifiable, and the presupposed cement of trust between citizens is lost. No society can operate effectively for any length of time under such conditions of suspicion. Segundo concludes that: 'Even though its protagonists may have no such intention, that kind of war undermines those basic rules of human and social existence'.[58]

Segundo's primary contribution to our discussion is that he provides a thoroughgoing analysis of the phenomenon of violent revolution on the Latin American continent. His sentiments lie quite clearly with the revolutionary cause; yet he is at pains to alert us to the extreme ravages that such a prolonged conflict visits upon a society. He warns that guerilla warfare over an extended period of time is exceptionally costly. Such ravages to the social ecology are to be weighed carefully by those who resort to the path of violent revolution.

## CONCLUSIONS: LIBERATION, VIOLENCE AND SOUTH AFRICA

Violence, as liberation theology consistently maintains, must only be taken up when there is no other viable alternative to overcoming institutionalised violence. It is here that the response of the Medellin Conference becomes realistic: violence may be regarded as theologically legitimate — but it is more desirable to attain justice by the 'awakening and organisation of the popular sectors' in non-violent strategies to attain it. This, as already observed, is the position adopted in the 1986 Vatican document and it is ultimately the theological position affirmed by the Christian church through the centuries. Nevertheless, given the crisis of the Latin American situation, liberation theology does give theological legitimation to violent revolution. But this is no blind baptism of violence; rather it is the result of painful experience and earnest deliberation, which leads to the growing realisation that the structures of injustice in Latin America, 'violence number

1', are so entrenched that revolutionary violence must be a part of the struggle to destroy such structures, if liberation and justice are to be achieved.

Christian theology, through its history, has been frequently subverted to serve the cause of the ruling class, particularly when the dominant groups within the church have belonged to the ruling class. In such situations theology has functioned as a powerful ideological legitimation for the state; sanctioning the institutional and represssive violence of the state and condemning the revolutionary violence of the oppressed. Yet adjacent to this dominant *misuse* of theology there exists a persisting and high tradition of church theology which has consistently recognised the appropriate use of revolutionary violence in one way or another. The other essays in this book make precisely this point.

Seldom if ever, however, in Christian history, has revolutionary violence on such a large and enduring scale been regarded as theologically legitimate by such a broad consensus of Christians as in Latin America today. What makes the treatment of the question by Latin American liberation theologians different, is the analytical moment in which this kind of violence is shown to be both inevitable and legitimate in an oppressed situation. The critical factor in this difference is that in liberation theology, theology is done from the perspective of the poor and oppressed, with their class interests in mind, rather than the class interests of the rich and the powerful. Liberation theology takes a preferential option for the poor, an option it regards as being faithful to the option which Christ took; an option which, according to liberation theology, clearly leads to greater justice and humanisation in society.

Violence is theologically legitimate when it is used in the service of justice, and when non-violent means alone are inadequate to end injustice. If revolutionary violence is legitimate in Latin America for these reasons, then the question needs to be raised as to whether under similar conditions, revolutionary violence in other parts of the world is legitimate or not. The parallels between the South African situation and the Latin American situation need not be exaggerated for us to see that the lessons which come out of Latin America are remarkably appropriate for the South African crisis. One of the most forceful challenges that comes from liberation theology to the South African church is that it should test its class alliances and determine whether its ambiguous stand on violence in South Africa bolsters up the status quo of injustice or not. The careful, considered response to violence by South African Christians is critical; a response which looks at both forms of violence; number 1 and number 2, assesses the cost of revolutionary violence, and then makes a courageous judgement for justice against injustice.

# NOTES

1.  J.G. Davies, *Christians, Politics and Violent Revolution*, (Orbis: Maryknoll, N.Y., 1976), p.88.
2.  E. Dussell, *A History of the Church in Latin America*, (Eerdmans: Grand Rapids, 1981), p.127.
3.  Dussell identifies the Mexican revolution of 1910 as the precursor to the popular revolutions of the 1960s. The Mexican revolution, he says, 'signalled a new economic, cultural and political reality, namely the emergence of a new proprietor of power... that is the proletariat created by industrialisation and the rural workers together with the student population and some from the middle class.', *A History of the Church*, p.25.
4.  G. Gutiérrez, *A Theology of Liberation*, (Orbis: Maryknoll, N.Y., 1973), p.89.
5.  L. and C. Boff, *Salvation and Liberation*, (Orbis: Maryknoll, N.Y., 1984), p.24.
6.  J.L. Segundo, 'The Shift within Latin American Liberation Theology', in *Journal of Theology for Southern Africa*, 52, 1985, pp.17-29.
7.  *Ibid.*, (1985), p.24.
8.  *Ibid.*, (1985), p.23.
9.  For an extensive survey of the debate about violence from a theological and ethical perspective, see Davies, *Christians, Politics and Violent Revolution*, pp.132-187.
10. Davies, p.129.
11. D. Dorr, *Option for the Poor*, (Orbis: Maryknoll, N.Y., 1983).
12. See the two documents issued by the Congregation for the Doctrine of the Faith, (1984 and 1986).
13. Dorr, *Option for the Poor*, pp.37-49.
14. *Ibid.*, pp.87-116.
15. *Ibid.*, p.102.
16. *Ibid.*, p.146.
17. M. Walsh and B. Davies, (eds.), *Proclaiming Justice and Peace*, (Documents from John XXIII to John Paul II), (Collins: London, 1984), p.141.
18. J.L. Segundo, *Faith and Ideologies*, (Orbis: Maryknoll, N.Y., 1984), p.284.
19. Dorr, *Option for the Poor*, p.199.
20. J.W. Douglass, *The Non-Violent Cross*, (Macmillan, N.Y., 1968), pp.81-89.
21. Dussell says that what took place at Medellin 'was of imponderable importance for Latin America. It was not only the moment of the application of the Second Vatican Council, but also of the discovery of the real Latin America and the transition to a clear commitment to liberation', *A History of the Church*, p.143.
22. *The Medellin Conclusions* 2, p.16. My italics.
23. H. Camara, *Spiral of Violence*, (N.J.: Denville, 1971), p.29.
24. G. Gutiérrez, *The Power of the Poor in History*, (Orbis: Maryknoll, N.Y., 1984), p.28.
25. This is spelt out in detail in section 2:8-10 of The Medellin Conclusions.

26. This adoption of Marxist analysis has generated a very negative response from the Vatican. See especially the 1984 document of the Congregation for the Doctrine of the Faith, section VII.

27. Gutièrrez, *A Theology of Liberation*, p.115.

28. *Ibid.*, p.138.

29. C. Villa-Vicencio, *Between Christ and Caesar*, (Eerdmans: Grand Rapids, 1986), pp.137-143.

30. The usual assertion that the Church is pacifist emerges again. In the light of what the bishops are to say later in the document, this is obviously a relative pacifism.

31. As Dorr, *Option for the Poor*, p.161 points out, this reverses the order of the statement in Paul VI's *Populorum Progressio*.

32. The English edition was first published in 1973.

33. Gutièrrez, *The Theology of Liberation*, pp.108ff. The distinction between these two types of violence is central to liberation theology, as we noted above with Camara's 1st and 2nd violences.

34. *Ibid.*, p.103.

35. *Ibid.*, p.104.

36. *Ibid.*, p.49.

37. *Ibid.*, pp.91,113.

38. *Ibid.*, p.48.

39. *Ibid.*, p.262.

40. *Ibid.*, p.272.

41. J. Sobrino, *The True Church and the Poor*, (Orbis: Maryknoll, N.Y., 1984), p.163.

42. *Ibid.*, pp.171-185.

43. *Ibid.*, p.178.

44. *Ibid.*, p.172.

45. *Ibid.*, p.170.

46. *Ibid.*, p.181.

47. *Ibid.*, p.181.

48. *Ibid.*, p.181.

49. *Ibid.*, p.181.

50. Segundo has published extensively. Here we are concerned with two of his more notable works, *The Liberation of Theology*, (1976), and *Faith and Ideologies*, (1984).

51. Segundo, *The Liberation of Theology*, p.157.

52. Segundo, *Faith and Ideologies*, p.295.

53. *Ibid.*, p.282.

54. *Ibid.*, p.282.

55. *Ibid.*, p.128.

56. By 'social ecology' Segundo means 'the whole system of relations existing between human beings and their context or environment', *Faith and Ideologies*, p.285.

57. As Segundo expresses it: 'The problem immediately becomes more complicated, even when the battle is armed and visible, when it takes place between fellow citizens divided by antagonistic political ideologies', *Ibid.*, p.289.

58. *Ibid.*, p.287.

# The Ecumenical Debate: Violent Revolution and Military Disarmament

## CHARLES VILLA-VICENCIO

One of the major challenges facing humanity in the latter part of this century is the need to cope with both technological and political revolutions. Neither one can be resolved without resolving the other. Faced on the one hand with the reality of having the military capability to destroy the world, humankind is also confronted with political liberation and the right to national self-determination — rarely realised without war — as the non-negotiable political imperatives of our time. In response to these two revolutions, the ecumenical church has repeatedly called for military disarmament, while affirming the right of oppressed people to resort to revolutionary war as a means to throw off the bonds of oppression. Is there a way beyond this apparent theological contradiction? How, in an ecumenical church, does one respond to the need for both disarmament and armed rebellion? It is here that the priorities of the theological agendas of the North, of First World countries and of the major industrial powers, are at variance with those of the South, of Third World countries and of oppressed nations. If the threat of nuclear annihilation determines the mindset of Washington, Moscow and Bonn, the will to political power shapes the perspective of Soweto, Managua and Kabul.

If there be a common agenda for the two hemispheres, it is found in the underlying *causes* of violence, rather than in a single-minded response to the problem of violence itself. In the words of the World Council of Churches' recent study on political ethics, the global issue facing humanity is *'how* to confront illegitimate powers which create injustice.'[1] It is around this question that theological consensus emerges. The Second Vatican Council recognises that peace 'is more than the absence of war'. It cannot be realised by a balance of power between enemies and it cannot be brought about by dictatorship. 'Instead, it is rightly and appropriately called "an enterprise of justice" (Is.32:7)',[2] and a recent encyclical by the Vatican has again allowed that violence be used as a last resort to attain this end.[3] Dean C. Curry, in turn, expresses the desire of a conference of 1 400 evangelical Christians meeting in 1983 to respond to the threat of the Nuclear Age: 'The nuclear peril is real. Christians, therefore have an urgent responsibility, as children of the God of peace, to work at constructing a more peaceful world'.[4] Many different perceptions were expressed at that conference as to what kind of peace is possible in this world, but none questioned the inherent biblical link between justice and peace.

In a revolutionary situation such as that which prevails in South Africa and other parts of the globe, it is becoming clearer that the best way to eliminate revolutionary violence is to remove institutional violence. What this consensus fails to do is to tie up the many loose ends of the debate. Are weapons of mass destruction permissible? Is it theologically justifiable to risk total conflagration in the quest for political liberation? These are the questions that require the just war theory to be rewritten. The consensus is further challenged by the pacifist tradition which it excludes. This tradition, often forgotten by the mainstream churches, continues prophetically to haunt even the most erudite and cautious theologies of violence. It has only rarely been tested in human history, and in its most celebrated form by a Hindu thinker. Yet this too is a costly tradition, and those who abuse it as a means of trying to escape paying the price demanded for the eradication of injustice, need to hear the challenge of Mohandas Gandhi's judgement that if cowardice is the only alternative to violence, it is better to choose violence.[5]

## FROM DESCRIPTIVE ETHICS TO PROPHETIC CHALLENGE

The documentation of the response of the ecumenical church to the threat of militarisation and to the armed rebellion of oppressed people is readily available, and this history need only be referred to in passing.[6] The devastation of World War II and the dawn of the atomic age in the bombing of Hiroshima and Nagasaki awakened the church to the urgent need for disarmament. Pius II called the people of God to pray for peace, conscious that

> technology has introduced and prepared such murderous and

unhuman weapons as can destroy...innocent children with their mothers, those who are sick and the helpless aged. Whatever the genius of man has produced that is beautiful and good and holy, all of this can be practically annihilated.[7]

The WCC Amsterdam Assembly in 1948 similarly condemned the indiscriminate destruction wrought by atomic weapons, arguing that 'the tradition of a just war, requiring a just cause and the use of just means, is now challenged. Law may require the sanction of force, but when war breaks out, force is used on a scale which tends to destroy the basis on which law exists'.[8]

Appalled as both the WCC and the Vatican were by the destructive power of modern military technology, they did not simply demand disarmament but went on to address the connection between peace and justice in their eager pursuit of a nuclear-free world, or with a world in which weapons of mass destruction would be strictly controlled. Yet it was primarily Pope John XXIII who showed up the two violations to peace in the most devastating and stark contrast, as he pointed to the necessity of resolving the contradiction that exists between 'the spectre of misery and hunger' and the use of 'scientific discoveries, technical inventions and economic resources...to provide terrible instruments of ruin and death'.[9] Neither the Vatican nor the WCC were ready to prescribe answers, recognising essentially three broad positions within the church:[10]

*Firstly,* there is the position which allows that although participating in a war may be one's Christian responsibility in particular circumstances, the use of weapons of mass destruction as used in modern warfare can never be regarded as justifiable.

*Secondly,* there is the position of those who argue that it is the responsibility of Christians to resort to violence in certain extreme situations, whatever the cost involved. Some within this category may believe that the demise of the planet would not be too much to pay for the defence of their particular 'faith' whether it be the Western free-enterprise system or Soviet domination. Others are more realistically driven to concede that when all other options have been tried 'chains are worse than bayonets'.[11]

*Thirdly,* there is the pacifist position which affirms an absolute witness against all forms of violence, including war.

The common ingredient which ultimately haunts all people of goodwill who fit into any one of these positions is the recognition that on most occasions the church is required to minister in a situation where violence is already prevalent. In this context the question is how to reduce the extent of violence and how to humanise the means of conflict.

While the church has never completely moved beyond this descriptive phase to dogmatic prescription, the Second Vatican Council (1962-65) and the third assembly of the WCC (New Delhi, 1961) mark the beginning of a shift from a descriptive ethic to a more concrete prophetic ethic. 'The Pastoral Constitution on the Church in the Modern World' *(Gaudium et Spes),* addressed itself to both disarmament and social justice, giving attention to 'problems of special urgency' in politics and socio-economic existence.[12] The New Delhi Assembly called for a halt to the arms race, and prepared the ground for the ecumenical attack on all forms of poverty, disease, exploitation, ignorance and discrimination on the grounds of status, race, sex or creed.[13]

A further development in the ecumenical debate, directly related to our concerns in this essay, in which the church addressed the relationship between disarmament and social justice, emerged in the late sixties and early seventies. This is seen in relation to the Fourth Assembly of the WCC held in Uppsala in 1968 and the Second Vatican Council. It is, however, perhaps most clearly focused in the meeting of the WCC Commission of the Churches on International Affairs (CCIA) in West Berlin in August 1974, which directly considered the effects of militarisation, militarism and the arms race on human rights and socio-political development.[14] The acceptance of this report by the WCC Central Committee, led in turn, to the Nairobi Assembly adopting a statement entitled 'The World Armaments Situation'. This gave rise to a new level of commitment to disarmament, an ecumenical program against militarism and the arms race, and a renewed determination to eliminate racism and oppression in the world. At the same time it was resolved that 'the Program to Combat Racism, including the Special Fund ... be strengthened and its scope increased'.[15] And in some ways it was the reality of this program together with its concern, through the special fund, to supply humanitarian aid to liberation armies fighting for the overthrow of *de facto* minority governments in southern Africa (to be discussed in more detail later) which forced the churches to take seriously the relationship between disarmament and violent revolution.

A shift had taken place from abstraction to specificity and from analysis to prophecy. The focus of the ecumenical church was now on the major revolutions in both technology and politics.

## DISARMAMENT

The resolutions and declarations of the WCC, together with the papal encyclicals and instructions of the Vatican, demonstrate a definite contextual approach followed during the period under consideration. Specific political and military global flash-points have been addressed and proposals made concerning arms sales and the testing of nuclear weapons.

The Nairobi Assembly, as already suggested, introduced a new sense of urgency into the debate, drawing attention to the ambiguities of the technological revolution.[16] Phillip Potter, addressing the United Nations' First Special Session on Disarmament, in turn introduced a qualitatively new set of elements into the disarmament debate by pointing out the use of science and technology by the intellectual élite in alliance with business, political and military sectors, to manufacture weapons at an ever accelerating rate. Arms production has become a significant part of the national economic infrastructure of developed countries, with foreign trade dimensions of this resource contributing directly both to the promotion of armed conflicts in the Third World and to the dependency of client states on supplier nations. Access to these kinds of sophisticated arms and surveillance equipment, in turn, becomes a major contributing factor to the existence and survival of military dictatorships and police states in both First and Third World countries. Finally, Potter refers to future generations of even more destructive conventional and nuclear weapons which can only lead to a proliferation of militarised states and a lowering of the nuclear threshold.[17] These developments make disarmament not only a necessary strategy for survival, but an integral part of the larger struggle for a 'just, participatory and sustainable society'. It is furthermore this gathering of resources, as increasingly used in police and military states, which makes revolutionary violence appear as one of the last options for removing a government from power.

Pope Paul VI's message to the United Nations' General Assembly at a Special Session on Disarmament in 1978 raises many similar issues.[18] Subsequent Vatican addresses to heads of state and political groups, together with its response to different world crises show an ecumenical consensus on disarmament and social justice which extends well beyond the confines of the WCC. This point becomes quite clear in the Message adopted by the *Life and Peace Christian World Conference* held in Uppsala in

1983. The Message reads: 'For the victims of injustice the struggle for peace makes little sense, unless linked to justice'. Then, giving special attention to the contribution by oppressed people at that conference, the potential division within the ecumenical debate on disarmament is addressed:

> The present catastrophe of millions starving to death and suffering injustice is of a higher priority for the poor and the oppressed of the world than the impending nuclear catastrophe. The peoples of the Third World remind us that the struggle for peace involves more than overcoming the perils of violent conflict. It means taking initiatives to create a world in which relationships between nations are based on a more equitable economic and moral order.[19]

At the 1982 World Alliance of Reformed Churches' conference, a delegate from an African country poignantly identified the place of justice in the disarmament debate. Referring to a statement handed out at the conference, he said: 'In this document, the word "nuclear" is used a number of times, but I don't even see the word "hunger". In my village, the people will not understand the word "nuclear", but they know everything about hunger and poverty.'[20] The high-water mark of the ecumenical debate emerges when disarmament is discussed in relation to political and socio-economic justice. When disarmament is debated in isolation from justice, the debate is limited to the North Atlantic. Said a participant in the Uppsala Peace Conference: 'While First World Christians talk of beating swords into ploughshares, Third World Christians are compelled to turn ploughs into swords and pruning-hooks into spears'. However, when disarmament is debated in relation to militarised rule and related demands for justice, the disarmament debate takes on direct significance, for oppressed people in both hemispheres. Bernard Criek, writing in *In Defence of Politics* identifies what he perceives to be an inherent link between technology and totalitarianism, which he defines as 'probably the only distinctively modern type of rule and form of violence' which is in direct contradistinction to normative participatory politics.[21]

This awareness of the threat that the technological revolution poses not only to life itself, but also to democratic politics and the freedom of individuals soon spills over into a specific dimension of the disarmament debate — namely, the various calls for nuclear deterrence and disarmament. Such proposals have not only generated extensive debate in political and theological circles, but have intensified the determination of the major military powers to maintain their nuclear capabilities and, in specific areas, to expand these resources. In so doing politicians have maligned the churches and nuclear disarmament groups and lobbies for alleged naïveté, while often ignoring the cautious proposals made by many of these groups. The U.S. Catholic Bishops have, for example, affirmed multilateral nuclear disarmament as an *ultimate* goal. Yet, they support deterrence as a necessary *immediate* strategy, provided there by a serious movement by the nuclear nations towards the goal of ultimate disarmament.[22] It can reasonably be assumed that other churches share a similar two-fold response to the challenge of nuclear weapons. The different dimensions of the ecumenical debate are well documented in the record of the Public Hearing on Nuclear Weapons and Disarmament organised by the WCC.[23] What emerges from this debate is not only the place of nuclear weapons in war as such, but as a means to world domination. When one relates this to the refusal of certain smaller countries, including South Africa, to sign the nuclear non-proliferation treaty, the continuum between conventional and nuclear weapons in both global and national institutionalised oppression becomes apparent.

Dom Helder Camara's description of the spiral of violence makes self-evident the necessary link between the ecumenical church's commitment to disarmament and its cautious support for revolutionary violence.[24] He identifies structural violence or injustice as the beginning of the spiral. Revolutionary violence by the oppressed, he argues, is an inevitable response to this kind of institutionalised oppression, and the consequent repressive violence of the state is, in turn, almost as inevitable a response to revolution. When the disarmament debate is related to the eradication of the root cause of violence, which is maintained by military and police oppression, what could be a debate not overtly related to the perceived needs of oppressed people takes on obvious and pertinent significance. In this moment the importance of this ecumenical debate and the political significance of the unity of the church is rediscovered.

## ARMED REVOLUTION

The period between the WCC's New Delhi Assembly (1961) and Uppsala (1968) was one of intense political activity. The official report on the 1968 Assembly set the stage for a new phase in the ecumenical struggle against racism: 'The struggle for racial equality, dignity and self-respect... is rapidly reaching a climax. The ominous events which have taken place since New Delhi, 1961, oblige us to promote new efforts to eliminate racism'.[25] During this period the world had witnessed successful liberation struggles in various parts of Africa, but also the intensification of the war against Portuguese colonialism in what was then Portuguese Guinea, Moçambique and Angola.

The Civil Rights Bill had been passed in the United States, while Martin Luther King, who was to have delivered the opening sermon in Uppsala, had been assassinated. Sharpeville, taking place shortly before the New Delhi Assembly, had incurred intensified brutality and oppression. Albert Luthuli was banned, and Nelson Mandela and others imprisoned. The African National Congress (ANC) and the Pan-African Congress had been forced underground, and *Umkhonto We Sizwe* (the armed wing of the ANC) established. This period of intensified African nationalism which witnessed an explicit incorporation of the armed struggle into a hitherto non-violent struggle is described in an essay elsewhere in this volume.

In the meantime the number of WCC member-churches from the Third World had increased from 42 in 1948 to 103 out of a total of 253 member churches in 1968. There were 41 African member churches, with the majority coming from independent Africa. The stage was set for a changed World Council.[26] Issues of social justice and the unquestionable right of peoples to self-determination and political liberation were to be addressed in a decisive manner.

The WCC's involvement in South Africa had also taken a decisive turn. In December 1960 WCC representatives met with delegates of South African churches, including three white Dutch Reformed churches. The conclusions of the consultation, cautious as they were, called into question the theological legitimation of apartheid. H.F. Verwoerd, Prime Minister at the time, reprimanded the DRC theologians for their part in the proceedings, and soon these churches withdrew their membership from the WCC. The English-speaking churches continued their membership, but ultimately found themselves trapped within the racist socio-political structures of South African society. The world church, in turn, committed itself to intensify its fight against apartheid.

The New Delhi Assembly had sent a message to South African Christians to fight all forms of discrimination both in the churches and in society. An important turning point in the ecumenical debate came at the Mindolo Consultation on Church and Society in 1964, when it was recognised that the refusal of various governments and colonial powers in Africa to negotiate with African peoples, together with increased military repression, had resulted in a situation in which many African leaders saw no alternative to armed revolution which 'was never desired nor sought'.[27] This event was followed by a World Conference on Church and Society in Geneva held in 1966. Here it was recognised that the 'mere sentimental harmonizing of conflicting groups' in situations such as those prevailing on the African continent was not enough. The church was called on to show *solidarity* with the oppressed in their struggle against the oppressor.[28]

The stage was set for Uppsala, and for the emergence of the Program to Combat Racism (PCR).[29] The Uppsala Assembly confessed it had done 'too little too late' to eliminate racism, and committed itself to the 'elimination of racism throughout the world'. A Consultation on Racism held at Notting Hill near London in 1969 proposed the establishment of the PCR, and the WCC Central Committee endorsed this proposal the same year. With this a new phase in ecumenical relations emerged, and the WCC committed itself to political, economic and social pressure on those recalcitrant regimes in Africa and elsewhere, as identified at the Mindolo Consultation, who refused to negotiate with their oppressed peoples — driving many of their leaders to armed revolution. Then, in 1970, the crunch came. A list was published of those organisations which would receive financial aid from the Special Fund established to fight racism. Among these were liberation movements committed to an armed struggle to overthrow the colonial minority governments in several southern African states. The South African white establishment initiated a cry which was picked up around the world: 'The WCC has committed itself to support terrorism!'. The explanation of the WCC that their funding was 'for humanitarian purposes consonant with the aims and policies' of the world body was lost in the heat of conflict. Perhaps the most soul-shattering realisation for white South Africans with feet firmly planted in the church was the realisation that those whom they had been led to dismiss as 'communists' and 'terrorists' were being affirmed by the world as Christians. The near-paranoid response from South African member-churches need not be discussed here.[30] Suffice it to say that despite renewed and sustained pressure from the South

African government on these churches to resign from the WCC they refused, to their credit, to do so.

The WCC regarded the grants in question as a 'combination of political judgement and support for humanitarian programs of a particular group or movement'. While stating that violence is inherent to the maintenance of oppressive regimes, 'the WCC does not and cannot identify itself completely with any political movement, nor does it pass judgement on those victims of racism who are driven to violence as the only way left to redress grievances and so open the way for a new and more just social order'. The WCC was not 'attempting to show another better way to liberation'. It argued that it would amount to gross insensitivity and paternalism to prescribe to oppressed people how to behave, after they had for generations tried other ways to attain liberation, and reluctantly now felt compelled to take up arms as a last resort. Yet, careful not to surrender prophetic independence, the General Secretary of the WCC in referring to a decision of the WCC Central Committee taken in Addis Ababa in 1971, expressed the position of his Council: 'As always our support is to be seen as a sign of *solidarity* which should be clearly distinguished from *identification* with a movement'.[31] Kenneth Kaunda, who had taken Zambia to independence less than a decade earlier, articulated the sentiments of many black South Africans when he called the decision to fund liberation movements 'the WCC's visionary action ... which may well be seen in the future as decisive for the church's fate in southern Africa'.[32]

Any hesitation which might have existed in the WCC concerning support for the liberation movements was dispelled with the banning of a number of individuals and organisations by the South African government in 1977. The world saw this as a further indication of the unwillingness of the South African government to allow legal, non-violent protest and political opposition in the country.

An equally important milestone concerning the funding of political movements occurred with the much publicised decision by the WCC to exclude those black nationalist movements which had joined the so-called 'internal settlement' of the Rhodesian conflict. Henceforth it would be only the Patriotic Front under the joint leadership of Robert Mugabe and Joshua Nkomo that would receive funds allocated for humanitarian aid to liberation movements fighting against the Smith regime. Criticism of this political decision by the WCC culminated in outrage from some member churches, particularly in the United States, Britain and the Federal Republic of West Germany. The Salvation Army and the Presbyterian Church in Ireland suspended their membership of the WCC, and the Church of England, with the 1978 Lambeth Conference in session, decided to review its membership. This resulted in a special background paper on South Africa which identified the key theological and ethical criteria operative in the PCR grants, and discussed some of the issues and dilemmas evident in the debate at the time.[33] A series of consultations on combatting racism were held throughout the world in the 1980s, and several important papers were produced on the theological and ethical nature of the program.[34] The outcome was an international consultation on racism held at Noordwijkerhout in the Netherlands, which endorsed both the PCR and the special fund established to fund liberation movements, one consequence being a significant change in attitude by member churches to a program that was regarded by some member churches in the West as 'anathema'. At the 1983 Vancouver Assembly of the WCC the debate on the PCR passed without rancour or much debate and a new era for the church's funding of liberation movements given to the violent overthrow of oppressive governments had apparently dawned.

Much has happened since then. In 1985 a 'partial' State of Emergency was declared, and 1986 saw the proclamation of a general State of Emergency in South Africa which has continued into 1987. Violence spread throughout the country, the freedom of the press was severely curtailed, leaders detained and organisations restricted in their work. As the options for peaceful change are reduced, it becomes increasingly difficult to censure people who affirm the 'last resort' criteria of the just war theory which allows Christians to take up arms. The theological significance of this cautious step by the WCC in recognising the legitimacy of armed revolution continues to be debated.

On the Roman Catholic side a similar trend has developed. Pope John XXIII heralded a new era in Roman Catholic social teaching with the publication of *Mater et Magistra* in 1961, although all that was to follow was in continuation with the dominant tradition of the church as articulated by Thomas Aquinas and others. The Pope's next encyclical, *Pacem in Terris,* published during Vatican II, took the debate a step further:

> 'Government authority', he insisted, '... is a postulate of the moral order and derives from God. Consequently, laws and

decrees passed in contravention of the moral order, and hence
of the divine will, can have no binding force in conscience,
since 'it is right to obey God rather than man'. Indeed the
passing of such laws undermines the very nature of authority
and results in shameful abuse.'[35]

The Vatican II documents addressed this theme more
specifically, arguing that 'where citizens are oppressed by a public
authority overstepping its competence ... it is legitimate for them
to defend their own rights and the rights of their fellow citizens
against abuse of this authority ....'[36] Roman Catholic teaching on
revolution became even more explicit when Paul VI encouraged
the Latin American bishops to relate the doctrinal renewal of the
church to their own situations.[37] In his opening address to the
General Conference of Latin American Catholic Bishops meeting
in Medellin in 1968, he sought for 'another way', rejecting violence
as an unacceptable remedy to injustice, because it gives rise to
worse evils, while allowing that there might be certain rare
exceptions to this general guideline. The Medellin Conference
changed the papal emphasis, allowing firstly that revolutionary
insurrection might sometimes be legitimate, and *then* warning
that it generally gives rise to new injustices.[38] As in the case of the
WCC response through the PCR to revolutionary violence, so the
Roman Catholic debate on revolutionary violence has continued.
Again, this debate cannot be pursued here. It is enough to note
that the recent *Instruction* of the Vatican's Congregation for the
Doctrine of Faith reaffirms the traditional and formal ethical
criteria of the church, allowing for 'armed struggle, which the
Church's magisterium admits as a last resort to put an end to an
obvious and prolonged tyranny which is gravely damaging the
fundamental rights of individuals and the common good.'[39]

As in the case of the disarmament debate, an ecumenical
consensus has also emerged in relation to a theological response
to revolution. It is a cautious consensus which does not promote
revolutionary violence but seeks rather to understand it as an
inevitable response to a situation where violence is already part of
the existing order. It is a consensus which recognises that the
institutional church, so often removed from the actual point of
conflict, is not in a position to dictate to those who bear the brunt
of a violent regime, nor is it in a position to pass moral
judgement on a revolution engaged in as a last resort. Its task is
rather to stand in solidarity with the oppressed, and from this
position to exercise both a pastoral and prophetic ministry in the

situation. This ministry must necessarily include a continuing critique of all ideological persuasions and programs of action, including the commitment to armed rebellion. For the church to fail to do this is to drift into either implicit or explicit legitimation of the revolution. Such action must ultimately be counter-revolutionary, and every bit as ideologically oppressive as the age-old legitimation of the ruling class which the church has accomplished with such skill.

The ecumenical church, at least at the level of theology if not praxis, has sought to affirm precisely this distinction: While having admitted the necessity of being on the side of the oppressed people of the world, the church has maintained a careful distinction between 'solidarity' and 'identification'. The tragedy is that large sectors of the institutional church have not tried to show any kind of solidarity with the poor.

## WHERE PEACE AND JUSTICE MEET

The dual ecumenical realisation that disarmament and socio-political equity, or peace and justice, cannot be separated is grounded in theological as well as political reality. Biblical and traditional theological teaching on peace and justice is grounded in the sense of well-being, wholeness, health and human dignity portrayed in the Hebrew word *shalom*. This is a concept which includes individualised 'personal peace' but never promotes it at the cost of the biblical promise of corporate peace and justice. This vision of peace and justice always incorporates an eschatological dimension which impinges in both grace and judgement on any particular manifestation of social justice in a particular nation. Yet, it is always more than a future hope. It is a quality of life realisable in the present through Christ whose gift is peace, abundant living and good news to the poor.

So powerful a motivation is this biblical incentive to peace with justice that history provides ample evidence for suggesting that the dominant political problem facing the world is not violence but the need to confront those illegitimate powers which are responsible for injustice and deny peace. The dominant consensus of the church is that non-violent means should be used if at all possible to accomplish this end. However, as is clear from all that has been written in this book, when such methods fail, the consensus also allows that restrained violence for a specific just end be permitted. Absolute pacifism has never been more than a minority theme within Christendom, although always one that haunts the more dominant tradition of reluctant if justified violence.

This is not to suggest that the violence versus non-violence debate is not a major issue in political ethics. Pertinent questions arise concerning the extent to which the means of a process are inherent to its end. To what extent does a violent war of liberation carry violence into the new society? What does violence do to the character of the person who carries it out, and how does it affect the values of a society born from such violence?

These are painful questions which *must* disturb anyone concerned about the quality of a post-revolutionary South Africa, but the central query remains: Does history provide any evidence of a *less* costly means to liberation when fighting against a ruthless oppressor? Fate seems to compel many leaders of the oppressed to resort to the use of force against injustice. When such leaders stand within a tradition which counsels them to love their neighbours and to turn the other cheek, their torment is terrible. Non-violent ways to radical peaceful change appear to be effective only against regimes which find their authority in a commitment to justice and tolerance, rather than in ruthless tyranny.[40] Such ways are also only likely to succeed where the hegemony and self-determination of the rulers is not about to be wrest totally from them. In India, only Britain's colonial power was at stake, while home-rule was never in question when Gandhi's non-violent resistance achieved its aim, and in the United States the black population constituted only ten percent of the entire American population when Martin Luther King's passive resistance campaign achieved its desired effect. It would also be naïve not to recognise that other 'violent' factors, including the presence of more militant revolutionary leaders, contributed significantly to the non-violent means employed by Gandhi and King. Above all it would be naïve not to recognise the cost in lives which such 'non-violent' struggles exacted. In South Africa more than colonial power is at stake, with whites recognising that their privileged 'way of life' cannot survive in a new South Africa. It is 'home-rule' that is threatened. In fact there is no obvious historical evidence of a privileged ruling class ever having surrendered power without blood being spilled in armed revolution. South Africa is involved in more than a civil rights struggle; the very socio-economic identity of the country is at stake.

The inherent link between disarmament and social justice is

nowhere more clear than in the recent highly-publicised exchange of views between Nelson Mandela and P.W. Botha. Botha announced that he was prepared to consider Mandela's release from Pollsmoor provided he gave a commitment not to:

> ...make himself guilty of planning, instigating or committing acts of violence for the furtherance of political objectives. It is therefore not the South African government which now stands in the way of Mr Mandela's freedom. It is he himself. The choice is his. All that is required of him now is that he should unconditionally reject violence as a political instrument.[41]

Mandela's reply was uncompromising:

> ...I am surprised at the conditions that the government wants to impose on me. I am not a violent man. My colleagues and I wrote in 1952 to Malan asking for a round table conference...
>
> When Strijdom was in power, we made the same offer. Again it was ignored.
>
> When Verwoerd was in power we asked for a National Convention for all the people in South Africa to decide on their future. This, too, was in vain.
>
> It was only then when all other forms of resistance were no longer open to us that we turned to armed struggle.
>
> Let Botha show that he is different to Malan, Strijdom and Verwoerd. Let him renounce violence. Let him say that he will dismantle apartheid....Let him guarantee free political activity so that the people may decide who will govern them.[42]

Simply stated, the renunciation of violence by the ANC is simply not realistic while the government has access to what is arguably the most sophisticated military force in Africa to maintain power. Yet, it is also clear that the South African regime cannot commit itself to a multilateral program of demilitarisation and open political activity without surrendering power. In this situation the options are threefold:

— An escalation of war as both sides in the conflict vie for victory. The likely consequence is a situation in which there is little left for either side to inherit.

— A second option is a protracted process of piece-meal reform. While some argue that this could lead to certain basic changes taking place over an extended period of time, the intensity of the present conflict is such that 'time' is simply not available.

— The third option consists of negotiations between the two

sides leading to a mutually acceptable, even if compromised, settlement.

It is this last option, aimed at bringing the South African government and the ANC to the negotiation table, which is presently being pursued by a variety of groups, including the ecumenical church, both inside and outside the country. For this to happen it is clear that the government will have to be persuaded by various forms of political, diplomatic and economic pressures to negotiate a new dispensation which will satisfy the basic needs and aspirations of the black majority in the country. The liberation movements, in turn, need to be persuaded that it is in *their* interest to negotiate. In other words, that there is sufficient likelihood of such a process bringing about the transfer of power to a majority government in spite of the guarantees demanded by the white minority.

The point being made here is the obvious one: peace is simply not possible without justice. If the ecumenical church pursues either its disarmament program or its support, however cautious, for movements compelled to resort to violent revolution, without giving due attention to the other position, it would be in danger of destroying the realistic basis of peace and justice incorporated in the biblical ideal of *shalom*. It would also be in danger of losing sight of a tried and tested piece of political realism which teaches us that people have over the years been prepared to pay a devastating price in the pursuit of justice. It is also necessary to recognise that the ideals of justice are all too often lost sight of in violent conflict. This realisation makes justice an absolute political priority. Yet, ultimately it is *political realism* itself, which makes justice a non-negotiable pre-requisite for peace, that needs to be sought. President Kaunda's observation in this regard, grounded in his own participation in African liberation politics, is worth noting:

> ...just stopping the war would leave all the major issues unresolved.... The result of an unlikely conversion to non-violence must be paralysis rather than peace because the hard questions are left hanging in the air. Once a war of liberation has begun, it must be fought through to a verdict — anything short of that must leave the *status quo* with the advantage and the freedom forces, because they are invariably less well equipped, will pay a heavy price for little return.[43]

Violence simply cannot be suspended without a celebration of justice for all who are involved in the conflict.

## TOWARDS A PROGRAM FOR PEACE

The ecumenical church has come to recognise that to affirm the ministry of Jesus as the Prince of Peace can never be merely an abstract goal. The biblical doctrine of peace always implies more than an absence of war and a reluctance on the part of the oppressed to resist. The pursuit of peace in fact often involves both war and resistance. It involves the elimination of those structures of injustice which prevent the hungry from being fed, the naked from being clothed, prison doors from being opened and the oppressed from being set free.

This pursuit of peace requires an ecumenical commitment to destroy the forces of oppression. The involvement by the churches in disarmament programs aimed at the elimination of militarism is part of this commitment. This involvement has direct implications for South Africa. The exchange of military technology, the sale of nuclear skills to South Africa and the expanding military build-up is possibly the single most important factor militating against democratic rule in this country. The End Conscription Campaign in South Africa, so severely restricted by government action, represents at another level not only the refusal of individuals to involve themselves in the military might used against neighbouring countries and in black townships to entrench the apartheid regime, but also a potential undermining of the morale and military strength of the country. The call for economic sanctions against South Africa, sports boycotts, cultural and academic boycotts and related programs all represent attempts by people of goodwill inside the country and around the world to eliminate the structures of oppression in non-violent ways. The ecumenical church has held on with resolve to non-violent options for change in South Africa, even in the face of the most convincing evidence against the likely success of these options. This basic theological commitment, coupled with a human reluctance to pay the price of possible mass destruction, is too often deliberately ignored by those reactionary forces committed to entrench the church on the side of the dominant class.

A careful consideration of the decision to provide humanitarian aid to liberation armies fighting a recalcitrant and oppressive South African regime allows for no more than a limited and reluctant realisation that there comes a moment in the history of people when those who suffer most feel compelled to resort to arms. It is also a realisation that in this situation the church is

obliged to minister to those who suffer most. What is significant is
that this cautious decision by the WCC is criticised most heavily
from the left in the black community in South Africa. It is still
regarded, almost twenty years after Uppsala, as 'too little too late'.

## AN UNCONCLUDING POSTSCRIPT

> Jesus came closer to the city, and when he saw it, he wept
> over it, saying, 'If you only knew today what is needed for
> peace! But now you cannot see it. The time will come when
> your enemies will surround you with barricades, blockade you,
> and close in on you from every side. They will completely
> destroy you and the people within your walls; not a single stone
> will they leave in its place, because you did not recognise the
> time when God came to save you.' (Luke 20:41-44)

The church is no less blinded by ideology from *seeing* what
makes for peace than the state. Yet the church which is obedient
to the gospel of Jesus is compelled to hear the cries of the
widows and orphans, the sick and the lame, prisoners and
oppressed people — those who are marginalised by the powerful
and the strong in society. This is not because the weak are
inherently less avaricious, potentially less exploitative, or
intrinsically more egalitarian than the powerful. It is rather because
social and historical circumstances are such that they are
prevented from being avaricious, exploitative and class-dominant.
The prophetic tradition of Judeo-Christianity emphasises that it is
the task of a prophetic church to represent those whose interests
are not adequately accounted for in the political equations of
society. This is primarily because in situations where the poor are
excluded from the political process, there is no one else to
represent them. The church also knows that peace is not possible
until the injustices of society are redressed.

The ecumenical commitment to support disarmament has to
do with the powerful learning to trust not in violence but in justice
for legitimate authority. The cautious support for those resorting
to violence as a means of resisting oppression is an affirmation of
the God-given right of the oppressed to be free. The commitment
to both disarmament and social revolution is a challenge to
promote social change without violence.

Yet it is a realistic challenge which recognises that justice may
not be possible without violence. This reluctant realisation has
caused some to suggest that the only remaining type of violence
which can possibly warrant the title of a 'just war' — if there be

such a type of violence at all — is revolution by a disciplined liberation army fighting against a tyranny.[44] This is a conviction grounded in the realisation that institutionalised violence, however disguised by legislation and custom, is ultimately intrinsically more evil than revolutionary violence. If for no other reason, this is because the latter is an attempt to destroy existing evil while the former is designed to entrench it, and ultimately because institutionalised violence always precedes and precipitates revolutionary violence.

The task of the Christian, called to be a peace-maker, is to diminish the power of the oppressor as a means to eliminate the major source of evil. The commandment to love one's enemies and to respect the sanctity of life demands that this be accomplished with a minimum loss of life. This theological qualification leaves some revolutionaries arguing that they are ready to dialogue and collaborate with the church, but not treat it as an equal partner in revolution.[45] It can also be argued that the gospel protects the revolution from ultimately devouring its own children.[46] Such a gospel is more revolutionary than anything the most militant revolutionary can offer.

## NOTES

1. Koson Srisang (ed.), *Perspectives on Political Ethics*, (Geneva: WCC Publications, 1983), p.31.
2. *Gaudium et Spes*, in Michael Walsh and Brian Davies (eds.), *Proclaiming Justice and Peace*, (London: Collins, 1984), pp.81-140.
3. Congregation for the Doctrine of the Faith, *Instruction on Christian Freedom and Liberation*, (Vatican City, 1986), p.47.
4. Dean C. Curry (ed.) *Evangelicals and the Bishops' Pastoral Letter*, (Grand Rapids: Eerdmans, 1984), p.209.
5. John J. Ansbro, *Martin Luther King, Jr.*, (Maryknoll: Orbis Press, 1982), p.139.
6. *Peace and Disarmament: Documents of the World Council of Churches and the Roman Catholic Church*. Published jointly by the World Council of Churches' Commission on International Affairs and the Pontifical Commission 'Institutia et Pax', 1982. For PCR resolutions see *inter alia*, *PCR Information: WCC Statements and Actions on Racism 1948-1979*, (Geneva: WCC Publications, 1979).
7. *Peace and Disarmament*, p.109.
8. *Ibid.*, p.15.
9. *Ibid.*, p.110.
10. *Ibid.*, p.15. Also *Violence, Non-Violence and Civil Conflict*, (Geneva: WCC, 1983), p.11.
11. The Victorian writer, Douglas Jerrold, quoted in Kenneth D. Kaunda, *Kaunda On Violence*, (London: Collins, 1980), p.168.
12. In Walsh and Davies, *Proclaiming Justice and Peace*, pp.81-140.
13. W.A. Visser 't Hooft, *The New Delhi Report*, (Geneva: WCC, 1961).

14. *Peace and Disarmament,* pp.72-75.
15. David M. Paton (ed.), *Breaking Barriers: Nairobi 1975,* (London: SPCK; Grand Rapids: Eerdmans, 1976), pp.179-182; 305-308.
16. *Ibid.,* pp.119-141.
17. *Peace and Disarmament,* pp.86-7.
18. *Ibid.,* pp.206-214.
19. See the published *Message* of the Conference, April 20-24, 1983.
20. Allan Boesak, 'Jesus Christ the Light of the World', in *Journal of Theology for Southern Africa,* No.45, December 1983, p.52.
21. Bernard Criek, *In Defence of Politics,* (London: Penguin Books, 1964), p.19.
22. Philip J. Murnion (ed.), *Catholics and Nuclear War: A Commentary on the Challenge to Peace. The U.S. Catholic Bishops' Letter on War and Peace,* (New York: Crossroad Publishing Co., 1983).
23. Paul Albrecht and Ninan Koshy (eds.), *Before It's Too Late,* (Geneva: WCC, 1983).
24. Helder Camara, *Spiral of Violence,* (London: Sheed and Ward, 1971).
25. *The Uppsala Report: The Report of the Fourth Assembly of the World Council of Churches,* (Geneva: WCC, 1968), p.241.
26. Elisabeth Adler, *A Small Beginning,* (Geneva: WCC, 1974), p.5.
27. *Ibid.,* p.6.
28. See the *Official Report: World Conference on Church and Society,* (Geneva: WCC, 1967).
29. For a full discussion of the emergence of the Programme to Combat Racism see Elisabeth Adler, *A Small Beginning.*
30. See C. Villa-Vicencio, 'Why Are We Afraid of the PCR?', *South African Outlook,* February 1982.
31. Quotations are from a letter written by the General Secretary of the WCC, Dr P. Potter, to the Netherlands Reformed Church, dated 2 November 1978. For the Addis Ababa statement see *WCC Statements and Actions on Racism 1948-1979,* pp.32-34.
32. Kaunda, *Kaunda on Violence* p.121. Also pp.131-132 for Kaunda's response to the distinction made between humanitarian and arms aid.
33. *PCR Information: Reports and Background Papers,* (Geneva: WCC), No.1/1979, p.17ff.
34. *Ibid.,* No.4/1980.
35. John XXIII, *Pacem in Terris,* in Walsh and Davies, *Proclaiming Justice and Peace,* pp.48-76.
36. *Gaudium et Spes, Ibid.,* pp.81-140.
37. E. Dussel, *A History of the Christian Church in Latin America Colonialism to Liberation.* (Grand Rapids: Eerdmans, 1981), p.140.
38. D. Dorr, *Option for the Poor: A Hundred Years of Vatican Social Teaching,* (Maryknoll: Orbis Books, 1983), p.161.
39. Congregation for the Doctrine of the Faith, *Instruction on Christian Freedom and Liberation,* (Vatican City, 1983), p.161.
40. David Bandey, 'Violence and the Christian Conscience', in *Journal of Theology for Southern Africa,* No.4, September 1973, p.49.
41. *Cape Times,* 1 February 1985.
42. *Weekly Mail,* 15 February, 1985. A report on a gathering held in the Jabulani stadium in Soweto on February 10 to celebrate the award of the Nobel Peace Prize to Desmond Tutu, at which Zinzi Mandela read out her father's reply to Botha's speech.

43. Kaunda, *Kaunda on Violence* p.86.
44. Bandey, ' Violence and the Christain Conscience', p.48.
45. Gonzalo Arroyo, 'Christians, the Church and the Revolution', in John Eagleson (ed.), *Christians and Socialism,* (New York: Orbis Books, 1975), pp.228-246.
46. Paul Lehmann, *The Transfiguration of Politics,* (New York: Harper and Row, 1975), pp.41-48.

# Women, Violence and Theology

DENISE ACKERMANN

Do women, as women, have an alternative option to offer our divided and increasingly violent society? In grappling with this question, I have become convinced of the validity of one of the basic insights of the feminist movement, namely that the personal and the political are intrinsically connected. This insight is the basis for the following discussion on women and violence in South African society. Violence has many facets and occurs in myriad forms. Certain aspects of the violence engendered by apartheid which affect the lives of women will be dealt with. After analysing a few areas relevant to women's situation in our society, a feminist theological option will be sought which may offer hope and direction in our present impasse.

Feminist theology starts with the naming of women's experience. The act of naming is public, exposing the evil of patriarchal structures to the world. This immediately makes it a political act. Feminist theology cannot view redemption as exclusively private or exclusively social and systematic: self and society are bound together in close dialectic. Putting people before society has been called a 'delusion of evangelicalism'.[1] Feminist theology stands for the interconnectedness of everything and against splitting and separateness.

When this insight is applied to the connection between politics and military violence on the one hand, and the personal violence of wife- or child-battering on the other, it means that the politics of peace have to take both 'private' and 'public' into account.[2] As Andrea Dworkin has written: 'If you want real peace (meaning an end to rape as well as war) ... you know that there must ... be real justice (meaning for women and children as well as for men)'.[3]

Naming our experience implies that we women have to raise our level of awareness by recounting our stories to each other, by listening one to the other and by manifesting sincere respect for the humanity of the other in our exchange. Consciousness-raising is a subversive activity because it is not satisfied with the mere subjective exorcising of hurt and twisted images. It seeks to liberate and restore by examining the social praxis in which we find ourselves. The structures in the group and in society that exclude or discriminate against us, depriving us of rights, are investigated and new models for partnership involving equal participation by men and women are constructed. A critical analysis by women of our own race and class is needed, which takes cognisance of the fact that women of all races and classes share oppression, but that the nature of such oppression differs. Women are divided against each other by belonging to both the oppressed and oppressor races and classes. This leads to different emphases in feminism; ways of overcoming contradictions and tensions must be found in mutual support. A last stage, which is consistent with women's concern for the unity of all creation, calls for the acknowledgement of human interdependence with the world in which we live. Raised feminist consciousness perceives that the present ecological crisis, in which our resources are dwindling and nature is being irreparably damaged, threatens our very life systems.

As violence escalates in our country, those who are the most vulnerable become more dependent, while those who dominate become increasingly authoritarian. Because women, who are at the receiving end of much violence, view the personal as political, what happens to them has far-reaching implications.

> Our bodily life and personal experience are a kind of a prism through which we know ourselves in relation to others. Women's own experience, and its imprint on their bodies, is a resource for reflection, knowledge, care, and action about political issues. Women cannot avoid the fact that 'the personal is political', that institutional policies and behaviour do help, or hinder, women's health.[4]

Since we all have our own point of departure determined by our particular context, I am aware of the fact that my situation, as a white middle-class South African woman, is fraught with contradictions. I belong to the race and class of people who, though a minority, oppress the majority of citizens of this country. I am both oppressor and oppressed. Simone de Beauvoir commented that the basic problem for women is one of identity. How and where do I find mine? My experience of the South African situation has shown me that issues of racism and sexism are inseparable. From the moment of my birth, three factors have determined my destiny — my nationality, my whiteness and my being born female.[5] The search for my own identity brings me into confrontation with my own racism. As I begin to understand the parallels between sexist and racist oppression and react to the former, I am compelled to dig deep into my own cultural and historical layers of racial prejudice, to name them and to exorcise them. I am confronted daily with the exploitative assumptions of my own class and race and how they separate me from my black sisters.

I believe that the search for my identity as a white feminist liberation theologian impels me to make choices, choices which have theological, social and political implications. The search demands a theology in which there is a place for all women (and men) who are truly concerned with the gospel promise of freedom and newness, and its implications for and in our context now. It is an endeavour which can only benefit from the input of both white and black feminist theologians, with one compelling proviso — that the white women who take part in this exercise stand in solidarity with their black sisters. Being both oppressor and oppressed has its own tense dialectic. Insights gained from critical reflection on this tension should be able to offer us white women a way out of the guilt and fear which paralyse so many of us, as well as the opportunity for making our own contribution from our own perspective to the liberation of women in South Africa.

## OUR SITUATION

It is appropriate at this stage to tell the following stories. They illustrate the experience of violence resulting from the practice of apartheid suffered by three women in differing places in our community.

> We were standing in the street. Jacob was on the other side a bit further down when the Casspirs came. They broadcast that everyone must go inside immediately. Jacob started to run away. I shouted to him but he was too afraid to hear. They shot him. I saw him fall in the street. I tried to go to him, but they chased us into the houses. They would not let us reach him. He just lay there and nobody picked him up. I don't know when he died — he was only ten. Do these people not have children? They shoot and kill our children.

> I knew they were coming for me. You see, our political

organisations are enemies. I saw the signs. A man came to 'interview' me. I knew he was a sham. There were people watching my house. I felt restless that Friday evening and decided to take my daughter to stay with family. I could not sleep so I cleaned the house. I lay down for a bit. They came at 4 am. I heard them and peeped out between the curtains. Within seconds they had broken in. I just prayed to God. I am in your hands, I said. I don't know why but I quickly ran into my friend's bedroom. There they found me. 'Where is X?' they demanded. Calmly I replied, 'She has gone away for the night'. They had a photograph of me but it was taken a long time ago and confused them. They started to argue. I heard one say: 'We don't want to burn the wrong one'. One of them then blew some grey powder in my eye. It burnt terribly. Then they started to beat me and dragged me outside. They showed me the tyre, petrol and matches. I knew they wanted to take me to a vacant lot nearby. Suddenly I got angry and grabbed one of the youngsters. He started to scream as he too received the blows. The neighbours appeared and eventually they decided to leave me in the street. By then I was barely conscious, but I managed to crawl to a friend's house. They took me to hospital. I spent three weeks there. I have lost the sight of my eye and my hearing in my one ear. I am grateful that I am alive. I bear no grudges. God has been good to me.

We were coming home from church — like we do every Sunday. The children were singing on the back of the pick-up in front of us. We were talking about the drought and how we needed to hire extra grazing when I heard the terrible explosion. I saw the pick-up in front of us lift into the air — dust, pieces of metal. I heard myself screaming. I fell out of the car and rushed forward. He was just a heap of clothes and blood. I knew he was dead. I heard Katie crying and saw her lift her head out of the grass. She had been thrown far from the road. I went to her. Thank God she was only scratched. It was a miracle. As I bent to pick her up, I saw one of Gerrie's shoes lying in the grass. It was terrible — just murder, cold-blooded murder. Don't they care that children die?

Each of these three women has her different perception in a different context, yet all share the common experience of pain and loss as a result of violent deeds. In the face of such polarized experience, is it possible to analyse the situation of women in our country? Although it is a difficult task, I believe that it should be attempted. Our situation of escalating violence and confusion also makes the need for social analysis very necessary.[6] The strategic planning for new visions of humanity cannot take place otherwise.

We have to look closely at the interlocking injustices of our system and analyse them using the critical principle of feminist theology — the promotion of the full humanity of women. When women claim this principle for themselves they may not simply reverse the sin of sexism. Because of the holistic thrust of feminist theology, women 'must reach out for a continually expanding definition of inclusive humanity — inclusive of both genders, inclusive of all social groups and races'.[7]

Oppression is multidimensional. Separating out the areas in which it occurs does not imply that they do not overlap; in fact, their interlocking reinforces the very mechanisms which maintain them to the advantage of the oppressors. Nevertheless, for the sake of clarity in social analysis, it is necessary to distinguish some areas of oppression. The nature of this contribution precludes anything more than a somewhat truncated analysis of women's situation.[8]

In the first place, women in South Africa, whether white or black, are subjected to an undisguised exercise of patriarchal power. *Patriarchy* is the privilege of all males in our society, regardless of their race or class. The socio-cultural conditioning of white males, and more particularly the Afrikaner, is rooted in a dualistic world view which rests comfortably on patriarchal structures. The man is seen as head of the family; the women's place is in the home. Men lead; women follow. Black male patriarchy, which existed long before the whites arrived at the Cape, is built into much of black culture and tradition. It is interesting to speculate on the extent to which white patriarchy has reinforced black patriarchy and vice versa. Perhaps one of the few things that black and white men in this country have in common on the political front is their belief that patriarchy, or the patriarchal social order, is the only viable foundation for society. Both appear committed to maintaining male-dominated political regimes.

Secondly, it is not surprising therefore that women in South Africa have been subjected to patriarchal power structures in the *religious sphere*. Historically, the South African churches have been patriarchal for centuries. It is not uncommon that churches which take strong official stances on questions of social justice deny women ordination. Even the *Kairos Document* contains sexist undertones and does not specifically address the question of women's oppression.

If the church in South Africa is to become more demonstrably

a sign and sacrament (instrument) of union with (that) God
and of the divinely willed community of humankind, it cannot
with integrity attack the external oppression of apartheid and
ignore the glaring internal contradiction presented by its
treatment of women as unequal members of the Body of
Christ.[9]

Has patriarchy in the churches played a role in their notable
lack of concern in regard to problems caused by aparthied — for
instance those relating to forced removals of people? Writing on
the church's role in this regard, Margaret Nash states:

Church responses at local and national level have however
scarcely scratched the surface of the problems relating to past
and threatened removals, and have had too little feedback
effect on main-stream priorities and structures... These
churches claim to be the body of the One who in his earthly
life broke through the conventions and prejudices of his time
and culture. From the gospels it is clear that he developed a
quality of relationships with women, both respectable and
outcast, that restored their dignity as co-created with men in
the image of God. As a class, women in resettlement areas
(and 'illegals' in squatter camps) carry perhaps the severest
burdens of all apartheid's victims. If anyone needs the grace of
God made known in Christ they do. But if, as the gospels
testify, the presence of Jesus Christ is most surely found in and
among those who are most sorely afflicted, perhaps these
women have a very special contribution to make to the
church.[10]

In the third place the majority of women in South Africa are
*economically* oppressed, providing the cheapest form of labour in
factories and in the agricultural and domestic sectors. The
situation of most working women is exacerbated by the fact that
after the day's wage earning they are expected to bear the sole
responsibility for domestic work at night.[11] Fourthly, the majority
of women in our country have no *political* rights and therefore no
say in the running of the country. Representation in the corridors
of power for white women who do have the vote is negligible.
Black women in the so-called 'homelands' have no voice in their
administration and those who live in the so-called white areas are
totally disenfranchised. In the fifth place, the majority of women
bear the *social* burden of the apartheid system with all its horrors.
Decades of apartheid legislation, such as the laws pertaining to
influx control, have wrought havoc in black family life. Countless
black women have had to shoulder the sole responsibility of
rearing children and providing for their families while the men are

away working in white areas as cheap labour. Margaret Nash notes that for nearly 350 years we have lived in a land divided and despoiled by a dominant minority, 'among people who have been denied their humanity, uprooted from the earth that nourished their communal life, and are being straitjacketed in bantustan asylums'.[12]

In surveying the South African scene it becomes apparent that racism and sexism go hand in hand in maintaining oppressive structures in the labour field. Firstly, they justify the cheap labour status of blacks and women relative to whites and men. Secondly, they divide the population, making it difficult for those who are oppressed to unite for better wages and conditions of employment. Thirdly, sexism in particular saves capitalism untold amounts in unpaid labour performed in homes, in raising children and maintaining present and future generations of workers.[13]

No attempt at analysing the South African context would be complete without mentioning the growth of *militarisation* — a factor which has made the position of women even more threatened and vulnerable. A community which favours military priorities usually favours and benefits the role of men in society.

> Violence takes many forms, but it is always characterised by the increasing dependence of the most vulnerable partner and the increasing authoritarianism of the dominating partner. Militarism is manifested as 'power over' and when that power is frustrated, it is often domestically targetted against women and children.[14]

The sons of white mothers are compelled to do at least two years of military service; white fathers up to the age of 55 years can be drafted into the so-called 'Dad's Army'; increasing numbers of white women are voluntarily joining the armed forces. The defence of the country against Marxist atheistic forces is seen as the moral duty, indeed as the calling, of every Christian in South Africa. One is tempted to wonder about the links between orthodox Christian attitudes and militarism. Research has, in fact, shown that certain types of devout Christians who have strong religious attitudes tend to be 'more warlike, less democratic, more punitive, less tolerant, more conservative, less world-minded, more repressive, and less humanitarian than non-Christians'.[15] Some white mothers are active in organisations for 'our boys on the border', while others connive at keeping secret the whereabouts of their sons who are either evading the draft or who are on the run to escape being arrested in terms of the Emergency regulations.

Black mothers have little hope of seeing their sons and daughters who have 'crossed over', i.e. have crossed the borders of our country and joined the forces arraigned against the South African government. Others have seen their children hanged as traitors, while yet others have had their sons and daughters wounded or killed in the townships or so-called 'homeland' areas. For South African women there is no escape from the violence and horror of war. The ideologies of nationalism and militarism in our country have become increasingly costly. The 'maintenance of law and order', the 'national interest' and our defence against 'the total onslaught' are shibboleths proclaimed daily over our government-controlled news media. Some churches speak in terms of a just war. It can be argued that the large annual expense on defence is money diverted from education, housing and welfare, and that women and children are the class of people most deprived in these respects.

The following perceptive statement, made by a Muslim, challenges Christians to give account of their attitudes towards women.

> The fact that the oppression of women does not make the headlines or that their suffering is condoned by our indigenous cultures and religious institutions does not make it any less real or less painful. Lamenting the constraints that racist capitalism had placed on our perception of justice and peace is one thing. Allowing these constraints to persist is quite another thing and will only lead to the further diminishing of our own humanness. All people genuinely committed to the establishment of a non-racial and democratic South Africa must face the issue of women's oppression squarely in the face. The shackles around our wrists will never be completely dismantled for as long as women are tied to their apron strings . . . The symbol of our people's struggle and hopes, the African National Congress, has only one woman on a national executive council of thirty people.[16]

If the simple analysis I have given above portrays women in South Africa as no more than submissive, voiceless victims of an unjust system, it fails to do justice to the sustained and courageous efforts women have made to resist oppression in our country. The Anti-Pass campaigns which started in the 1950s, the subsequent formation of the Federation of South African Women (1954) with its 'Women's Charter',[17] the formation of the Black Sash (1955) to protest against the Senate Bill, and the coming into being of Women for Peace after the Soweto tragedy (1976) are but a few examples of women's resistance to oppression, injustice and violence. Many black and some white women who have opposed apartheid have been ridiculed and harassed in their daily lives, detained without trial, imprisoned, banned, and forced into exile.

## A FEMINIST THEOLOGICAL OPTION

As there are many different articulations of feminist theology, the particular type congruent to our situation will have to be sought. In my view the one offering hope to both women and men in our context is a critical feminist theology of liberation. Feminist theologians can identify with Gustavo Gutiérrez's definition of the theology of liberation as attempting '. . . to reflect on the experience and meaning of the faith based on the commitment to abolish injustice and build a new society . . .' When, however, he continues, '. . . this theology must be verified by the practice of this commitment, by active, effective participation in the struggle which the exploited social classes have undertaken against their oppressors',[18] differences surface. Firstly, feminist theology as liberation theology is done by those who themselves belong to the 'exploited classes', and not on their behalf. Women reflecting on their faith belong to a world in which they have only marginal influence. There are no links to be established between 'us' and 'the poor': we are 'the poor'. Secondly, in contrast to many liberation theologies, feminist theology cannot be localised. Women (and men) live everywhere. Nationality, class and race offer no barriers.[19] The context of feminist theology is more universal than the class struggle of liberation theology. Yet it must become concretised in a women's movement for societal, political, economic and ecclesial change. Oppression is not limited to androcentrism or sexism. It is in fact a socio-political system and societal structure of graded subjugations and oppressions.[20]

The crucial question then: Can solidarity among women prevail over loyalty to race, class, church and economic status? Can feminist liberation theology bridge the gap between women in a South Africa so direfully in need of a new vision for humanity? Can women in this country cross the barriers set up by apartheid and meet as women? Has the church, in response to the call of women, the potential to renew its spiritual and theological foundation in order to become a community of genuine partnership, interdependence and reciprocity?

For the rhetoric of sisterhood to become a reality, white women have to face two facts squarely. Firstly, in a capitalist, racist state women as a group do not share the same social status. Black women do not enjoy the same socio-political and economic advantages that white women do. White women's 'experience' is not synonymous with that of black women and vice versa. Secondly, feminism in this country should not be allowed to serve the cause of white women at the expense of their triply oppressed black sisters.

> Is it not hypocritical that middle-class women, especially whites, fight to be free at the expense of working-class women and black women in particular? Is it not true that women from rich families (or the upper classes) employ and underpay poor (lower class) women so that 'they' can be free and compete with men? Is this not an act of betrayal and sabotage of the very struggle of women? [21]

It is my belief that a critical feminist liberation theology has a contribution to make towards bringing women together in our country and thus enabling us to resist violence. The following ingredients should play a role in this process.

Our theological reflections start with our experience of ourselves as women and our need for the recognition of our full humanity. Feminist theology therefore offers a view in which *anthropology* is central. Apartheid has been both responsible for and nurtured by a distorted anthropology, based on an hierarchical view of humanity. Whites have perceived blacks as not fully human, as 'the other', and we have in the process forfeited our own humanity. It is not surprising therefore that blacks view whites as inhuman, or certainly less than human. The feminist perspective seeks a transformative anthropological model; one which is neither hierarchical nor complementary.[22] Such a model is directed towards the attainment of full personhood for both men and women, whilst realising the simultaneous need for societal change. It derives from a more holistic impulse than the complementary model. Traditionally-defined masculinity is neither innately good nor innately evil; nor is traditionally-defined femininity. All, female and male alike, are victims of oppression; all need to be liberated from alienating and oppressive social systems to find their place as whole persons. Full humanity demands the simultaneous conversion of society.[23] Feminist theology rejects an anthropology based on the familiar 'separate but equal' dictum of apartheid and seeks one based on mutuality which will stretch across denominational, religious, cultural and racial boundaries. It is therefore also unreservedly concerned with inter-faith dialogue and with finding common ground for all women seeking full personhood.

Secondly, because a critical feminist theology rejects a *hierarchy in creation,* in which certain human beings are more important than others, it rejects *patriarchal structures* wherever they occur. The most familiar statement made by the 'benevolent' patriarchs of apartheid is 'we know what is best for you'. We are ruled by those who, knowing what is best for us, can sanction any form of oppression in the national interest, as the latter is synonymous with the interest of those who are at the top of the hierarchy. The institutionalised churches, in most cases, merely mirror the patriarchal society in which they find themselves. In many cases women are excluded from ordination and from decision-making bodies by hierarchies composed of men. As women are doubtless no more immune to what Letty Russell calls the 'pinnacle complex' than men are,[24] they will have to move circumspectly and not allow themselves to be co-opted into hierarchical systems. Affirming an attitude of *semper reformanda* in all spheres of life, feminist liberation theology seeks a partnership of equals for men and women in the whole of society.

Thirdly, in feminist liberation theology Jesus Christ is understood as the liberating paradigm for all humanity. Unfortunately a *Christology* emphasising the maleness of Jesus has been the doctrine most used against women and, in supporting the exclusion of women from the priesthood, it has ratified male domination. Feminist liberation theology starts with the message and praxis of the Jesus of the synoptic gospels. It examines his reversal of the system of religious status: 'the last shall be first and the first last'. In our context, it addresses the question: What ought the followers of Jesus to be doing in South Africa now? While accepting that the Jesus of the gospels did not articulate a deliberate strategy for structural change, his proclamation, by envisaging new dimensions in human relationships founded on the freedom to love and serve, implicitly subverted existing patriarchal-androcentric structures of oppression.[25]

Feminist liberation theology seeks *signs and symbols* which are inclusive. It wants to promote a heightened awareness with regard to our use and abuse of language. The cause of apartheid has been served only too well by the misuse of language — from the infamous 'Whites Only' signs and the tragi-comic juggling by whites with a variety of terms applying to blacks, to the constitutional double-speak of 'own' and 'general' affairs. There can be no people in the world more confused than ordinary South Africans, black and white, by the debasement of language in the interest of the reigning ideology.

Our faith language has also become impoverished, stripped of holism and empathy, truncated and one-dimensional. Most liturgies have not yet dealt effectively with sexist terms; hymns, sermons and prayers usually exclude women. Feminist theology seeks and encourages a language which takes the emotions, the faith, the characteristics and hopes of all humanity seriously. In our present violent situation, such an exercise could be both **defusing**, as it implies the ability to listen carefully to ourselves and to others, as well as **healing**, for it is committed to communication and is concerned not with alienation but reconciliation.

In the fifth place, feminist theology is opposed to the *dualisms* which have polluted western thought for centuries, fostering patriarchy, hierarchies, racism and sexism. A holistic feminist world view is one in which the personal can never be divorced from the political. Apartheid, a product of the most blatant dualistic thinking, has effectively separated South Africans into a myriad of splinter groups. Suspicion and mistrust of 'otherness' is rife. Can women, the common factor in all these groups, acquire a holistic view of human redemption, which will enable them to speak right across barriers and to draw people together in a common vision of freedom and human dignity? In order to do so they will have to be willing to be self-critical and to rise above licking their own wounds.

> When the dominant values, ideas, and attitudes of a society are not our own, but are the measuring rod for our humanity and our right to justice, we become self-haters and haters of others, for the eternal world refuses to confirm our existence. The oppressed learn to adopt the very system that is used to oppress us. Members of the dominant group create ideologies and institutions they use against all who threaten their system ... When we feel wrong within a prescribed system that proscribes us, we are ashamed of ourselves ... We fail to see that our self-hate leads us to devalue others. Hence, feminism has failed at many points to confront its own racism, anti-Semitism, classism, and Western imperialism. We identify ourselves solely as the victim. Then, rather than seeing the

damage our fear does to ourselves and others, we place all
responsibility elsewhere on a one-dimensional 'enemy'.[26]

Lastly, in this process of seeking a new vision for humanity,
women will find the *feminist base community* both necessary and
helpful. It represents an autonomous, self-gathered community
that takes responsibility for reflecting upon, celebrating, and acting
on the understanding of liberation as redemption from sexism.[27]
Rosemary Ruether finds such communities having both an
internal and an external mission. Internally they are directed
towards growth in human potential through mutual empowerment
and externally they are concerned with a vision of a transformed
society 'beyond all the alienating '-isms' of exploitation and
alienation', with issues ranging from battered women to the
nuclear holocaust.[28] Women, meeting as women in such base
communities, can from a position of unity and strength, address
the problem of violence and plan to resist it.

We must have no illusions — yearnings for mutuality and for
oneness are threatening to a patriarchal society. For those who
have perfected the human system of separateness, feminism is no
welcome prospect. It is therefore not surprising that many white
South Africans who support apartheid and enjoy its 'fruits', resist a
feminist liberation perspective which advocates equality and
togetherness. Black women need to raise their voices against their
exclusion by black men from the liberation struggle.

> On the other hand it is shocking that those who claim to be
> involved in the liberation struggle, who agonize about their
> oppression and exploitation by the South African Apartheid
> Regime (which is based on Racial Capitalism), can retain and
> continue oppressive and exploitative structures against their
> womenfolk.[29]

The way forward ultimately entails making choices — probably
the most threatening aspect of the feminist theological option in
the present South African context. Black and white women alike
will have to opt for the cause of poor and oppressed women. This
means standing side by side with the women of the shanty towns,
of Crossroads, of Winterveld, of the drought-ridden rural areas.
This choice will mean having to take sides in structural conflict; it
will mean being wherever women suffer. This is both a
challenging and dangerous path to walk in South Africa today.
Those who are threatened by such a choice will claim that it is a
political one and not one for the gospel. Our community abounds
with organisations of women and men dedicated to the cause of

peace and reconciliation as *the* true Christian option, but who do not yet see that apartheid cannot be reconciled with the gospel and that *their* choices must also inevitably be political.

In the words of Albert Nolan, feminist liberation theology calls on oppressed women to 'take a clear option for their own cause, for the cause of all the poor and oppressed'. He continues:

> An option to become upwardly mobile by oneself or with a small group that abandons the rest of the oppressed is not an option for the poor but an option to join the oppressing and exploiting classes ... An option for the poor is an option against every form of oppression and exploitation. An analysis of the relationship between the various forms of oppression is helpful here. But a Christianity that does not challenge the poor and oppressed themselves, including women, to take an option and join in the struggle for liberation is simply unbiblical ... One of the more serious emotional obstacles is based upon the fact that we do not experience the same daily sufferings and insecurities as the poor.[30]

In conclusion, a few remarks on the connection between feminism and peace. The tendency among some feminists to believe that the violence perpetrated against them by men can only be met with violence needs to be rejected. In my view, it would be impossible to denounce patriarchal violence while at the same time advocating feminist militancy. In addressing this problem, Rosemary Ruether writes of the necessity for a new mode of human selfhood that could transcend both aggressive dehumanisation of others and timid acquiescence to or support of individual or collective violence. This resistance to violence is based on one's own value of oneself as a human being.

> Violence toward others, far from being an expression of self-worth, is based on repression of one's sense of vulnerability which then translates into hostility toward others ... An empowered self will not accept its own degradation, or that of others. At this point, it becomes possible to forge new links between feminism and peace. Feminism fundamentally rejects the power principle of domination and subjugation. It rejects the concept of power which says that one side's victory must be the other side's defeat. Feminism must question social structures at every level ... We seek an alternative power principle of empowerment in community rather than power over and disabling of others. Such enabling in community is based on a recognition of the fundamental inter-connectedness of life, of men and women, blacks and whites ... humans and

the non-human community of animals, plants, air, and water. Nobody wins unless all win.[31]

A feminist theological option calls women to be converted to a new sense of self in the confidence that a personal conversion has far-reaching implications for the society we live in. Armed with the self-knowledge that we are no less immune to racism, militarism and hierarchical structuring than men are, we can move forward together and claim with confidence a better future for ourselves and our children than the one which faces us at present. Our confidence rests on the gospel, on the truth that sets us free. This truth will not allow us to bow to violence or to assent to it.

## NOTES

1.  R.R. Ruether, 'Feminist theology and spirituality', in J.L. Weidman (ed.), *Christian Feminism: Visions of a New Humanity*, (San Francisco: Harper and Row, 1984), p.26.
2.  Recently I was told by a social worker that there has been a marked increase in the incidence of wife-battering by affluent white males. Her preliminary research shows a clear correlation between this phenomenon and the violence, fear and uncertainty pervading our society.
3.  M.C. Segers, 'The Catholic bishops' pastoral letter to war and peace: a feminist perspective', *Feminist Studies*, 11, 3, (Fall, 1985), p.642.
4.  C.F. Parvey, 'Re-membering — a global perspective', in Weidman (ed.), *Christian Feminism*, p.165.
5.  Cf. B. Hooks, *Ain't I a woman: Black women and Feminism* (Boston: Boston Southend Press, 1981), p.12.
6.  J. Cone in *For my People: Black Theology and the Black Church*, (Johannesburg: Skotaville, 1985), p.97, comments: 'But I believe that the gospel combined with social analysis provides Christians with insight into evil that others often overlook. That is what creates prophets: the gift of God's grace combined with critical interpretation'.
7.  R.R. Ruether, *Sexism and God-talk: Towards a feminist theology*, (Boston: Seabury Press, 1983), p.20.
8.  Cf. J. Holland and P. Henriot, *Social analysis: Linking faith and justice*, (Washington: Orbis, 1983), p.xix.
9.  M. Nash (ed.), *Women — A power for change*, Report of the 17th annual national conference of the South African Council of Churches, (Johannesburg: SACC, 1985), p.2.
10. M. Nash, 'Black uprooting: agenda for the churches', *Journal of Theology for Southern Africa*, 50 (March, 1985), pp.57,62.
11. A remarkable account of the suffering of black women is contained in J. Barrett, *et al, Vukani Makhosikazi: South African women speak*, (London: CIIR, 1985). See pp.19-55 on 'Women at work'.
12. M. Nash, *Journal of Theology for Southern Africa*, p.56.
13. N. Bancroft, 'Women in the cut-back economy: Ethics, ideology and class', in B.H. Andolsen (ed.), *Women's consciousness, women's conscience*, (Minneapolis: Winston Press, 1985), p.27.

14. Parvey in Weidman (ed.), *Christian Feminism*, p.163.
15. E.W. Russell, 'Christianity and Militarism', *Peace Research Review*, 4, 3 (November, 1971), p.39.
16. Maulana Faried Esack from the Second Desmond Tutu Peace Lecture for the World Conference on Religion and Peace Johannesburg Chapter, (September, 1986), p.4.
17. Commenting on the charter, Cherryl Walker, *Women and Resistance in South Africa*, (London: Onyx Press, 1982), p.156, says: 'The charter ... identified the women's movement completely with the national liberation movement, as represented by the Congress Alliance group, in its struggle to overthrow the white supremacist government in South Africa. Since roughly 80 per cent of all South African women were black, it regarded the removal of the political, economic and social inequalities suffered by blacks as of overriding concern for any broad women's political movement. But it was also explicit on the need for change in the position of women within society. It dealt gently with the "ancient and revered traditions" by which the continued subordination of African women, in particular, was justified, conceding that "no doubt" these had once served "purposes of great value". Nevertheless, it declared, those days were past ... It went on to add that women had shared in these developments — large numbers of women were in fact the sole bread-winners for their families — but despite these changes the law has lagged behind ... it no longer corresponds to the actual social and economic position of women.'
18. G. Gutiérrez, *A theology of liberation: History, politics and salvation*, (New York: SCM, 1973), p.307.
19. C.J.M. Halkes, 'Feminisme en theologie: Enkele notities als nawoord', in C.J.M. Halkes and D. Buddingh (eds.), *Als vrouwen aan het woord komen: Aspecten van de feministische theologie*, (Kampen: J.H. Kok, 1977), p.126.
20. E.S. Fiorenza, 'Feminist biblical interpretation', in Weidman (ed.), *Christian Feminism*, p.37.
21. From the ICT's report of the Feminist Theology Conference, *Women's struggle in South Africa*, (Johannesburg: ICT, September, 1984), p.10.
22. C.J.M. Halkes, *Vrouwen — mannen — mensen*, (Baarn: Ambo, 1984), p.12.
23. D.M. Ackermann, *Women and ministries: A feminist perspective*, (thesis submitted for the degree of Master of Theology, University of South Africa, 1985), p.5.
24. L.M. Russell, 'Women and ministry: problem or possibility?', in Weidman (ed.), *Christian Feminism*, p.87.
25. Ackermann, *Women and ministries*, p.65.
26. R.N. Brock, 'The feminist redemption of Christ', in Weidman (ed.), *Christian Feminism*, p.61.
27. Ruether, in Weidman (ed.), *Christian Feminism*, p.28.
28. *Ibid.*, p.31.
29. From report, *Women's struggle in South Africa*, p.10.
30. A. Nolan, 'The option for the poor in South Africa', *New Blackfriars*, 67, 787, (Johannesburg: ICT, January, 1986), p.13.
31. R.R. Ruether, 'Feminism and peace', in Andolsen (ed.), *Women's consciousness*, pp.72-73.

# Radical Pacifism — An Option For Peace?

SHEENA DUNCAN

Can pacifism be regarded as an option for peace when injustice is the very fabric of a political system imposed and maintained by the use of violent force? What are pacifists to do when pacifism can no longer be held merely as a theoretical position, but is challenged by a society in which war, militarisation and violence are part of daily and personal experience as is the case in South Africa at the present time?

The pacifist position cannot be abandoned, whatever the circumstances, when it has been arrived at out of the conviction that in the crucifixion Christians have been shown how they must act when confronted by injustice and violence. None of the arguments about 'just war' or 'just revolution' or the 'justified use of violence', however persuasive and rational, can shake a deeply-held belief that the sacrificial death of Jesus is the way we are commanded to go. We are commanded to love even unto death.

We have been taught that men and women are made in the image of God. If we really believe this, it is unthinkable that we should in any way, for any reason, deliberately kill or injure another person. But to love as we are meant to love also means that we have an obligation to work for justice and to strive to put a stop to evil-doing. Christian pacifists cannot merely sit back wringing their hands and refuse to participate in violent action. Christian pacifism cannot mean inactivity and withdrawal. It has to mean committed and sacrificial action to build a just and righteous society, to prevent violence wherever possible, and to intervene in violent confrontations. It has to mean showing a better way of resolving conflicts.

## THE CHURCH'S WITNESS

The church in South Africa has on the whole failed to do these things. There have been some shining examples when individual church members have demonstrated a brave commitment to non-violent action and there have been a few occasions when the church itself has stood firm, notably in opposition to the 'church clause' in 1957.

The bishops of the Church of the Province then acted forthrightly. Archbishop Clayton's letter to the Prime Minister, so dramatically highlighted by the former's sudden death immediately after signing it, has been buried in the history books. We need to remind ourselves of his words:

> We recognise the great gravity of disobedience to the law of the land. We believe that obedience to secular authority, even in matters about which we differ in opinion, is a command laid upon us by God. But we are commanded to render unto Caesar the things which be Caesar's, and to God the things that are God's. There are therefore some matters which are God's and not Caesar's, and we believe that the matters dealt with in Clause 29(c) are among them.
>
> It is because we believe this that we feel bound to state that if the Bill were to become law in its present form we should ourselves be unable to obey it or to counsel our clergy and people to do so.
>
> We therefore appeal to you, Sir, not to put us in a position in which we have to choose between obeying our conscience and obeying the law of the land.[1]

The church clause became law but it was not enforced. It was impossible for the government to do so.

Would that church leaders had since then given such a lead. It is tragic that the church has over so many years perceived its duty to act only in relation to a narrowly-defined concept of religious freedom. There has been an inadequate response from the church to much legislation which directly contradicts Christian teaching.

As Christians we have been content to pass resolutions, to make statements and to send delegations to Ministers of State on issues such as migrant labour and the consequent destruction of family life, the uprooting and removal of millions of people in the interests of the separation and division of racial and ethnic groups, detention without trial, and the many other violations of human rights which are part and parcel of the apartheid system. When our approaches have failed we have meekly accepted defeat.

We have said that we do not approve but we have not often acted to prevent such things or to defy them.

Even when religious freedom was directly denied we have failed to act. We said we did not like the Mixed Marriages Act. We condemned it in the strongest terms but why did we continue to allow our ministers to act as agents of the state in performing marriages? We could very easily have separated the legal requirements for marriage from the sacramental. It would have been costly, yes, but it would have prevented the long years of complicity with an intolerable law. What kind of support did we give to those few ordained ministers who refused to comply and sent back their licences as marriage officers? Why did we allow them to be so isolated? We can take no credit for the repeal of this legislation after so many years of suffering and wrong-doing.

Why have we allowed military chaplains to wear uniforms and follow the orders of the generals instead of the bishops? We talk endlessly about our obligation to minister to all people wherever they may be placed in the war in which we are engaged, but we have not had the courage to insist that this ministry be fully exercised under the direction and control of the church. As militarism has taken hold in our society with the creeping tentacles which now bind us all, we have failed to act in time to try to prevent it. We condemn violence from our pulpits but we bless military flags and glorify war. In white parishes each 11 November we pray for those 'who laid down their lives for us' but rarely ask how and why we took their lives away from them.[2]

Sadly, all this has meant in the past in South Africa that pacifists have had to act in isolation. There has been no groundswell of support for non-violent direct action in the churches, except spasmodically. There is no general commitment to non-violence on the part of those who condemn violence. Those leaders who have in our history led movements of non-violent resistance have mostly had to do so without the support and active involvement of the organised church. That they have so often failed to achieve their objectives is our failure, not theirs.

We have to accept a large part of the blame for the fact that so many South Africans now say: 'we have tried non-violence and negotiation so often in the past that there is now no alternative but to take up arms'.

If we are to put our past failures behind us and to start afresh, how are we to begin? How are we to move beyond protest, beyond resistance, to take the future into our own hands to be moulded and formed by positive and creative rather than reactionary actions?

## NON-VIOLENT DIRECT ACTION

We have to recognise that there are very few pacifists. It is an isolated position. Most people are not pacifist. However, many people do believe that violence should be undertaken only as a last resort and that every other possibility must be explored before violent means are adopted. The problem is that the 'everything' falls far short of being *every* possible means short of violence. The acceptance of the justification for violence as a last resort leads to a short circuiting of the long hard road which is the only way for the committed pacifist. The discouragement of repeated failures and indiscernible progress leads the 'not-yet-violent' to resort to arms before *everything* else has been tried.[3]

It is the responsibility of pacifists to convince the not-yet-violent that non-violent action and a total rejection of violent means *can* achieve the desired end. It is also the responsibility of pacifists to demonstrate that non-violent action is a more effective, more certain and less costly way (in terms of human lives) of achieving justice and peace than violence can ever be. Means do shape ends. Violent and armed struggle in South Africa will, indeed is, bringing about change but the end result is unlikely to be a just peace.

Pacifism has too often presented itself as being only non-violent protest about, or resistance to, injustice and violent acts. It is imperative that pacifists in South Africa try to find ways in which protest and resistance can be transformed into action which will change things, end injustice, and create a just and peaceful society.

This all seems impossibly idealistic in our present situation. The violence used by the state to enforce its will on the people is now being answered with counter-violence and many of the campaigns of non-violent action such as rent, school and consumer boycotts are now often being enforced by violent intimidation. As violent conflict engulfs people in many communities and violence escalates throughout South Africa it seems ridiculous to talk of non-violence. Nevertheless, violent conflict may not be taking us along the road to a just peace.

Non-violent direct action is not merely protest. It is carefully targeted, carefully planned and carried out in order to bring about specific changes. It goes beyond response and resistance to creativity. It does not necessarily involve civil disobedience. Indeed, for the pacifist, civil disobedience is the last resort, only to be undertaken out of deep respect for the idea of Law and when all other means have failed to achieve the desired end.

Non-violent direct action is not an easy option. It begins with certain basic principles best summed up in Gandhi's word *satyagraha*, coined by him in South Africa in 1906.

> Truth *(satya)* implies love, and firmness *(agraha)* engenders and therefore serves as a synonym for force. I thus began to call the Indian movement *Satyagraha*, that is to say, the Force which is born of Truth and Love, or non-violence, and gave up the phrase passive resistance.[4]

Love encompasses love of the opponent, the desire to convince him of the rightfulness of one's cause, to save face for him, to bring him over to one's side. There should be no defeat and no victory, only atonement and reconciliation.

Non-violent direct action demands deep thought, detailed planning, proper preparation and training, discipline, organisation and trust, patience, commitment and sacrifice. The basic steps are summed up in the See, Judge and Act method. Identify the problem; analyse its structures, causes and vulnerable points; plan a campaign to resolve it.

The campaign will be dictated by the nature of the problem but will usually include the following ingredients:

— information and publicity in order to gain as much sympathy and support for the cause as possible. This may necessitate symbolic and high-profile public actions;
— canvassing of support from specific influence groups and lobbies such as trade unions, churches, business people, press, diplomats, women's organisations and so on;
— the testing of the law relating to the issue. Can the law help? Is application to the courts likely to assist?
— dialogue with the authorities concerned in order to establish whether there are any possibilities of negotiated resolution of the problem.

The next steps may involve refusal and withdrawal of co-operation, or civil disobedience. There must always be firmness and resolution, even when faced with the threat of death or injury. Non-violent direct action will not work at all unless the participants are convinced of the rightfulness of their cause, united in determination to resolve the problem and agreed upon the methods to be used.

There are whole libraries of books in South Africa on the strategies and techniques of non-violent direct action.[5] Perhaps the most helpful approach in this short article would be to describe a successful campaign.

## THE DRIEFONTEIN CAMPAIGN

The people of Driefontein bought their land in the Eastern Transvaal in 1912 before the 1913 Land Act made such purchases by black persons unlawful. The threat that they would be uprooted and removed from their land hung over them from the 1960s onwards, but became an imminent reality in 1980.

> But later in 1980 the government sent people to Driefontein telling the people should be moved away, so my brother Saul started looking for the door to consult who are these people who want to move the people of Driefontein. When he got the door, which was the Development Trust, he wrote a letter to Dr Koornhof telling him about Driefontein . . . .[6]

These attempts to negotiate continued throughout the next five years, in spite of there being no willingness on the part of the government to enter into any consultations. Dr Koornhof's attitude to the community was similar to that expressed by all the goverment ministers and officials with whom they had to deal:

> He says we are squatters: we said, 'Can you tell us the difference between a squatter and one who privately owns his land in freehold?'
>
> He says, 'You are squatters you black people. You don't have a right'.
>
> And he even mentioned to us that there was no man in South Africa in the beginning. 'You are all coming from Africa, from the East. There was no man here. Only the first man came in 1497, Vasco da Gama'. And he said the second man was in 1652 which was van Riebeeck, so he feels it's nobody's land.[7]

The freeholders never faltered in reasonableness and in their preparedness to enter into negotiations.

Saul Mkhize, the leader of the community, 'began to realise that what he had thought was a battle of title deeds, minutes and meetings, permits and lawyers, publicity and special pleading, was something quite different and that he had taken on a ruthless and implacable foe'.[8]

The Driefontein Council Board of Directors used the whole range of strategies open to them. They consulted lawyers and discovered how limited was the law's ability to help them. They sought out resource agencies in Johannesburg. They invited members of the press and the diplomatic corps to visit

Driefontein. Most important of all, they decided to demonstrate their determination to remain on their land.

They began to tackle local problems. They explored the rights concerning old-age pensions which were being quite unlawfully denied to old people in Driefontein and intervened in individual cases. They concerned themselves with the problems of farm workers in the district. They learnt how to deal with administrative wrong-doing and established a legal clinic which operated monthly, when lawyers came to Driefontein to handle the cases which the community had not been able to resolve.

They made plans to rebuild the medical clinic on the farm and to employ a full-time resident nursing sister to deal with day-to-day health problems. They enlisted the active support of Mr Enos Mabuza, the Chief Minister of Ka Ngwane, who took an unprecedented step for a homeland leader when he refused to co-operate with the plans for removal.

Finally, they won the support of one of South Africa's largest business enterprises, Barlow Rand, which made land available as compensation for the land flooded by the rising waters of the Heyshope Dam. Had it not been for this offer, the settlement eventually reached in August 1985 might never have taken place as it was out of the question for the government to expropriate white farmers in order to compensate black families whose land had been flooded. The Driefontein people's understanding of this reality was evident throughout the whole process of resistance. They never made demands which would be impossible for the South African government to accede to.

Throughout the years of their resistance the people were subjected to the whole gamut of official tactics designed to divide the community, to weaken their determination and to force compliance with the removal plans: the delay or withholding of services, pensions, permits and licences, a constant intimidatory police presence, searches and assaults, and attempts to set up 'stooge leaders'. Saul's son, Paris, was badly assaulted.

On 2 April 1983, Easter Saturday, Saul Mkhize was shot dead in the school yard by a policeman, Constable Nienaber. A meeting had been called to discuss progress in the campaign against the removal. The police maintained that the meeting was illegal. A year later Constable Nienaber was found not guilty of murder.

> What we cannot understand is that Nienaber admitted that he
> shot Mkhize, he actually agreed to that, and yet the Judge left

him to go free. They said that Mkhize was killed because it was
an illegal meeting. How could they say that? They shot him
before the meeting even began, so how could they know what
the meeting was going to be about or that it was an illegal
meeting? They came with five guns and three teargasses which
shows that they were planning violence before they even got to
Driefontein. The Judge asked about the Council Board of
Directors and the removal in the trial — why did he do that?
The trial was about one man killing another, not about these
things. In fact they wanted to say that Mkhize was guilty not
Nienaber.[9]

It is impossible to say categorically that it was Saul's death that
was the turning point in the people's battle to remain where they
are. How can one estimate the importance of such things? If Saul
Mkhize had not died perhaps he and his people might have failed.
He did die, however, and from that time the people's
determination was voiced in a different way.

> Why did they come prepared to kill Mkhize? Because he was
> our leader and we loved and respected him. So they thought
> that if they killed him we would leave Driefontein. But we never
> will, unless they wake up Mkhize and he leads us out of this
> place. Otherwise if they are so desperate for our land, they
> better shoot us all dead here and then take it for the whites.[10]

> Mr Saul Mkhize said he would die at Driefontein and he did
> die at Driefontein. I will die at Kwa Ngema farm like Mkhize
> died at Driefontein. I will never move from Kwa Ngema, never
> before I die.

> If the government can listen to us, we will say thank you to
> Saul Mkhize who died for us. But if the government doesn't
> listen gentlemen, we'll die, all of us there. We'll never leave
> Mkhize, because they killed Mkhize. He has the key of the car,
> and the car will never move without a key. Mkhize died with the
> key of the car, and they will never move that car, never.[11]

It was after Saul Mkhize died and after the acquittal of the man
who shot him that the people of Driefontein, led by the women,
began to plan to dig their own graves at Driefontein. They were
ready for the removal squads. They said they would stand beside
their own graves and be shot dead before they would allow
themselves to be removed.

In the end a settlement was reached which has allowed them to
remain on their land with more land being given to them and
their neighbours at Kwa Ngema. This was finalised at a meeting
between themselves and Deputy-Minister Ben Wilkens on 26
August 1985. They have succeeded. Many others have failed.

Pacifism *can* be an option for peace but we are all too reluctant to make the necessary commitment. There is no power on earth that can force us to do what we refuse to do. But over and over again we co-operate with our own destruction.

> After this, he said to his disciples, 'Let us go back to Judea'. 'Rabbi', his disciples said, 'it is not long since the Jews there were wanting to stone you. Are you going there again?' Jesus replied, 'Are there not twelve hours of daylight? Anyone can walk in day-time without stumbling, because he sees the light of this world. But if he walks after nightfall he stumbles, because the light fails him.' (John 10:7-10)

# NOTES

1.  Alan Paton, *Apartheid and the Archbishop*, (Cape Town: David Philip, 1973), p.170.
2.  The Revd. Arnold Hirst — sermon 11 November 1979, St. George's Church, Parktown, Johannesburg.
3.  The Revd. Rob Robertson — see his unpublished papers, Justice and Reconciliation Division, SACC, for discussion of the concept of 'not-yet-violence'.
4.  Mohandas K. Gandhi, quoted in John V. Bondurant, *Conquest of Violence*, (California: University of California Press, 1967), p.73.
5.  SACC Division of Justice and Reconciliation; SACBC Justice and Peace Commission, Diakonia, in Durban, IFOR, ECC, and so on.
6.  Pickson Mkhize in *Sash*, Vol.26, No.2, August 1983.
7.  *Ibid.*
8.  Jill Wentzel in the editorial of *Sash*, Vol.26, No.1, May 1983.
9.  Driefontein spokesman in *Sash*, Vol.27, No.1, May 1984.
10. *Ibid.*
11. Moses Ngema, *Sash*, Vol.26, No.2, August 1983.

# Conscientious Objection: The Church Against Apartheid's Violence

LOIS LAW, CHRIS LUND AND HARALD WINKLER

Since 1974, conscientious objection has been a major point at which church and state have confronted each other over the issue of violence in South Africa. In any theological history of violence in this country, therefore, conscientious objection becomes a central area of debate. It is a point at which the church, drawing on its theological heritage, confronts the state on the violent mismanagement of its own human resources. Further it is a point at which a connection can be made between this violent mismanagement and the broader injustices of apartheid South Africa.

This essay will approach conscientious objection in the following way. Firstly we will discuss the 1974 SACC resolution on conscientious objection. We will then trace the historical development of the issue to the end of the 1970s. Attention will then be given to the broadening of the war resistance movement through the Conscientious Objector Support Groups and the new legislation affecting both the duration of national service (1982) and the plight of conscientious objectors (1983). This will be followed by a discussion of the emergence of the End Conscription Campaign (ECC) as a 'proactive' response to growing militarisation. Finally we will raise some of the important issues facing the churches and the war resistance movement at present.

## THE BEGINNINGS OF WAR RESISTANCE IN THE CHURCHES

### SACC RESOLUTION: THE SPARK

Conscription was originally introduced in 1912, but was suspended during the two World Wars and only re-introduced in

1967. By 1972, the initial national service period had been
increased from 9 to 12 months with an additional 19 days service
annually for the 5 years following initial training. These new
conscription laws were related directly to the changing political
climate in southern Africa. The independence of Angola and
Mozambique had the effect of drawing the border between white
rule and popular government closer to apartheid South Africa.
And the 'border-consciousness' was further stimulated by the war
in Namibia in which the SADF had played an aggressive role.
This changing political climate led to a shift in the South African
government's strategy. In 1974 the state developed the concept of
'total strategy' which provided the justification for the intense
militarisation which was to follow.

The churches were slow to respond to this process of
militarisation, firstly because of the traditional Protestant problem
of getting involved in things 'political', and secondly because of
the failure among whites to see the connection between military
structures and apartheid. In 1974, the SACC at its annual
conference at Hammanskraal, tabled a resolution which marked
the first concrete statement by churches (apart from the peace
churches) on the issue of military conscription. In debate at the
conference, Douglas Bax, a Presbyterian minister, stood up and
remarked that

> ... neither the churches nor the SACC has been in the lead of
> doing something practical to change the status quo in South
> Africa. Isn't it time for us to consider seriously whether the
> SACC should challenge young men on the score of
> conscientious objection?[1]

After some heated discussion and several amendments, a
motion proposed by Bax was passed unanimously by the
conference. Because this resolution forms the groundwork for
much of the conscientious objection debate in the years that
followed, we shall look at it in some detail here.

In its preamble, the resolution invokes scripture to assert the
sovereignty of God over all human powers:

> 'we must obey God rather than men' in those areas where the
> government fails to fulfil its calling to be 'God's servant for
> good' rather than for evil and oppression (Acts 5:29;
> Rom.13:4).[2]

Several points are then noted:

1. 'That Christians are called to strive for justice and the true
   peace which can be founded only in justice ....'
2. That the conference does not see that it is automatically the

Christian's duty to obey his/her nation's call to commit violence.

3. That both Catholic and Reformation theology justify taking up arms, but only in order to fight a 'just war'.
4. That 'the theological definition of a "just war" excludes war in the defence of an unjust and discriminatory society . . . '.
5. That the Republic of South Africa is a fundamentally unjust and discriminatory society.
6. That the South African military forces are defending this society.

The conference therefore:

1. 'deplores violence as a means to solve problems . . . .'
2. 'Calls on its member churches to challenge all their members to consider in view of the above whether Christ's call to take up the cross and follow him in identifying with the oppressed does not, in our situation, involve becoming conscientious objectors . . . .'
3. 'Commends the courage and witness of those who have been willing to go to jail in protest against unjust laws and policies in our land'.[3]
4. Requests the SACC to investigate methods of non-violent action for change.
5. Prays for the government and rapid steps to change.

The SACC resolution was a dramatic departure from previous church statements. It located the question of individual moral decision in the context of the justice of the cause being fought for. The context of apartheid, and not war in itself was being questioned. There is virtually no pacifist tradition in South Africa, apart from a small group of Quakers and Jehovah's Witnesses.[4] The Hammanskraal statement was therefore not primarily a pacifist statement, but drew more strongly on elements of the just war theory. As a result of the resolution, those churches which had previously not faced or discussed the issue were challenged to formulate their own positions on conscientious objection.

## THE CHURCHES TAKE UP THE ISSUE

The resolution provoked a strong reaction. The government condemned it outright, with Prime Minister Vorster and Minister of Defence P.W. Botha issuing warnings and threats of possible legal action. White political opposition from Vause Raw (NRP) and Van Zyl Slabbert (PFP) was also critical. White opinion was not supportive. In a survey conducted by *The Argus*, 81 percent of whites interviewed thought that South African citizens should not be allowed to refuse to do military service. To back this up, the English and Afrikaans press, with the exception of the *Rand Daily Mail*, condemned the SACC statement. Clearly the notion of conscientious objection had raised sharply the question of patriotism for whites. The connection between military service and oppressive apartheid structures had not been made clear.

Within the church a split occurred between those who supported the resolution and those who did not. The Dutch Reformed Church was quick to condemn the statement, and attack the SACC. In October 1974, it formally recognised the right and privilege of every citizen to defend his/her fatherland. The Baptist Union of South Africa (BUSA) responded similarly, and passed a resolution disassociating itself from the SACC resolution. The Executive Commission of the Presbyterian Church of Southern Africa (PCSA) also disassociated itself, and at least two Presbyterian congregations followed suit. But these responses were from the (almost entirely white) minority of the church. Black sections of separated churches (for example the Presbyterian Tsonga congregation) came out in support of the resolution, as did all the multiracial denominations. The Church of the Province of South Africa (CPSA) responded favourably — in September the Johannesburg Diocesan Council passed a resolution supporting the SACC statement. In October, the Evangelical Lutheran Church (ELC) of Namibia passed a resolution unanimously supporting the SACC statement. The Transvaal region of the ELC in addition announced its support. The Roman Catholic Church, too, made clear its support, perhaps most explicitly in the following statement from Archbishop Hurley:

> In the South African situation, conscientious objection should be adopted as a principle by the churches. I believe that the churches should adopt this view, even at the risk of open confrontation with the government. Confrontation has to occur some time.[5]

Hurley was right in stating that confrontation between church and state over this issue was inevitable. The Nationalist government's immediate response to the SACC was to insert a new section into the Defence Further Amendment Bill at the time under debate in Parliament. It was to become section 121(c) of the 1957 Act. The section

> ... provided that a person commits an offence if he/she uses

any language or does any act or thing with intent to recommend to, encourage, aid, incite, instigate, suggest to or otherwise cause any other person or category of persons or persons in general to refuse or fail to render any service to which such person or a person of such category or persons in general is or are liable or may become liable in terms of this Act.[6]

This section of the Act had the immediate effect of uniting both 'pacifist' and 'just war' positions in the church, and of further alienating the church from the state. Numerous people and organisations condemned the Act, and the administrative board of the Southern African Catholic Bishops' Conference (SACBC) declared that if the bill became law, the SACBC would be bound by conscience to disobey it and would encourage clergy and lay members to do the same. So far no one has been charged under 121(c), but at the very least it has been a major inhibiting factor in the debate on conscientious objection. This is borne out by the immediate effect the Act had on the churches. Only the Methodist Church of Southern Africa (MCSA) attempted to follow the SACC lead and provide guidance to its members on the issue of conscientious objection. In response to the new legislation, many churches let the war issue slide to the agendas of backroom committees. Even at the SACC conference in 1975, a motion proposing new action and thought on conscientious objection was shelved. At the 1976 conference the issue was only referred to in passing.

Against this trend, in February 1976, the SACBC initiated an investigation into the generally accepted attitude to conscientious objection, and explored the possibility of an ecumenical support group to safeguard objectors. But it was the broader social and political issues which proved to be the most powerful forces against church inertia. The wave of strikes which had spread from Durban in 1973 had already moved the church to re-evaluate its social witness. And the rise of Black Consciousness and the 1976 Soweto uprisings had a further radicalising effect on the church. White church hierarchies were coming under more and more pressure from their black bases to confront the state on a number of issues, among them conscientious objection. But the church moved slowly. In September 1976, the Natal Diocesan Synod of the CPSA called on the government 'to investigate and establish "additional alternatives to military service" in the form of community service which would benefit all South Africans'.[7] It then encouraged all people to make a clear moral choice on the use of violence to uphold or change the status quo. And it recognised the right of each individual to obey his/her conscience, and the subsequent responsibility of the church for that person. In February 1977, as a result of pressure from Catholic youth and student groups, the Roman Catholic Church became the second major denomination to declare its support for the right of individuals to object to military service on the basis of conscience. The SACBC statement was subsequently endorsed by the CPSA in April 1977, and by the Methodist conference and the United Congregational Church of Southern Africa in October of that year.

## THEOLOGICAL RESOURCES

The theological traditions on which the various denominations drew were major resources in the establishment of this stand. The Catholic bishops appealed to authoritative Catholic teaching on the issue. Vatican II, in *Gaudium et Spes*, held that those who conduct military service for their country fulfil a role of upholding the long term peace and security of that country. But it also held that

> ... it seems right that laws make human provisions for the case of those, who for reasons of conscience, refuse to bear arms, provided, however, that they accept some other form of service to the human community.[8]

Both Pope Paul VI in 1967 and the Roman Synod of Bishops in 1971 endorsed this, recognising the right to object conscientiously to military service, and the need for alternative forms of national or community service. The Anglican and Methodist churches reversed this process, using their experience of the South African situation to influence their international bodies, which in turn endorsed their actions. The Anglican church, however, seemed to be acting in the spirit of the 1978 Lambeth conference, which had made a clear statement on war and violence (though not dealing specifically with conscientious objection). It condemned violence and its many forms — exploitation, open war, misdirection of resources:

> ... in the face of the mounting incidence of violence today, and its acceptance as a normal element in human affairs, we condemn the subjection, intimidation, and manipulation of people by the use of violence and the threat of violence.[9]

Though the churches had defined their positions more clearly on principle, their responses still did not match developments in the broader 'secular' community or even among their own members. With conscription a growing controversy, the churches would soon have to respond with concrete programs of action.

Towards the end of 1970, the Presbyterian Church of Southern Africa issued a statement:

1. It called for the repeal of section 121(c) and for debate on the issue;
2. instructed every presbytery to appoint someone to introduce the issue to the congregations, and provide counselling;
3. condemned punishment of conscientious objectors.

At the same time the Baptist Union recognised the right of individuals to object on the grounds of conscience, and called for an easing of the law affecting objectors, so that their service to the community could be channelled in another direction. The UCCSA proposed an almost identical set of resolutions and added a call for discussion of the issue amongst congregations. In October at its annual conference, the MCSA made a concrete proposal to the Minister of Defence that 'a commission of enquiry, comprising 'a fair cross-section representative both of the church and the Department of Defence' be established to test the convictions of any person claiming to be a conscientious objector'.[10] In November the CPSA provincial synod accepted the right of individuals to fight on the side of the liberation movement.

It also endorsed many of the other churches' statements. These statements formed a firm public acknowledgement that the churches had a duty to take up the issue of war, and would not be intimidated into ignoring it. But the churches had now also provided concrete ways in which the issue could be discussed.

In many instances, however, the education programme did not go as far as hoped. Much work was eventually left to unofficial church groups, composed mainly of ministers, members of the major denominations and several conscientious objectors. Although relatively autonomous, a degree of contact between these groups occurred on a national scale. They formed several functions — conducting research into the issue, acting as support groups for objectors, calling for alternative service, and campaigning for effective action within the church. A conscientious objection movement within the Christian community was clearly forming.

## THE MOVEMENT GAINS MOMENTUM

The churches, as is evident from their declarations and

statements, had drawn attention to the role of compulsory military service in South Africa. They argued that the SADF was becoming identified with the maintenance of law and order. The SADF was also involved in neighbouring countries — notably Namibia, Mozambique and Angola. Since 1966, South Africa had been involved in armed conflict with the Namibian liberation movement, SWAPO. This involvement amounted to an occupation of that country. The partisan nature of the SADF activities was more and more evident. From the perspective of the churches, conscripts faced a crisis of conscience in that they were involved in a situation where their intrinsic right to freedom of conscience was ignored and overruled. The call of the churches for the recognition of the validity of conscientious objection was a call for the individual's right to conscience to be respected. Significantly, this call embraced both universal pacifists as well as selective conscientious objectors.

In 1976 and 1977, mass popular resistance to apartheid rule swept across South Africa. SADF conscription was increased — initial national service was doubled from 12 to 24 months. Defence Force activity was no longer limited to the country's distant borders combatting the 'external threat', but had become extensively involved in containing internal resistance to apartheid rule. The SADF had begun to move to the center-stage of apartheid politics. The voice of the churches had been prophetic and the growth in resistance to apartheid had occurred simultaneously with the development in SADF activity. The case for selective objection to participation in the SADF was fast gaining legitimacy. The defence of apartheid — a particular expression of violence — had become the issue. Clearly this was not only a matter for Christian conscience. Rather it was a dilemma confronting all those called to serve in the armed forces. Freedom of conscience, declared the churches, must at all times and in all situations be respected.

Since the mid-1970s a growing number of conscripts had exercised their right to individual conscience and had refused to serve in the SADF. Religious reasons — with increasing 'political' content — had been advanced by these objectors. The witness of conscientious objectors Peter Moll, Richard Steele, Charles Yeats, Neil Mitchell, Billy Paddock, Pete Hathorn and others was to challenge other conscripts. Pacifists and selective objectors, religious and non-religious — all were united in their refusal to serve in the SADF, their demand for recognition of their right to refuse to serve, their solidarity with other objectors, and their commitment to working for a just and peaceful society.

The stands of these 'pioneer' objectors gave substance to the call for the recognition of conscientious objection. One of the first of these objectors was a Baptist, Peter Moll. Church leaders declared that 'he was a conscientious objector to military service in the present situation in South Africa because he was convinced that South African society is fundamentally unjust and that military service would involve him in violent conflict with citizens of South Africa who suffer under the prevailing injustices'.[11] Although Moll was initially only fined, his trial in September 1979 focused church and general public attention on the issue of conscientious objection. Subsequently, Moll was called up again, refused to serve again, and this time was sentenced to 18 months in detention barracks. The public outcry raised against this sentence put sufficient pressure on the court to reduce the period to 12 months.

The stand taken by objectors such as Peter Moll provided a basis for organisations focusing on the increasing militarisation of South African society. The debate was no longer confined to the churches, but had become more secular. This secularisation of conscientious objection was closely linked to the growing militarisation of South Africa. The debate that had begun within the churches had spilled over into the wider society.

## CONSCIENTIOUS OBJECTORS SUPPORT GROUPS

The small groupings of friends and supporters of conscientious objectors broadened to include a wide range of people concerned with the importance of conscientious objection and the militarisation of South African society. The statements made by conscientious objectors at their respective court martials were used as a basis for publicity and educational work. Military court martial proceedings were the primary medium for communication with the public.

These groups were formalised into Conscientious Objectors Support Groups. Branches were formed in all the major centers and soon a national movement had emerged. In March 1978, the then Deputy Minister of Defence accused conscientious objectors of 'undermining national service and frustrating the defence of the country in the long run as a consequence'.

The wider political context had a great effect in changing the course of resistance to the military. In 1982, the Defence Act was amended. The length of camps — ie, time in addition to the two years initial service — was increased from 240 to 720 days. After completing their camps, white males could still be drafted into 'Dad's Army' up to the age of 55. These changes were made in response to the upsurge of guerilla activity and the anticipation by the authorities of increased resistance at a 'local area' level. This in turn forced the war resistance movement to change its strategy.

The statements made by objectors became more politicised — focusing on the aggressive and destabilising role of the SADF. Objectors also applied the 'just war' theory to the conflict in southern Africa. Objector Billy Paddock said at his court martial:

> The just war doctrine has validity only when it is applied within the context of a socio-economic and political analysis which then gives the criteria meaning . . . . I cannot enter the SADF because of the role it plays in defending the structural violence of the South African system . . . . I choose to object because once I have sided with the oppressed and exploited it becomes virtually impossible to speak of strategic involvement in the military because I would then be siding with the oppressor . . . . I believe objection is a very valid option today because whites need to take sides and need to be seen to be taking sides. I believe this is one clear way of joining the struggle for a democratic South Africa.[12]

From 1982 then, a second strand of resistance began to emerge alongside the support work for objectors. Campaigns were organised around objectors and through high-profile campaigns, meetings, education programs, publications, the national newsletter of the Conscientious Objectors Support Group, *Objector*, the issues of conscription and militarisation were raised. Objection to military service was expected to further increase if conscription were extended to the 'Coloured' and Indian communities, as was being mooted by government ministers. Increasing numbers of young men, many of them students, were leaving the country to avoid military service. Conscientious objection was recognised by many as a valid and even necessary response to the reality of political violence in South Africa.

Objectors had repeatedly emphasised their willingness to serve the country by participating in a non-military national service. This call for an alternative national service was echoed by the churches and was taken up by the Conscientious Objectors Support Groups. The various denominational hierarchies were called upon to take action concerning war resistance and provide support for such groups.

The government was petitioned to introduce a non-military form of national service. Up until this time only members of the 'peace churches' had been effectively recognised as conscientious objectors. Most of these objectors were imprisoned for one year for refusing to obey military call-ups. A larger group obtained permission to do their military service as non-combatants on pacifist grounds.

The state's response to the call for alternative national service was the 1983 Defence Amendment Act. This legislation made provision for alternative service, but only on religious grounds. A distinction was made between those objectors who were religiously motivated, and those morally or politically motivated. According to the Act's definition, all objection based on the traditional just war position of many churches would fall into the latter category. The Act made provision for 'community service' in a government department, for a period of one-and-a-half times the full period of service owed. This was granted only to religious universal pacifists. The conditions of service were to be laid down by the State President. The penalty for all other objectors was up to six years in civilian prison.

The 1983 amendment was ambiguous in that it appeared to broaden the category of people recognised as objectors and granted religious universal pacifists the possibility of six years alternative service. On the other hand, the prison sentence of political, ethical, or philosophical objectors was lengthened from two to six years. The amendment was an attempt to defuse and minimise conscientious objection as a political issue by offering a significant concession to religious pacifists, while making objection by non-religious or non-pacifist objectors prohibitively costly. The options offered to objectors were unattractive — exile, prison or lengthy community service. The repressive aspect of the new legislation was revealed in the case of Brett Myrdal. Myrdal had been preparing himself for a court martial in November 1983, expecting one or two years imprisonment under the old system. The day before he was due to appear, his call-up was withdrawn and re-issued for July 1984. Suddenly, he fell under the new system and faced six years in jail rather than two. Like many others after him, he was forced to reassess his options.

Objector Pete Hathorn, having spent a year in prison, said on his release:

> The legislation has changed. It now stipulates a maximum six year prison sentence. But the basic principles stay the same. If you participate in the military you must accept that you are fighting for apartheid. The costs have changed, but the facts remain the same.[13]

The Act forced the debate, once again, onto purely religious terrain. Conscience, according to the Act, was an exclusively religious issue. Non-religious moral convictions and decisions of conscience related to current political issues were excluded. The Act took a blatantly political stance expressed in religious terms. While rejecting non-participation in the SADF on political grounds, it assumed participation in the armed forces to be a non-political activity.

The Defence Amendment Act comes nowhere near realising the churches' demand for the recognition of conscientious objectors and the provision of genuine alternative service. The churches found it completely unacceptable. As a Congregational Church statement declared:

> . . . the churches cannot accept a law that provides solely for religious objectors while it imposes severe penalties on others. To do so would amount to condoning privileges for the religious and persecution of the non-religious — a complete anomaly in a state which is opposed to religious discrimination.

The complex legal situation now surrounding objection prompted the emergence of advice bureaus on military conscription in many of the major centers. Largely under the auspices of the Conscientious Objectors Support Groups, advice bureaus were set up to inform conscripts about the limited options open to them.

The provisions of the Defence Amendment Act brought into focus the need for a different approach. The emphasis could no longer be on the individual objector.

## THE EMERGENCE OF THE END CONSCRIPTION CAMPAIGN

The idea for a campaign with a program intended to educate the white community about the military issue was set out in a motion passed at the Black Sash conference in March 1983. The motion demanded 'that the South African government abolish all conscription for military service'. To many, the demand seemed idealistic, but the Black Sash motion offered a vision of a campaign built around a bold demand — an end to conscription.

The decision to launch such a campaign was taken at the annual Conscientious Objectors Support Group conference held in Durban in mid-1983. The campaign was to unite the broadest possible front of organisations around opposition to conscription. As a single-issue campaign, the ECC needed to take no clear position on broader political issues. Anyone who opposed the system of conscription into the SADF, whether on religious grounds or not, whether as a pacifist or just-war proponent, whether liberal or radical, could join ECC. This broad appeal was reflected in the range of groups which formed ECC, including NUSAS, the Young Christian Students, UDF Area Committees, the Black Sash, the Quakers, the social action groups in the Methodist and Anglican churches, the Civil Rights League and eventually the Young Progressives.[14] It was also a rallying point for opposition to apartheid within the white community. Conscription affects white youth, and thereby everyone in the white community in a personal, direct way.

## THE ROLE OF THE CHURCHES
Prior to the formation of ECC, the churches had played a seminal role in the formation of the war resistance movement, and had in the process grappled with the issues involved. However, much of the activity even in that period had been limited to the passing of resolutions rather than the creation of structures within the churches to actively take up the military issue. With the emergence of the ECC as a secular organisation, the churches again showed reluctance to take up the issue in their own structures. With a few notable exceptions, synods seemed content to pass resolutions concerning support for or rejection of positions already established in ECC. Much of the earlier initiative seemed to have been lost.

## A DECLARATION TO END CONSCRIPTION
In the first phase of the ECC's history, attention was focused on building up the organisation by affiliating as many organisations as possible. ECC committees were established in Cape Town, Durban and Johannesburg. In the first few months, ECC operated exclusively as a broad front for sympathetic organisations. Much work was further needed to establish links with other organisations, opening channels of communication with important persons in the church, and lobbying for international support as well. This process culminated in the launching of the *Declaration to End Conscription* at the end of 1984, endorsed by a wide

range of organisations. The declaration called for an end to conscription and for a just peace in our land. The campaign and the meetings to launch the declaration also drew support from individuals not belonging to ECC's front organisations. Sub-committees were set up for people wishing to join ECC directly, the first being the Media Committee in Cape Town in August 1984. In this period, ECC also engaged in extensive surveys to gauge the feelings of conscripts on the military issue.

The first campaign run around a specific military issue was the 'No War In Namibia' campaign in mid-1984. This focus on the external role of the SADF in destabilising neighbouring countries was soon to be overshadowed by the presence of troops in the townships.

## TROOPS OUT OF THE TOWNSHIPS

On 7 October 1984, troops moved into Soweto and Joza (near Grahamstown), and on 23 October a massive operation involving 7 000 troops was carried out in the Vaal township of Sebokeng. This marked the start of a new phase for the ECC. It was a phase characterised by large high-profile public campaigns. It also saw the extension of the ECC beyond the three major centers, with branches being established in Grahamstown, Pietermaritzburg and Port Elizabeth in 1985.

At the first national conference held at Botha's Hill early in 1985, the ECC formally adopted a constitution, and plans for a national campaign were worked out. The Peace Festival held in Johannesburg in July 1985 received strong international support, with Carol Tongue from the British Campaign for Nuclear Disarmament a prominent speaker. Another invited guest, Cardinal Arns from Brazil, was refused a visa.

August 1985 saw the declaration of a 'partial' State of Emergency but this did not halt the ECC campaigns. That same month, ECC presented evidence to the Geldenhuys Committee, which was investigating *inter alia* conscientious objection. The evidence outlined the limitations of the present legislation and the activities of the Board for Religious Objection.

A campaign calling for 'Troops Out of the Townships' was launched. The following month meetings focusing on the role of the troops in the townships were organised around a 'Fast for a Just Peace'. The right not to serve in the townships was the immediate demand of the campaign. This demand was part of ECC's general call for freedom of choice to be given to conscripts

— whether or not to serve in the SADF at all. On the final day of the fast, the public was invited to participate in the fast. The campaign was widely supported, and drew support from most churches. In Cape Town, 4 000 people packed the City Hall for the closing meeting of the campaign.

Another successful national campaign was entitled 'Working for a Just Peace'. Conceived at the second national conference in Durban in January 1986, it posed positive alternatives to military service in the form of projects which helped the community.

The first half of 1986 also saw the extension of the ECC into three more regions. A committee was established in East London, and also on the Afrikaans university campuses in Pretoria and Stellenbosch.

## ECC UNDER THE STATE OF EMERGENCY

In the regulations pertaining to the second State of Emergency (June, 1986), the ECC was singled out in a clause that prohibited statements

> ... calculated to have the effect or likely to have the effect ... of inciting the public or any person or category of persons to ... discredit or undermine the system of compulsory military conscription.

This legislation made the open campaigning around conscription — which had marked the previous phase — virtually impossible. The ECC began to experience increased repression. Meetings were banned, many members of the organisation were detained, others threatened with deportation orders or placed under restriction orders.

In the face of this wave of repression, the ECC initially was chiefly concerned with surviving as an organisation. But as soon as the cohesion of the organisation had been ensured, a new campaign was launched — 'Let ECC Speak/*Laat ECC Praat*'. Regions engaged in separate campaigns which were subject to continual harassment from the police, and the detention of key activists continued.

The ECC currently finds itself severely constrained by political and legal restrictions. The central issue of conscription can no longer be addressed directly. Yet at the same time, the support base of the ECC is widening.[15] Support has come from the Afrikaans communities in Stellenbosch and Pretoria, as well as from Afrikaans school pupils in Johannesburg. The ECC has shed its student image, with the establishment of a Parents Group in Cape Town, and wide-spread organised opposition to registration for 'Dad's Army'. The participation of Jewish community organisations has further broadened the front. Thus it is clear that the repression which the state has levelled at the ECC has not succeeded.

## THE CHURCH AND THE FUTURE OF THE MOVEMENT

Conscientious objection thus remains an important source of church-state conflict. In the 1970s, it was the primary source of that conflict, but since then there has been a broader reawakening of social concern within the English-speaking churches, and the issue of conscription has not received the attention that it should. There are two reasons why the churches should continue to grapple with the issue of the military in apartheid society. Firstly, the issue affects white members of the churches more directly than any other group. Secondly, while many churches hesitate to take a clear position on broader political issues, the churches have already taken a definite stand on the issue of conscription. Now those positions, expressed in synod resolutions, need to be put into practice. The churches need to move from speaking to acting.

The right of conscience, long asserted and defended by the Christian churches, has always been premised by the assumption of an informed conscience — that is, a conscience fully aware of the options and choices available. The responsible ministry of the churches to conscripts must therefore involve the provision of information, the creation of opportunities for discussion and prayerful reflection, and, crucially, the development of support structures. There must be a correspondence between church statements and concrete action.

Beyond utilising existing church structures, the churches could create special groupings to deal with this vital issue. Chaplains could be made available to counsel conscripts before they went into the army. Information could be made available in the form of books or articles.

The present context of the State of Emergency demands more urgently than ever that the churches take up the issue more effectively. The choices facing young white males become increasingly problematic as the civil war escalates. The legal space available to ECC is severely circumscribed, and the organisation has been subject to intense State harassment. The prospect of the banning of ECC — or an alternative strategy which would have the effect of a banning — is becoming more likely. Thus it is important that the churches continue to lend their public support to the ECC and the campaigns.

The churches must persist in questioning the justice of defending an unjust society. The struggle against conscription has, in a short space of time surged forward — opposition to the call-up has been broad-based and vocal. Increasing repression has been the consequence. But the struggle against conscription must be carried on and carried forward if a just peace is to be realised — and the churches have a vital role to play in this process.

## NOTES

1.   Catholic Institute for International Relations (CIIR) and Pax Christi, *War and Conscience in South Africa: The Churches and Conscientious Objection,* (London: CIIR, 1982), p.28.
2.   *Ibid.,* p.78.
3.   *Ibid.,* pp.78-9.
4.   J. de Gruchy, *The Church Struggle in South Africa,* (Cape Town: David Philip, 1979), p.14.
5.   MCSA, *Church and Conscience: A Collection of Church and Other Statements on Conscientious Objection in South Africa,* (Cape Town: Christian Citizenship Department of the Methodist Church, unpublished, 1986).
6.   CIIR, *War and Conscience in South Africa,* p.34.
7.   *Ibid.,* p.47.
8.   MCSA, *Church and Conscience,* p.5.
9.   *Ibid.,* p.8.
10.  CIIR, *War and Conscience in South Africa,* p.53.
11.  *Cape Times,* 5 December 1979.
12.  Billy Paddock, *Why I Object to Service in the SADF,* unpublished pamphlet, 1982.
13.  *Objector* interview, August 1984.
14.  For a full list of affiliates see the evidence submitted to the Geldenhuys Committee.
15.  See the 'Let ECC Speak' advert in the *Weekly Mail* of September 5-11, 1986 for the breadth of support.

# BEYOND DEBATE

# Where the Debate Ends

## FRANK CHIKANE

The debate about violence and non-violence in South Africa is an old one — particularly within the church. This debate has intensified since the 1960s when local liberation movements went underground and resorted to armed struggle, believing that this was the only way to force the racist South African regime to abandon the violent system of apartheid. This historical decision is best explained in Nelson Mandela's famous statement from the dock during his trial:

> At the beginning of June 1961, after a long and anxious assessment of the South African situation, I and some colleagues came to the conclusion that as violence in this country was inevitable, it would be unrealistic and wrong for African leaders to continue preaching peace and non-violence at a time when the goverment met our peaceful demands with force....

> This conclusion was not easily arrived at. It was only when all else had failed, when all channels of peaceful protest had been barred to us, that the decision was made to embark upon violent forms of political struggle.... We did so not because we desired such a course, but solely because the government had left us with no other choice.[1]

Elsewhere in the court records Mandela says that he did not plan sabotage in a 'spirit of recklessness' nor because he had 'any love of violence'. He says that he planned it as a result of a 'calm and sober assessment of the political situation that had arisen after many years of tyranny, exploitation and the oppression of my people by the whites'.[2] He further advances his argument with the words of Chief Albert Luthuli:

> Who will deny that thirty years of my life have been spent knocking in vain, patiently, moderately and modestly at a closed and barred door? What have been the fruits of moderation? The past thirty years has seen the greatest number of laws restricting our rights and progress, until today we have reached a stage where we have almost no rights at all.[3]

Mandela advances two reasons for resorting to armed struggle.

301

The first is that 'as a result of government policy, violence by the African people had become inevitable and that unless responsible leadership was given to canalise and control the feelings of our people, there would be outbreaks of terrorism which would produce an intensity of bitterness and hostility between the various races of this country which is not produced even by war'.[4] The second reason was that without violence there would be no way open to the African people to succeed in their struggle against the principle of white supremacy.

It was this agonising decision of the 1960s that intensified the debate on violence and non-violence. The debate has been further intensified as the violent conflict between the forces of the apartheid regime and the oppressed masses escalated in recent years.

## THE ABSENCE OF SPACE FOR DEBATE

The intention of this paper is not to participate in the violence — non-violence debate but to raise some questions about the debate itself. My submission is that *the debate about violence and non-violence reaches a point at which it simply must end.* There is a point beyond which such a debate is no longer possible. There may be times when there is a space within which the debate can take place but there is a time when this space is so violated that it is no longer possible to engage in the debate. Circumstances or events at a particular stage in life can so 'squeeze' or constrict this space that it ceases to exist.

I shall elucidate this point by means of three theses.

My *first thesis* is that the only space within which the debate on violence and non-violence can take place is one where there is no war or where the war does not directly involve the participants in the debate. This space is a state of affairs in which the participants experience no immediate threat to their lives. It is a state of comfort and relative peace, a state of privilege. People in the black townships of South Africa consider this 'a luxury' of which they have been deprived. This condition, which is the only condition conducive to this type of debate, exists only in theological seminaries, universities and church conferences, isolated from social reality, and at conference centers where the participants are not exposed to violence or likely to have their debate disrupted by violence.

My *second thesis* is that this space can also be an artifically 'created space', a space that has been created by violence. This is the space within which many people operate under the illusion that they at least are non-violent. Others know that it is only by violent means that this space can be created to enable them to talk about non-violence. Most white people in South Africa and some privileged blacks dwell within this space, condemning the violence of the townships, and expressing their abhorrence of all violence as if they were not involved in violence themselves. The fact of the matter is that this class of people is 'protected' by the violence of security forces and without this 'protection' they would not be able to engage in any debate about violence and non-violence. Violence is being perpetrated on their behalf to enable them to masquerade as non-violent and peace-loving people. This is a privilege that the ordinary person in Soweto does not have. In most cases it is those whose privileges are secured by violence who are able to debate violence and preach non-violence to those without privileges or protection.

This then is the 'created space' that exists only for the privileged and dominant classes and oppressive regimes. P.W. Botha, for instance, occupies this 'created space'. It is the space created by his brutal and violent apartheid forces that enables him to condemn what he calls the violence of the ANC while he prohibits the victims of violence from engaging in this or any other debate. The debate on violence and non-violence is a debate in which only one party in the conflict can participate. The other party is deprived of the necessary space.

Most of the disciples of non-violence in South Africa also have to make use of this 'created space' in order to continue with their ideal of non-violence. The recent case of Mrs Coretta King was a classic example. In order to undertake her mission of peace in South Africa in line with the non-violence tradition of her husband Martin Luther King, she had to be protected by security police.

With regard to my own non-violent stance, the contradictions began to appear after I was released on bail during the treason trial in 1985. My house and my family were attacked with petrol bombs and my name was discovered to be on a hit list. At the time, I was preaching non-violence and preparing my case to show how peaceful I was, while the community organised itself to protect me from those agents of the apartheid system who were threatening my life. I was confronted with the reality of armed people who were committed to preserving my life and the lives of my family. I was obliged to admit that I was only able to continue preaching non-violence because others were prepared to use violence to create this space for me. There comes a time when one cannot preach non-violence without recognising the hypocrisy of enjoying a security provided by violent means.

My *third thesis* is that there is a point, particularly for the dominated classes in society, beyond which it is no longer possible to participate in the debate about violence and non-violence. For the oppressed masses of South Africa the space for debates of this kind simply no longer exists. These people live in a situation in which this space has been completely eliminated. It is a situation where meetings are prohibited and discussions about non-violent strategies are outlawed; where peaceful protests and non-violent demonstrations are forbidden by law, strikes by workers are crushed and where boycotts are seen as sabotage. It is a state of war in which townships and schools are occupied by the apartheid army, some areas are under siege, the sound of gunfire has become part of daily life and teargas fills the atmosphere at regular intervals. It is a situation where hit squads and 'balaclava-men' attack the community indiscriminately. Vigilante groups are formed, with the evident backing of the apartheid security forces, to attack innocent people.

Faced with this reality one can either run for one's life or fight back in self-defence. That is why people of the townships are now forming 'Defence Committees' or 'Street Committees' to enable them to defend themselves. At this point the debate comes to an end and action becomes the only option. There is no time or space to talk about the problem of violence. There is time only for responding to the violence of the system. The only way in which one could create the space to engage in a debate about violence and non-violence would be to mobilise a strong enough army to keep the apartheid army at bay, but this too has serious implications. All of which brings one back to the contradiction of created space as a space created by violent means in order to discuss and condemn violence.

The question is: how should the church handle the reality of a violent war? It is a war which is going to become more brutal as time goes by and will result in incalculable harm and untold suffering, pain and misery. What makes the situation even more critical for the church is the fact that the majority of the people involved on both sides of the conflict claim to be Christians. The *Kairos Document* expresses this dilemma succinctly and poignantly:

> Both oppressor and oppressed claim loyalty to the same

Church. They are both baptised in the same baptism and participate together in the breaking of the same bread, the same body and blood of Christ.

The Kairos theologians conclude this paragraph by proclaiming: 'The Church is divided and its day of judgment has come'.[5] In the words of Leonardo Boff:

The faithful in the Church occupy objectively different social positions according to their social class. They perceive reality in a way that corresponds to their social conditions, and so they interpret and live the gospel message out of the needs, interests and behaviour of their particular class. Thus actions that are possible, tolerable, recommended, necessary or demanding vary from one social class to another.[6]

## THE VIOLENCE DEBATE

It was this fact of a divided church that led the Kairos theologians to critically examine the official theology of the mainline missionary churches, and especially their theology of non-violence. We first need, however, to clarify something that critics of the *Kairos Document* have said about violence and non-violence. The *Kairos Document* has not entered into the debate as to whether or not Christians could justifiably take up arms in our situation. This is not an issue in the document nor did it arise in any of the preparatory discussions leading to the publication of the document. In the face of the battle raging in the townships at the time, such a question would have been simply irrelevant. What was of paramount importance in all the preparatory discussions was the search for the *causes* of violence, the *causes* of the war being fought in the townships. And the reason for this interest in causes was quite simply the overwhelming concern of the Kairos theologians to stop the war. They had no desire to talk about the relative merits of violence and non-violence or to make any decisions about it. We simply wanted to stop the violence already existing.

What concerned the Kairos theologians about the stance of the official church was that church theologians were talking about the morality of the use of violence in the war instead of doing something to stop the war by tackling its causes. This point has not been generally understood and as a result the *Kairos Document* has become the centre of the very debate on violence and non-violence — a debate that the Kairos theologians had no intention of entering into. But perhaps this misunderstanding is inevitable, since it is a misunderstanding that arises out of a particular social position or class. Those critics who accuse the Kairos theologians of promoting violence, murder, terrorism or communism all come from a particular social class. They are simply incapable of appreciating the concerns of the Kairos theologians.

The fundamental question raised by the Kairos theologians goes beyond the violence and non-violence debate. It starts a 'debate' about the debate itself. It starts a debate about the way in which the church responds to the issue of violence in South Africa. The document contends that the church's response is subtly weighted against the victims of the system. And the reason for this is found in the underlying theme of the *Kairos Document*: the question of the legitimacy or illegitimacy of the South African regime.

## LEGITIMATE AND ILLEGITIMATE AUTHORITY

The supporters of the apartheid regime, the disciples of the ideal of non-violence and many of those among our church leadership always begin with the assumption that the existing political authority is legitimate. The Kairos theologians on the other hand, have argued that the present regime in South Africa is illegitimate and tyrannical. Consequently they approach the problem of violence and war in South Africa with a different premise. Until the critics of the *Kairos Document* recognise this radical difference of initial assumptions, they will never understand the radically different conclusion reached as to how the church should respond in this situation of crisis.

Social position plays an important role here. Someone who does theology from the heat of the struggle in Soweto will always come to different conclusions from someone who theologises from the luxury of a suburb in Johannesburg. As Leonardo Boff says: 'they will perceive reality in a way that corresponds to their social condition or class'.[7]

As perceived by the Kairos theologians, the problem is that the church usually starts with the assumption that the existing authority is a legitimate authority. This assumption needs to be seen in its historical context. Throughout its history since Constantine came to power in the fourth century the church has enjoyed a position of privilege and served to legitimate the activities of the ruling classes. After Constantine the church became what Leonardo Boff calls 'the legitimating religious ideology for the imperial social order'.[8] The persecuted church of the apostolic tradition (the early church) became the persecuting church; the suffering church became the accomplice in perpetuating the suffering of others; the church of the poor became the church of the rich, and the servant church became the dominating church.

During the period of colonisation, which was also the period of missionary expansion, the church, in order to secure its missionary activities, was bound up with the European colonial powers. It did not seem to matter how totalitarian or tyrannical these powers were. What mattered to the missionary church was the privilege of being allowed to preach 'the gospel'. This 'privilege' was granted by the colonial powers as a trade-off for legitimation. The church gave legitimacy to colonial expansionism and the colonial and imperalist powers in turn legitimated the church, so that the legitimacy of the church was no longer derived from its heavenly Lord but from the lords of this world.

It should therefore not surprise us when we observe that even today the church seldom questions the legitimacy of political authorities. The evils of the system can be condemned in the strongest possible terms but the legitimacy of the existing authority cannot be questioned. Thus the church will regret the 'excesses' of these 'legitimate' authorities while condemning the 'violence' of the victims of these authorities. What this means is that those in power have the legitimate right to use violence to keep law and order provided they do not exceed reasonable limits, while the victims of the system have no legitimate right to use violence to defend themselves against those who are in power. Once the legitimacy of existing authority is taken for granted, one is bound to view the violence of the victims as illegitimate.

If the church is to minister effectively to the oppressed in South Africa and if, in this war, the church is to exercise its pastoral responsibility in a credible manner, it will have to face up to the question of the legitimacy or illegitimacy of the present regime. If the church wants to participate meaningfully in the debate about violence and non-violence, it will have to begin by debating this question of legitimacy and illegitimacy in the light of God's justice and the coming Kingdom of God. On the other hand, if the church does not ask itself this question in the near future, it will lose its credibility in the eyes of the people and forfeit any legitimate right to participate in the debate about violence and non-violence or to condemn those who engage in violence to defend themselves against the violence of the system. In other words the church will lose its own legitimacy.

The consequences of a church statement that the present regime is illegitimate would be far-reaching. The church would then have to take appropriate action in solidarity with others to ensure that the tyrant would be removed from power and a legitimate political authority set up in its place. Whatever methods of doing this might be approved by the church, whether violent, non-violent or a combination of the two, they would have to be tried and tested. Thus if the church could approve only non-violent methods, it would have to lead the way in proving that non-violence could be effective in removing an illegitimate regime from power. But if the church stops short at the 'traditional' line where religion is said to end and politics to begin, if it does not cross this imaginary line in order to test its non-violent methods in the field, it will forfeit any legitimate right to condemn those who go further into the arena of life and death for the sake of justice. Once one recognises the illegitimacy of the regime one cannot hesitate in order to create the 'space' for a lengthy debate on violence and non-violence. One can only go forward with whatever methods are judged best to remove the tyrant.

## BEYOND DEBATE

What Emilio Castro has said of Latin America applies even more pertinently to our situation:

> In the urgency of the Latin American situation there is no time to lose in discussions on violence and non-violence. Those who are committed to non-violence should prove the efficiency, the validity of their approach, not by discussing it with those who do not share their conviction, but by struggling with the factors of oppression in society.[9]

In South Africa today there is no time or space left for discussion. At this critical point the debate ends and action begins.

## NOTES

1. T. Karis and G. Carter (eds.), *From Protest to Challenge*, Vol.3., (Stanford, California: Hoover Institution Publications, 1977), p.777.
2. Extract from the court record of the trial of Mandela held in the Old Synagogue court, Pretoria, from 15 October to 7 November 1962.
3. A. Luthuli, *Let My People Go*, (London: Collins, 1962), p.236.

4.  Extract from the court record of the trial of Mandela held in the Old Synagogue court, Pretoria, from 15 October to 7 November 1962.
5.  The Kairos theologians, *The Kairos Document,* (Johannesburg: ICT, 1985), p.5.
6.  L. Boff, *Church Charism and Power: Liberation Theology and the Institutional Church,* (London: SCM, 1985), p.111.
7.  *Ibid.,* p.111.
8.  *Ibid.,* p.113.
9.  E. Castro, *Amidst Revolution,* (Belfast: Christian Journals Ltd., 1975), p.68.